Families in Economically Hard Times

Families in Economically Hard Times: Experiences and Coping Strategies in Europe

EDITED BY

VIDA ČESNUITYTĖ

Mykolas Romeris University, Lithuania

GERARDO MEIL

Autonomous University of Madrid, Spain

emerald PUBLISHING

United Kingdom – North America – Japan – India – Malaysia – China

Emerald Publishing Limited
Howard House, Wagon Lane, Bingley BD16 1WA, UK

First edition 2020

Reprints and permissions service
Contact: permissions@emeraldinsight.com

British Library Cataloguing in Publication Data
A catalogue record for this book is available from the British Library

ISBN: 978-1-83909-072-1 (Print)
ISBN: 978-1-83909-071-4 (Online)
ISBN: 978-1-83909-073-8 (Epub)

Printed and bound by CPI Group (UK) Ltd, Croydon, CR0 4YY

ISOQAR REGISTERED
ISOQAR certified Management System, awarded to Emerald for adherence to Environmental standard ISO 14001:2004.
Certificate Number 1985
ISO 14001

INVESTOR IN PEOPLE

Table of Contents

Part II: Families' Strategies against Economic Hardships

List of Figures

List of Tables

List of Abbreviations

ADLs	Activities of Daily Living
A-MDS	Adapted Material Deprivation Scale
CAPI	Computer-Assisted Personal Interviewing method
CEE	Central-Eastern Europe
CES-D	Center for Epidemiologic Studies Depression scale
DF	Depressive Feelings
DI	Depression Index
ERC	European Research Council
ESA	Employment Support Allowance
EU	European Union
Eurostat	European Statistics
EU-SILC	European Union survey of Social Inequality and Living Conditions
EVS	European Values Study
FBS	Food Budget Standard
FSC	Family Social Capital
GDP	Gross Domestic Product
HBAI	Households Below Average Income
HRS	Health and Retirement Study
IADL	Instrumental Activities of Daily Living
IMD	Index of Material Deprivation
ISCED	International Standard Classification of Education
ISTAT	Italian National Institute of Statistics
JSA	Jobseeker's Allowance
LCFS	Living Costs and Food Survey
MD	Material Deprivation

MIS	Minimum Income Standard
NUTS	Nomenclature of Territorial Units for Statistics
OECD	Organisation for Economic Co-operation and Development
PiP	Personal Independence Payment
PRS	Parenting-Related Stress scale
SC	Social Capital
SD	Standard Deviation
SHARE	Survey of Health, Ageing and Retirement in Europe
UK	United Kingdom
UNECE	United Nations European Commission of Economics
WWII	Second World War

About the Contributors

Prof. Martina Brandt is Professor for Social Structure and Sociology of Ageing Societies at TU Dortmund (Germany). She was Assistant Coordinator (Research) of the European SHARE project and currently leads an international ORA project on inequalities in care and wellbeing. Her quantitative research focuses on ageing, family, health and social inequality.

Prof. Julia Brannen is Professor of the Sociology of the Family at the Thomas Coram Research Unit, UCL Institute of Education, and fellow of the Academy of Social Science (UK). She has an international reputation for research on methodology, the lives of children and young people in families, work–family life and intergenerational relationships. Recent books include *Fathers and Sons* (2015), and *Social Research Matters* (2019).

Dr. Benedetta Cappellini is a Professor of Marketing at the University of Durham (UK). Her research falls broadly into the areas of consumer culture, critical marketing and sociology of consumption. Topics she has recently studied include food cultures, meal practices, austerity, intensive mothering and domestic violence. She has published in journals such as *Journal of Business Research*; *Journal of Marketing Management*; *Consumption Markets and Culture*; *Sociology*; *Sociology of Health and Illness* and the *Sociological Review*. She has co-edited books on the practice of the meal and mothering and food consumption.

Dr. Vida Česnuitytė is Associated Professor of the Sociology at Mykolas Romeris University (Vilnius, Lithuania). With over 15 years in various positions she has participated in research projects. Main research interests concern family conceptualisation, family practices, family quality life, social policy, and social research methods. Individually or in co-authorship she has published over 20 articles, book chapters and books in Lithuanian and English.

Dr. Christian Deindl is Postdoctoral Researcher at the Institute of Medical Sociology at the Heinrich-Heine-University Düsseldorf (Germany). He is involved in projects involving the harmonisation of ELSA and SHARELIFE, employment in old age and inequality in care. His research covers intergenerational relations, family sociology, health, employment and life course research.

Prof. Diego Dueñas Fernández is Professor in the Department of Economics at the University of Alcalá (Madrid, Spain). He was awarded the prize for extraordinary doctorate in the year 2012 at the University of Alcalá. His line of research focuses on issues of gender in the labour market, topics of analysis regarding labour segregation and wage discrimination.

Dr. Vicki Harman is a Senior Lecturer in Sociology at the University of Surrey (UK). Her research interests include family life, gender, food practices and social inequalities. Her research has been published in journals including *Sociology*; *Sociology of Health and Illness; Families, Relationships and Societies*; *International Journal of Consumer Studies*; *Young Consumers*; the *European Journal of Marketing* and *Ethnic and Racial Studies*. She is the co-editor of *Feeding Children Inside and Outside the Home: Critical Perspectives* (Routledge, 2019).

Dr. Bettina Isengard is Senior Research Associate at the Institute of Sociology, University of Zurich (Switzerland) and a member of the research group 'LAbour, Generation, Stratification' (AGES). She has a PhD in Sociology of the University of Mannheim, Germany. Current research activities include studies about generations, social structure and inequality.

Dr. Abigail Knight is Lecturer in Sociology at the Thomas Coram Research Unit, UCL Institute of Education (UK). As well as teaching, she is a qualitative researcher with children and families and has researched and written widely on the lives of young people in care, children with disabilities and families living in poverty.

Dr. Ronny König is Graduate Research Assistant at the Institute of Sociology at the University of Zurich (Switzerland) and member of the research group 'LAbour, Generation, Stratification' (AGES). He has a PhD in Sociology at the University of Zurich since 2015. His main research interests are social inequality, stratification and intergenerational relationships.

Dr. Alessandra Marilli is a Post-Doctoral Researcher at the Department of Sociology and Political Studies, University of Florence (Italy). Her research interests are media consumption, media representation of gender and ethnicity and family consumption. She held various research and teaching positions at the University of Florence. She has just concluded a European Union–funded research project on the Italian media representations of immigrants.

Prof. Dr Aušra Maslauskaitė is Professor of Sociology at the Department of Sociology, Vytautas Magnus University (Kaunas, Lithuania) and Senior Researcher at Lithuanian Social Research Center. Her research interests include family demography and family sociology. She works on issues related to family formation and dissolution, causes and consequences of divorce, families and inequalities, gender and intergenerational relationships.

Dr. Sara Mazzucchelli is an Assistant Professor in Family Sociology at the Faculty of Psychology and collaborates with the Family Studies and Research University Centre (Italy). Her research focuses primarily on family–work reconciliation and corporate welfare; the socio-cultural transformations of the family; social policies and services for the family. She teaches Sociology of cultural and communication processes and Sociology of cultural welfare processes.

Prof. Gerardo Meil is Professor at Autonomous University of Madrid (Spain), and former President of the European Society on Family Relations. His research fields include family lives, balancing working and private lives, gender studies, domestic violence, new family forms, job mobility, social policies and family policies. His research has been funded in competitive calls by the regional government of Madrid, the Spanish Ministry of Education and/or Science, the European Union and private institutions. He has published scientific articles, book chapters and books in Spanish, English, German or French.

Prof. Almudena Moreno Mínguez is Professor in Sociology at the University of Valladolid (Spain). She is a specialist in family issues, welfare state, public policies and comparative research on gender. Her research work has been recognised with the International Award for Young Sociologists, given by the International Sociological Association.

Dr. Miriam Parise is Post-Doc Researcher in Social Psychology at the Family Studies and Research University Centre of the Università Cattolica del Sacro Cuore of Milano (Italy). Her research focuses primarily on the couple relationship, which she studies from a psycho-social perspective. She teaches 'Psychology of groups' and 'Psychology of educational contexts: juridical and social aspects' at the Faculty of Educational Sciences at UCSC-Brescia and UCSC-Piacenza.

Prof. Elizabeth Parsons is a Professor of Marketing at the University of Liverpool Management School (UK). She is interested in consumer culture and critical marketing. Recent topics include food poverty, food and family and marketplace exclusion. Her approach to research is interdisciplinary and she has published in *Sociology*; *Sociology of Health and Illness*; *Organization Studies* and the *Journal of Consumer Culture*. She is co-editor of the journal *Marketing Theory* which publishes critical and alternative perspectives on markets and consumption.

Ernesta Platūkytė is a PhD student in Sociology at Vytautas Magnus University (Kaunas, Lithuania) since 2013. In 2004, she graduated from Vilnius University, and obtained a Master's degree in Social Work. Between 2004 and 2006 she was PhD student in social work at Lapland University. Her research interests concern sociology of family.

Dr. Rebecca O'Connell is a Reader in the Sociology of Food and Families at the Thomas Coram Research Unit, UCL Institute of Education (UK). She is co author, with Julia Brannen, of *Food, Families, and Work* (2016) and Principal Investigator of the European Research Council–funded study, Families and Food in Hard Times.

Prof. Marc Szydlik has been a full Professor of Sociology at the University of Zurich (Switzerland) since 2004. He previously worked at the German Institute for Economic Research, the Max-Planck-Institute for Human Development, the Free University of Berlin and the University of Erfurt. He recently directs the research group 'LAbour, Generation, Stratification'.

Prof. Eric D. Widmer is Professor at the School of Social Sciences of the University of Geneva (Switzerland), and a member of the board of I-DEMO. His long-term interests include intimate ties, family and other interpersonal relations, life course research and social networks. Along with others, he has been developing for two decades research on families in configurational perspective. He is an active member of NCCR lives, and the author of numerous books and research papers.

Preface

The edited collection *Families in Economically Hard Times: Experiences and Coping Strategies in Europe* was initiated by the members of the European Sociological Association's Research Network 'Sociology of Families and Intimate Lives' (ESA RN13). The editors invited researchers to contribute their papers presented at sociological conferences, and also invited prominent authors who work on corresponding themes.

The book provides readers with novel knowledge on experiences and behaviour strategies of European families during the decade after the global economic crisis at the beginning of the twenty-first century. The research studies provide answers to the questions: how challenges emerging in an economically hard context influenced the way of life of European families? Which known and unusual behaviour strategies are specific to families of various configurations in solving vital issues caused by the latest economic crises? Research results focus on material deprivation, functional solidarity and practices concerning co-residence, sharing of money and food acquisition.

Authors from six countries (Germany, Italy, Lithuania, Spain, Switzerland and the UK) present original research results by developing and applying innovative theoretical and methodical approaches for a deeper understanding of phenomena. The most promising papers that best correspond with the book's aims, and give an integrated vision, are included in the collection. The editors of the book express special gratitude to Benedicte Brahic, Donatella Bramanti, Berit Brandth, Esther Dermott, Jacques-Antoine Gauthier, Detlev Lück and Claude Martin whose valuable comments enabled to significantly improve the quality of the book's content.

The main benefits of the book are the following: the novelty of findings, innovative research approaches and, finally, international dimension in terms of countries represented and compared in the empirical analyses. The editors hope that this edited collection will be a useful reading for researchers, teachers, students, professionals and others who are interested in scientific knowledge on the family in economically hard times.

Vida Česnuitytė & Gerardo Meil
Book editors

Introduction

Vida Česnuitytė and Gerardo Meil

Introduction

Social research studies conducted in the twentieth century revealed sensitivity and vulnerability of the family in terms of economic conditions. Eventually, the concepts like material deprivation, the burden of dependants, feminisation of poverty, social exclusion and others related to the phenomena were introduced into discourse. Nowadays, particular importance of the topic of family in economically hard times is determined by at least two main factors:

(1) Economically hard periods happen from time to time globally or at national level. Meanwhile, families' experiences and behaviours during recent economic crises may differ from the past since present reality is concomitant to late modernity characteristics marked by constant change, uncertainty, globalisation, mass migration, information society, etc.
(2) Even welfare state takes over some functions of the family including support to persons in need; researches reveal that family members still tend to rely on themselves or their close networks during periods of hardships. However, pluralisation of the family model entrenched in the last few decades influenced negatively the ability of the family to respond to its members' needs.

The purpose of the edited collection *Families in Economically Hard Times: Experiences and Coping Strategies in Europe* is to provide readers with a novel and unique sociological knowledge on European families' experiences and behavioural strategies in the decade after economic crisis that ensued at the beginning of the twenty-first century. The main questions that the book seeks to answer are the following: how challenges emerged during recent economically hard contexts influenced the way of life of European families? Which known and unusual behaviour strategies are specific to families of various configurations in solving vital issues caused by the latest economic crises?

In order to extend knowledge on purposive experiences and behaviour strategies, prominent scholars from Germany, Italy, Lithuania, Spain, Switzerland, and the United Kingdom joined efforts and created a volume based on their latest research study. The researches focus on hardships, functional solidarity and issues

Families in Economically Hard Times, 1–6

doi:10.1108/978-1-83909-071-420191002

of vital human needs, including practices of co-residence, sharing of money, food acquisition. Some investigations are conducted at national level, whereas others at international level. Quantitative and qualitative research methodologies, as well as international comparative perspective are used. Such multidimensional approaches enable us to identify both universal and unique experiences and behaviour strategies, and to ensure reliable results contributing to better understanding of the phenomena.

The edited collection consists of nine chapters divided into two main parts: *Economic Hardships Experienced by Families,* and *Families' Strategies Against Economic Hardships.* It also includes an Introduction and summarising Conclusions. At the end of each chapter, extended lists of references are given. For easier work with the book, at the end of it an Index of the main terms is provided.

Economic Hardships Experienced by Families

Over a long time, the family was the main and almost the only shelter protecting family members from various external forces (Robila, 2004). The family builds material and immaterial backgrounds for life in adulthood. So far, family in need presupposes particular ways of life, unlearnt some kinds of lessons and learnt other lessons, possible obstacles in life of the adult. The latter forms individuals bring as their attitudes and behaviour patterns into the community and society. Thus, sustainable economic and social foundations of family itself are guarantors of a further successful development of almost everyone at a micro level, and in society at a macro level (Campiglio, 2010). Cultivating interpersonal relationships creates an environment that makes our lives more protective against both material and immaterial poverty that is rather common, especially in urban contexts (Bramanti, 2015).

The latest processes in global economy have undergone a severe downturn; financial hardship has become a significant public concern in many European countries. The depressed economic climate increased the unemployment rate and is affecting families, where a lot of families live in severe material deprivation and other measures are decreasing their level of living. In Chapter 1, Mazzucchelli, and Parise analyse the possibilities of making savings from jobs available for families. Studied processes are linked to educational qualification and marital status. Much attention is paid on primary family social capital, trust in institutions and satisfaction with conjugal life. The question is whether dimensions that are both internal and pertain to the link between the family and the context in which it lives are influential in opportunities of families to make savings.

Previous research studies on different forms of functional solidarity have shown that family generations are strongly connected, and these ties are particularly strong between parents and (adult) children in most European societies (Haberkern & Szydlik, 2010), especially in economically hard periods. König, Isengard, and Szydlik in Chapter 2 focus on social inequalities at the micro, meso and macro level, and try to explain differences in family cohesion in general and intergenerational functional solidarity in particular. The chapter explores flows of support between generations: who receive, and who gives economic resources. Authors look for answers to the questions: what behaviour is specific to those with better economic opportunities? And in the opposite: what behaviour is related to those who have complaints concerning health, material conditions, etc.? What are the experiences of competing family members, e.g. siblings? How the process of intergenerational solidarity is effected by societal inequality at the macro level?

For better material maintenance of the family, involvement of men and women in the labour market may contribute. Notwithstanding, men and women are unequally incorporated into the labour market in European countries (Comisión Europea, 2009). Dueñas Fernandez and Moreno Mínguez in Chapter 3 present an analysis on the conditions for both participation in the workforce and the type of work they do for women from the families with children in the home. The analysis considers the correction factor introduced by the recession, which to some extent favoured women. During the recession, the size and composition of families have varied, with a reduction in the number of children in the second decade of the twenty-first century and, consequently, a reduction in the number of children less than three years of age. So, the question is how has the behaviour of women changed in respect to work, and care after children in the home? Whether these women in Spain are more actively involved in the labour market, or is it the opposite? How is it related to the type of employment and work contract?

Meanwhile, single-mother families in many countries are exposed to high risk of poverty, social exclusion and lower overall quality of life (Härkönen, 2017; Maldonado & Nieuwenhuis, 2015). Welfare state policies help these families cope with various disadvantages, and to strengthen their level of living. Often the latter are accumulated, or transmitted between generations, etc (McLanahan & Percheski, 2008). In Chapter 4, Maslauskaitė and Platukytė present research results on interrelation among household types, experiences of poverty and the social policy measures. Authors look for the answers on questions: what is the role of individual resources in managing the single-motherhood disadvantage? What are the outcomes for single mothers who are a heterogeneous group?

Families' Strategies Against Economic Hardships

Since the middle of the twentieth century, some of the family's functions were taken by the welfare state. Individuals became socially and economically independent from the family and community more than ever before. At the same time, the family institution changed drastically – became more open for new ways of living and daily life arrangements, family model became pluralistic and dynamic (Holstein & Gubrium, 1995; Stacey, 1991, 1993). In some cases, friends and others from beyond the nuclear and extended family replaced family members and their roles, including friendship, love, care and support. Nevertheless, researches reveal, in the periods of crises, as older, as young generations preferences give to the family (Pahl & Spencer, 2004). And then families meet challenges once changed families not always are able to satisfy vital needs of its members. On the other hand, those who live in the traditional nuclear or extended family, also, meet some challenges because of various factors, e.g. unemployment, burden or dependants, etc. Considering what is said above, the following questions emerge: how families cope with challenges and hardships in the periods of economic crisis? What strategies do they apply?

Everyday routine and family practices connect people and generate personal networks or community as an element of social capital. It may include not only members of the nuclear or extended family but, also, friends and other persons beyond kinship (Morgan, 1996, 1999; Silva & Smart, 1999). Česnuitytė and Widmer in Chapter 5 present research on interrelation among problematic situations experienced, personal network and practices of support sharing. The questions are explored: what types of help and support Ego received and gave in cases of various problematic situations experienced? Who from the personal network gave and who received particular help and support? Which family practices build such personal networks that are ready to support Ego in need? Types of help and support analysed: services and care, financial and other material support, and emotional support. Personal networks consisting of members from the nuclear and extended families, as well as persons from beyond are investigated. From numerous family practices, investments into various aspects of individual life are considered.

Personal network may serve as a shelter in economically vulnerable situations, though it is very dependent on number and kind of events in individual life course and kind of personal network available for the individual and the family. It is especially true in case of young families who just started to generate their personal networks. Even so, Deindl and Brandt in Chapter 6 focus on issues related to a safety net provided by families. When do family members support each other? What are the links between social inequality and transfers between middle-aged people, their adult children and older parents? What is intrinsic in respect to individual social and material deprivation, regional social inequality and intergenerational transfer patterns?

In previous works was shown a substantial effect of regional social inequality on transfer patterns: higher inequality goes hand in hand with lower social cohesion (Wilkinson & Pickett, 2010). That is, where to live is a matter. Geographical proximity or distance between parents and their adult children can be seen as fundamental in functional solidarity. Isengard, König and Szydlik in Chapter 7 analyse spatial proximity – an important aspect of residential mobility. The questions explored are: what issues determine decisions to change the residence? How financial hardships influence the decisions on relocation of adult children when they are ready to run their own family and household? How are these processes influenced by the facts of having a child, need for additional space, etc.?

The global economic recession, as well, influence higher food prices, and so-called 'austerity' policies in some European countries. That has made food less affordable for families. O'Connell, Knight and Brannen in Chapter 8 analyse proportions of the food budget standard available to families, particularly, the United Kingdom. How is it changed over time? How does it relate to type and size of family? How do the families manage to provide enough food with less than the food budget standard spendings? Issues on compromises in food quality and quantity, social participation and socially acceptable procurement are explored.

Similar questions, from a comparative perspective, are presented by Cappellini, Harman, Marilli and Parsons in Chapter 9. Cases of two single mothers, one in Italy, the other in Britain, are compared. In line with the discourse of intensive mothering where children are seen as 'beyond market value' (Lareau, 2003), additional efforts should be made to shield children from the impact of austerity. Thus, the following questions are analysed in the chapter: how do different cultural and social capitals contribute to everyday coping strategies in acquiring food? What are the roles of the emotional work and the everyday practices feeding the family in economically hard times? How much time and labour should be dedicated for stretching economic resources? How much creativity and effort should families invoke in the process?

Conclusion

To conclude, global economic crisis, recession and austerity that emerged at the beginning of the twenty-first century have made the lives of families harder and more complex for a long time. In some cases, intergenerational relationships, personal networks, collaborative consumption, strategies applied on issues of co-residence, sharing of money and food acquisition ensure the material provision for the family and its separate members during economically hard times. On the other hand, the processes are additionally influenced by the environment conditioned by the globalisation, spread of knowledge economy, mass migration, etc. Thus, there is evident need for novel knowledge on families in economic crisis. Authors in nine chapters ask according questions and provide answers that contribute as to benefit of the book, as to real life.

The main benefits of the book are the following: (1) the objects in study of families' experiences and strategies in economically hard times, (2) the novelty of empirical findings and (3) multidimensionality, including methods applied in analyses, and empirical evidence from 18 European countries represented and compared in the analyses. It is expected that the book meets the attention of its target group – scientific and academic communities. It can be useful for specialists working with issues related to families, as well, and may attract a wider society once it provides examples of problem-solving problematic situations. The International perspective presented in the book will lead to suppose worldwide interest in it.

References

Bramanti, D. (2015). Capitale sociale e ambiente amichevole: quali risorse per le famiglie con figli (0–13). *Sociologia e Politiche Sociali*, *18*(2), 130–151.

Campiglio, L. (2010). La ricchezza (economica) delle famiglie. In E. Scabini & G. Rossi (Eds.), *La ricchezza delle famiglie. Studi Interdisciplinari sulla famiglia* (Vol. 24, pp. 57–73). Milano: Vita & Pensiero.

Comisión Europea. (2009). *Gender segregation in the labour market. Root causes, implications and policy responses in the EU*. Luxemburgo: European Commission's Expert Group on Gender and Employment (EGGE).

Haberkern, K., & Szydlik, M. (2010). State care provision, societal opinion and children's care of older parents in 11 European countries. *Ageing and Society*, *30*(2), 299–323.

Härkönen, J. (2017). *Single-mother poverty: How much do educational differences in single motherhood matter?* (No. 714). LIS Working Paper Series, Stockholm: Stockholm University.

Holstein, J. A., & Gubrium, J. F. (1995). Deprivatization and the construction of domestic life. *Journal of Marriage and Family*, *57*, 894–908.

Lareau, A. (2003). *Unequal childhoods: Class, race, and family life* (Second edition with an update a decade later). Berkeley, CA: University of California Press.

Maldonado, L. C., & Nieuwenhuis, R. (2015). Family policies and single parent poverty in 18 OECD countries, 1978–2008. *Community, Work & Family*, *18*(4), 395–415.

McLanahan, S., & Percheski, C. (2008). Family structure and the reproduction of inequalities. *Annual Review of Sociology*, *34*, 257–276.

Morgan, D. H. J. (1996). *Family connections. An introduction to family studies*. Cambridge: Polity Press.

Morgan, D. H. J. (1999). Risk and family practices: Accounting for change and fluidity in family life. In E. B. Silva, & C. Smart (Eds.), *The new family?* (pp.13–30) London: Sage Publications.

Pahl, R., & Spencer, L. (2004). Personal communities: Not simply families of 'fate' or 'choice'. *Current Sociology*, *52*(2), 199–221.

Robila, M. (Ed.) (2004). *Families in Eastern Europe. Contemporary perspectives in family research* (Vol. 5). Bingley: Emerald Publishing Limited.

Silva, E. B., & Smart, C. (Eds.). (1999). *The new family?* London: Sage Publications.

Stacey, J. (1991). Backward towards the postmodern family. In A. Wolfe (Ed.), *America at century's end*. Berkeley, CA: University of California Press.

Stacey, J. (1993). Is the sky falling? *Journal of Marriage and Family*, *55*, 555–559.

Wilkinson, R. G., & Pickett, K. (2010). *The spirit level: Why greater equality makes societies stronger*. New York, NY: Bloomsbury Press.

Part I
Economic Hardships Experienced by Families

Chapter 1

What Are the Family Characteristics That Better Help to Cope with the Economic Crisis? Evidence from a Large Population Survey in Italy

Sara Mazzucchelli and Miriam Parise

1.1 Introduction

Over the past few years, the global economy has undergone a severe downturn, and financial hardship has become a significant public concern in many countries. The depressed economic climate is affecting many families: the ongoing high rates of unemployment have reduced families' standard of living and have also contributed to changes in several areas of family life.

Italy is the European country with the highest number of people living in 'severe material deprivation'. This emerges from the 2015 Eurostat data, which indicate a significant drop in the number of poor people in Europe, but only a marginal one in Italy. In 2015, 41,092 million poor people lived in Europe; the poverty rate fell to 8.2% of the total number of European citizens, from 9% in 2014. In Italy, by contrast, the poverty rate rose from 11.5% to 11.6%, i.e. a total of 6,982,000 of people living in overt poverty.[1] According to Eurostat (2015), these are people who cannot deal with an unexpected expense, afford a meal with meat every two days or maintain a home. The risk of poverty or the social exclusion indicator in Italy remains stable compared to 2013[2]: the decrease in the percentage of people in severely deprived families (12.3%–11.6%) is offset by an

[1]People at risk of poverty are estimated at 19.4%, while those from families with low work intensity represent 12.1% (ISTAT, 2015). The number is much lower in Germany (3,974 million), where the rate is just 5%, and also in France (2,824 million), with a rate of 4.5%, both countries more populous than Italy (Eurostat).

[2]The ISTAT data are from the survey on the household expenditure, which replaced the previous survey on consumption, sign of a broader consideration of this issue and a tighter connection with the family. The substantial changes introduced have made it necessary to rebuild the historical series of the main indicators since 1997.

Families in Economically Hard Times, 9–29

doi:10.1108/978-1-83909-071-420191004

increase in the percentage of people living in low work intensity families (from 11.3% to 12.1%). The poverty risk estimation is rather unchanged (ISTAT, 2015).

After two years of increase, the incidence of absolute poverty in Italy remains essentially stable: considering the sampling error, the decrease in the number of families and individuals in absolute poverty (6.3% and 7.3%, respectively) is not statistically significant compared to 2013. Absolute poverty is also substantially stable across the country: 4.2% in the north, 4.8% in the centre and 8.6% in the South.

The absolute poverty incidence falls with increasing educational qualifications: if the individual has a diploma, the incidence (3.2%) is almost one-third of that recorded for those with only a primary school certificate (8.4%). In addition, absolute poverty only marginally concerns families headed by entrepreneurs, self-employed people or executives (the incidence is less than 2%), is below average among families with people withdrawn from work (4.4%), increases to 9.7% in families of manual workers and has the highest value among those with a person seeking employment (16.2%) (ISTAT, 2015); finally, the poor are not only immigrants, the number of poor Italians is rising.

The economic crisis has increased the unemployment rate which also extends over time with a direct impact on income. The unemployed are people who turn most to charitable organisations, followed by the working poor and retired people, and people who do not earn enough money to make a meal every day. There are also new categories of poor: indebted, and single or separated mothers. The face of poverty is therefore changing: the crisis has introduced a clear discontinuity (Rovati & Pesenti, 2015).

The incidence of absolute poverty is a real emergency that puts Italy far below the European average – Italy is the country that, compared to 2007, has undergone a greater increase in the percentage of people experiencing food poverty – and without a unitary state project that would ameliorate the situation. In Italy, there are 17,000 charitable organisations working to combat poverty, but research shows that 66% of these institutions would not be able to handle an increase in requests for help (Rovati & Pesenti, 2015).

Interestingly, according to Eurostat (2015), in Italy the incidence of poverty decreases less after public policies in support of poverty, thereby indicating that Italian welfare is unable to intervene significantly. Thus, public policy interventions seem irrelevant: the State allocates an insignificant GDP percentage to family policies and refrains from either legitimising or countering socio-demographic trends. Although social legislation is quite advanced in certain areas in Italy compared with other parts of Europe, the social investments needed to make it effective are negligible. In particular, government policies in the last 30 years have allocated limited assistance to cases of extreme poverty, whilst ignoring the needs of medium-income families and the social cost of their children (Donati, 2010, 2013). In short, in Italy, the family supports the State, not vice versa. In light of this, a strategy to reduce poverty could be a more consistent investment in the family as suggested also by some eminent economists (Campiglio, 2010a, 2010b; Cunha, Heckman, & Schennach, 2009, 2010; Heckman, Humphries, La Fontaine, & Rodriguez, 2012; Heckman,

Stixrud, & Urzua, 2006; Heckman & Vytlacil, 2007). From an economic viewpoint (Campiglio, 2010a, 2010b), the family in fact is:

(1) The foundation of sustainable development (i.e. the continual increase in the country's assets);
(2) The guarantor, through its children, of continuity for the national and social community;
(3) A decisional unit, combining efficiency and fairness, merit and needs, thus reducing the factors likely to cause social imbalance and
(4) The producer of 'human wealth', and thus of 'wealth for the country' (both quantitatively and qualitatively).

What wealth are we talking about? James Heckman, winner of Nobel Memorial Prize in Economic Sciences (with Daniel McFadden) in 2000, 'translates' the theme of wealth in terms of investment (investing in our young people), not just an economic investment. The family generates 'human wealth' as cognitive (intellectual) and non-cognitive (socio-emotional) skills. The former (memory, speech, problem-solving, etc.) is shaped early in life, and the family plays a main role in their formation as the only agency present; the latter (resilience, self-confidence, character traits) are developed through childhood to adolescence, with the family as a main reference point. Investing in human wealth is crucial, as its nature is mostly irreversible and increases with time, unlike physical capital, which is subject to wear and tear (Cunha & Heckman, 2009; Cunha et al., 2010; Heckman et al., 2006, 2012).

According to this perspective, there is a primacy of family relationships paradigmatic of all others (Cigoli & Scabini, 2006; Donati, 2011; Scabini & Rossi, 2006). Moreover, the efficacy of family relationships can be seen in the long term, as a kind of sleeper effect (Scabini & Rossi, 2010): the wealth/generativity of family relationships consists of social capital (SC) (Campiglio, 2010a, 2010b; Rossi, 2010) and children (as the common good). The family provides, with its children, the continuity of the national and local community; moreover, the child, as part of a new generation, is an irreplaceable asset for the overall well-being of the human family (Heckman, 2010).

The theme of SC[3] is instead more complex and allows us to delve into the distinctive trait of the family relationship. The relational perspective allows us to see SC as the *quality of social relations:* its primary function, as a *sui generis* bond, is not instrumental, yet something which favours social relationality. From the

[3]The term SC refers to a multidimensional concept (Bagnasco, Piselli, Pizzorno, & Trigilia, 2001; Folgheraiter, 2004; Smith & Kulynych, 2002; Turner, 2000). Given its extreme complexity and its semantic ambivalence, a thorough analysis of the approaches to SC seems impossible. According to Donati (2007), the different paradigms show significant criticalities: a tendency to identify SC with those relationships which are useful to the individual to gain advantageous exchanges and favours; a conception which mixes individual action with structural conditioning and a lack of references and a reductive vision of the family.

relational perspective, SC is a competitive advantage not only for the individual who uses and consumes it, but also for the society that has to rely on it to regenerate itself. It is good that SC can be seen from the perspective of an individual, as a resource that individuals use for their actions, and from the perspective of our society, as a network of relationships (Donati, 2003; Donati & Prandini, 2007). In this approach, the concept of SC can be understood following four main dimensions (Mazzucchelli, 2007): *network, trust, reciprocity* and *cooperation*. We can thus refer to SC when we are dealing with relations that are simultaneously based on networks, reciprocity, trust and cooperation. The adverb 'simultaneously' shows that these four dimensions are necessary to discuss SC in a relational perspective even when variably present (the *quantum* should be verified). It is possible to distinguish two types of SC:

(1) Primary SC[4] is typical of social relations characterised by primary trust, interpersonal reciprocity as symbolic exchange (gift).
(2) Secondary SC[5] belongs to the sphere of the associations of civil society and is characterised by secondary trust and social reciprocity, and constitutes a 'civicness' factor.

Family SC (or FSC), a subtype of primary SC, is a quality of social relations which derives, even if unintentionally, from the ties among family members and assumes the character of living memory of those relations, conferring on them a distinguishing subjectivity (Prandini, 2007). However, FSC is contingent and depends on the interaction of complex factors, which cannot be predicted and must be carefully evaluated. It is responsible for the creation of reliable bonds, based on gift and reciprocity, which, in turn, are able to produce cooperation-oriented behaviour.

Nonetheless, FSC strongly depends on the real orientation and the nature of the relationships among family members: family relations do not automatically generate FSC, which is related to the quality of family relations, in particular to a well-functioning marital and parental relationship.

To summarise, we can state that family relations, characterised by trust, open to generativity, and ability to produce relational well-being, constitute primary SC (or informal, family kinship SC). When these features become catalysts of a chain reaction that pushes families towards open and greater solidarity, secondary SC (or associative SC) is created. The value of secondary SC increases with bonds that are not linked to a personal action code. They become a resource for the community and leave a mark on the well-being of society (civic or generalised SC). Here we will consider mainly primary and secondary SCs.

---

[4]FSC and kinship SC can be considered subtypes of primary SC; FSC is typical of the family in terms of reciprocal trust, help offered and received, and intensity of contacts, while kinship SC refers to the reciprocal support between a person and his/her family or extended family.

[5]Associative SC and generalised SC can be considered subtypes of secondary SC (Tronca, 2008): Associative SC identifies SC related to the participation in associations; generalised SC is related to trust and reciprocity in general and towards society as a whole.

1.2 The Present Study

In light of the above considerations, the present study does not aim to analyse how families are affected by the economic crisis but aims to identify which factors are likely to have the greatest impact in helping families to cope with these challenges. This goal is quite ambitious as the family nowadays tends to be considered as a burden on the economy, due to the fact that it conditions people's decisions regarding work and mobility, it hinders women's careers, it burdens women with stress, it condemns people to social immobility and it forces the State and companies to adopt legislative measures aimed at supporting work and family reconciliation. Thus, the economy appears to 'see' the family only as a function of consumption; actually, the family is scarcely recognised as a subject able to regulate and structure the market (Mazzucchelli, 2012).

Starting from such challenging statements, the present study intends to answer this research question: whilst financial and social difficulties are affecting a growing number of households, what is the role of the family? In other words, and more precisely, what are the family characteristics that help to better cope with the crisis? The underlying hypothesis is that the more the family is characterised by stability, commitment and intergenerational solidarity; can count on a solid marital and parental alliance and belongs to relational networks marked by reciprocity, trust and cooperation, the more it is able to cope with the crisis. We will try to verify this hypothesis focussing on the capacity to save money (vs fall into debt) as a marker of the ability to cope with the crisis; in particular, we will analyse whether and how some family structural and relational characteristics impact on this capacity.

1.2.1 Data

To answer these research questions, we relied on data from a large population survey on family relationships in Italy (Donati, 2012a, 2012b), carried out between March 2011 and April 2011 and financed by the Pontificium Consilium Pro Familia.[6] The survey was based on a probabilistic sample of individuals representing Italy's resident population, in a couple relationship, in the 30 to 55 year age bracket, classified according to gender, age bracket (30–35, 36–40, 41–45, 46–50, 51–55) and area of residence (Northwest, Northeast, Centre, South, Isles). The interviewees were selected by randomly digitising landline and mobile telephone numbers taken from the telephone lists of the sampled towns. Later, their eligibility for participating in the survey was restricted to individuals within the age bracket considered in the study and being in a couple relationship. A home appointment was made for each one for submission of the 40-question questionnaire created by using the computer assisted personal interviewing method. The opportunity to carry out face-to-face dialogue has led to the collection of reliable data, with very low rates of unanswered questions. The data were computerised, and 89 variables were obtained.

---

[6]The results were presented at the World Meeting of Families, Milan, 2012.

The sample (see Table A1), theoretically set to a maximum of 3,500 cases, was obtained through two-stage sampling. First, 21 towns were selected across Italy's five macro-regions (Northwest, Northeast, Centre, South, and Isles), then prospective interviewees were identified. Subsequently, the interviews were distributed across the selected towns considering the weight of each macro-area. For each area, the interviews were distributed equally among the different towns. The reference universe amounted to a total of 23,439,217 units, while the sample included 3,527 individuals[7] (Tronca, 2012).

Participants answered a series of questions on the following areas: socio-demographic aspects, solidarity and openness to the social context, SC, trust in institutions, couple relationship, parent–child relationship (if they had children), work–family balance and representation of their social context and of institutions (see Table A2).

For the purpose of this study, we decided to focus on the subsample of people with children ($N = 2{,}039$) in order to consider all the aspects covered by the questionnaire (including the parent–child relationship). In this subsample, 45.4% were men and 54.6% were women, while the mean age was 44 years (age range 30–55). As to the geographic distribution, 46.5% lived in the North, 18.6% in the Centre and 34.8% in the South of Italy. Cohabiting people made up 4.5%, 81.9% were married for the first time, 4.5% were married for the second time, 3.8% were separated single parents, 3.9% were separated parents who lived with a new partner and 1.3% were widowed. While 47.9% had one child, 42.5% had two children and 9.6% had three or more children.

1.2.2 Methodology and Data Analyses

As previously outlined, we focused on the capacity to save money (vs fall into debt) as a marker of the ability to cope with the crisis, analysing in particular whether and how some family structural and relational characteristics impact on this capacity.

In line with international big surveys (i.e. European Values Study – EVS), a variable was specifically devised to analyse this point: depending on the answer given to the question, 'With regard to your economic condition, at the end of the month you…', two groups were created: people who, at the end of the month, 'manage to save some money' (66.2%) versus those who fall into debt (33.8%) (Table 1.1). For the purpose of this study, we did not consider the group of people who did not have problems making ends meet.

We performed different types of analyses. In the first step, descriptive analyses such as Chi square tests and *t*-tests were used to get a description of these two groups in terms of structural characteristics[8] and relational characteristics.[9] We shall present here those characteristics that clearly differentiate the two groups.

[7]Please, see Table A1 in appendix for an in-depth description of the original sample.

[8]Geographical area; marital status; educational qualification; help received from the grandparents; job; sex; number and age of children; age cohort.

[9]Couple satisfaction; co-parenting; primary and secondary SCs; trust in institutions.

Table 1.1. Description of the Two Groups Created Depending on the Economic Condition (Save Money vs Fall into Debt).

Economic Condition: At the End of the Month You…	N	**Valid %**
Save some money	618	66.2
Fall into debt	316	33.8
Total	934	100.0

Logistic regressions were then used to identify those characteristics that are better associated with the ability to save money, and then to cope with the crisis.

1.2.3 Results

Chi square tests were performed to examine the relationship between the ability to save money or not and the following *socio-demographic characteristics*: sex; age cohort; geographical area; marital status/family composition; number of children; help received by grandparents; educational qualification, and job. *T-tests* were conducted to examine the association between the ability to save money or not and the following *relational characteristics*: couple relationship satisfaction; co-parenting; primary and secondary SC, and trust in institutions.

As for structural characteristics, the two groups differed significantly in terms of geographical area (χ^2 (2, N = 934) = 33.64, p = 0.000), marital status/family composition (χ^2 (4, N = 934) = 36.61, p = 0.000), educational qualification (χ^2 (3, N = 932) = 155.88, p = 0.000), help received from the grandparents (χ^2 (1, N = 928) = 12.37, p = 0.000) and job (χ^2 (1, N = 934) = 149.32, p = 0.000) (Table 1.2). No differences were found for gender, age cohort or number of children.

T-tests for independent samples were performed to examine the relationship between the ability to save money or not and the following relational variables: couple satisfaction; co-parenting; primary SC; secondary SC, and trust in institutions. The results showed that the groups differed significantly in terms of couple relationship satisfaction, co-parenting, primary and secondary SC, and trust in institutions. In particular, with respect to those who fall into debt, those able to save money reported higher levels of couple satisfaction (t (927) = −6.33, p = 0.000; save money: M = 8.31, SD = 1.55; debts: M = 7.62, SD = 1.62; Fig. 1.1), co-parenting (t (926) = −5.76; p = 0.000; save money: M = 7.88, SD = 1.79; debts: M = 7.24, SD = 1.52; Fig. 1.2); secondary SC (t (932) = −4.87; p = 0.000; save money: M = 6.56, SD = 1.39; debts: M = 6.06, SD = 1.56; Fig. 1.3), primary SC (t (932) = −6.68; p = 0.000; save money: M = 7.89, SD = 1.36; debts: M = 7.21, SD = 1.53; Fig. 1.4) and trust in institutions (t (930) = −6.06; p = 0.000; save money: M = 6.23, SD = 1.31; debts: M = 5.65, SD = 1.51; Fig. 1.5).

In summary, those who manage to *save money* live in Northern or Central Italy, are in their first marriage, have a high level of educational qualification, can

Table 1.2. Structural Characteristic of the Two Groups (Save Money vs Fall into Debt).

	Save Money	**Fall into Debt**
Where do they live?	North–Centre	South and Isles
Marital status/family composition	Married people (first marriage)	Separated/divorced people (single or in a new relationship) People at their second marriage Widow/widower
Educational qualification	High	Low
Help by the grandparents	Yes	No
Job	Employees (public and private sector) Self-employed – freelance professional	Unemployed Redundant workers Atypical workers

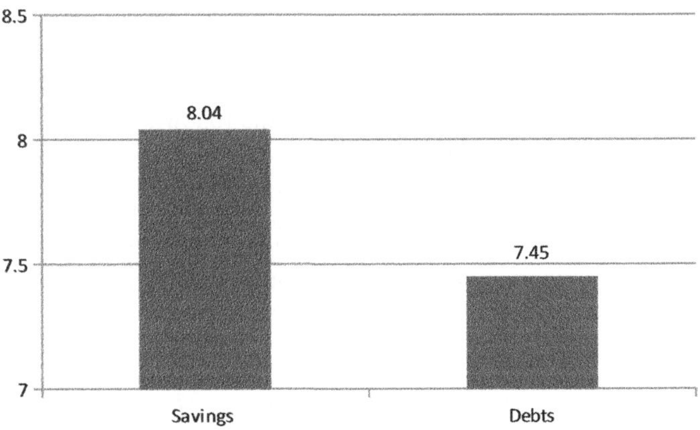

Fig. 1.1. Levels of Couple Satisfaction in the Two Groups.
Note: Couple satisfaction was assessed with the item 'To what extent are you satisfied with your couple relationship?' (Norton, 1983; Parise, Manzi, Donato, & Iafrate, 2017). Responses were given on a 10-point Likert scale: 1 = not at all; 10 = extremely.

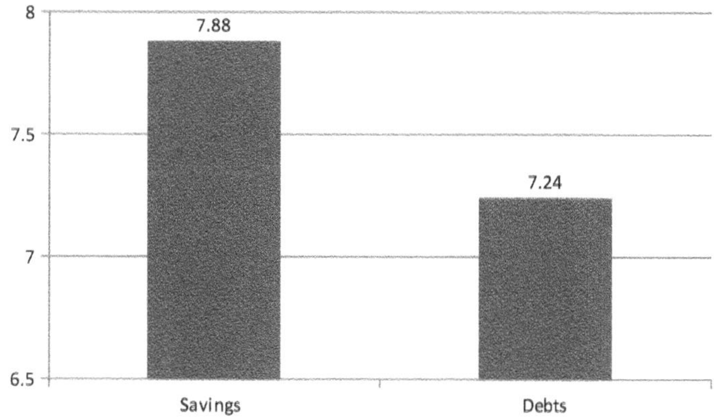

Fig. 1.2. Levels of Co-parenting in the Two Groups.
Note: Co-parenting was assessed with the item 'To what extent are you able to deal with the various educational and caring problems related to the growth of your children in a mutual agreement with your partner?' (Ranieri et al., 2016). Responses were given on a 10-point Likert scale: 1 = not at all; 10 = extremely.

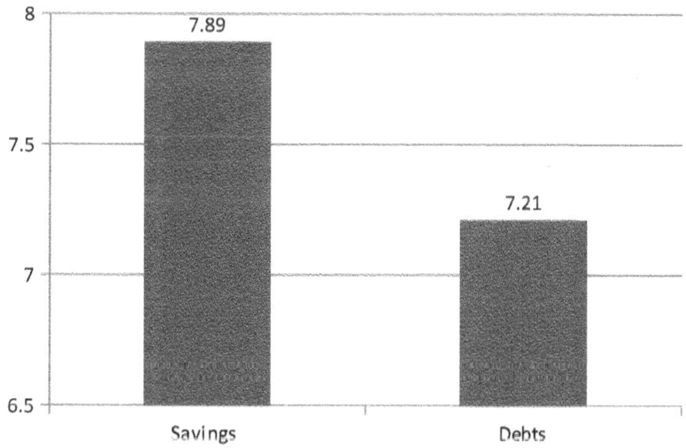

Fig. 1.3. Levels of Primary Social Capital in the Two Groups.
Note: To assess primary social capital, we computed a mean score with the following three items: 'In my family people are prone to help the other members of the family instead of claiming credits toward them', which was rated on a 10-point Likert scale (1= definitely no; 10 = definitely yes), and 'In case of urgent need, to what extent can you really count on your close kin?' and 'In general, to what extent in your family do you help each other?', which were rated on a 10-point Likert scale: 1 = definitely yes; 10 = extremely.

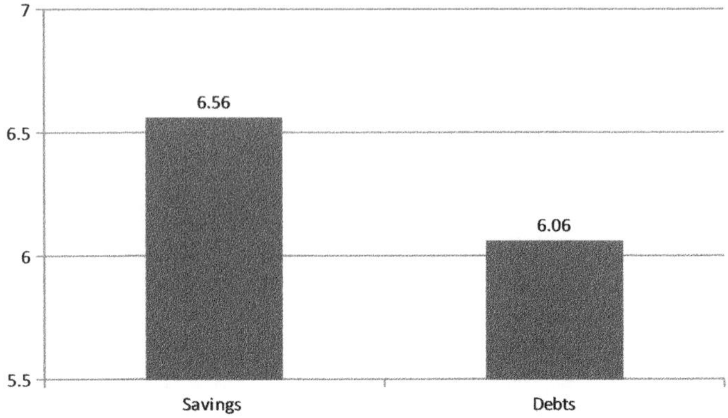

Fig. 1.4. Levels of Secondary Social Capital in the Two Groups.
Note: To assess secondary social capital, we computed a mean score with the following eight items: 'Generally, in my family there is a trustworthy attitude toward my neighbours', 'In my family there are members who dedicate their time to helping people who do not live in my family', 'In my family, there are members who participate in associative activities (social, cultural, religious, political)', which were rated on a 10-point Likert scale (1= definitely no; 10 = definitely yes), and 'How often do you participate as a parent in school activities or in other activities regarding your child (e.g. participating in meetings, knowing sport trainers or educators, knowing the other parents of groups attended by your child)?', 'How often do you and your close kin listen to people outside your family (e.g. friends or other people) and help them to overcome their problems?', 'How often do you and your close kin help people outside your family (e.g. friends or other people) to overcome their marital or family problems?', 'How often do you and your close kin help people outside your family (e.g. friends or other people) to care for their children (helping them to do the homework, hosting them)?', 'How often do you and your close kin help people outside your family (e.g. friends or other people) to care for elderly people?', which were rated on a 10-point Likert scale: 1 = never; 10 = very often.

count on the help from the grandparents, are employees both in the public and private sector, or self-employed. They report higher levels of relationship satisfaction, co-parenting, SC and trust in institutions. Those who are forced to fall into debt live in Southern Italy or in the Isles, are separated/divorced (single or in a new relationship) or in their second marriage or are widows/widowers, have a low level of educational qualification, can rarely count on help from the grand-parents and are unemployed, redundant or atypical workers. Moreover, they report lower levels of relationship satisfaction, co-parenting, SC and trust in institutions.

To find out whether a significant association exists between the ability to save money and the structural and relational-social variables presented above, we performed two maximum likelihood estimation logistic regressions. Logistic regressions have the goal of detecting, all other attributes controlled for in the

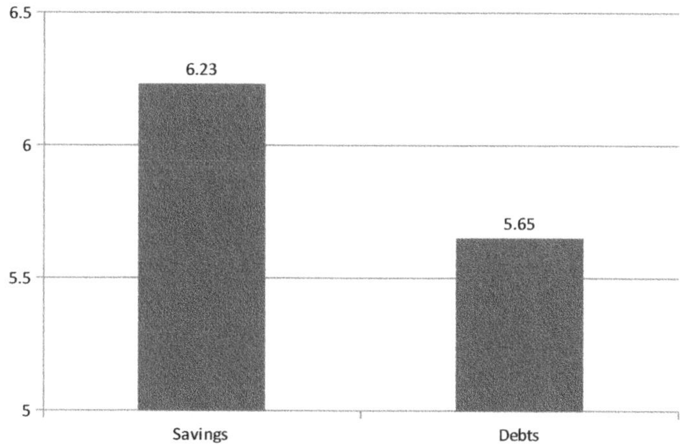

Fig. 1.5. Levels of Trust in Institutions in the Two Groups.
Note: To assess trust in institutions we computed a mean score with the following 10 items: 'To what extent, in your opinion, are these social institutions…[the church, the school and the university, the political system, companies and firms, banks, the family, the judiciary, the security force, the mass media, the public administration] able to contribute to the development of our country?', which were rated on a 10-point Likert scale: 1 = not at all; 10 = extremely.

model being equal, the odds ratio that a certain result (the dependent variable) may take place, depending on the independent variables (Lanzetti, Lombi, & Marzulli, 2008).

The ability to save money was set as a dependent variable. In the first regression, some structural characteristics were chosen as independent variables (Table 1.3): geographical area (North, Centre, South and Isles), help from the grandparents (yes/no), marital status (not cohabiting unmarried partners, cohabiting partners, married in first marriage, remarried or separated in a new relationship, separated/divorced or widowed), job (students, unemployed, redundant and atypical workers, housewives/retired, employees in the public sector, employees in the private sector, self-employed), and educational qualification (low, medium, high). In the second regression, some relational variables (i.e. couple satisfaction, co-parenting, SC and trust in institutions) were chosen as independent variables (Table 1.4).

In the first regression, we used a 'predictive' logistic regression model with dichotomous dependent variable and more multimodal independent variables by the method 'Enter' to see the odds ratio of all variables considered.

The results highlight that people who live in the North or in the Centre of Italy are more likely to save money than those who live in the South or in the Isles. Moreover, housewives and retired people, employees in both the public and the private sectors and self-employed are more likely to save money than students, the

Table 1.3. Results of Regression on Structural Characteristics.

	Exp(B)	Significance
Constant	0.004	0.000
Geographical area (ref. South and Isles)		
Centre	1.920	0.010
North	2.556	0.000
Help by grandparents (ref. No)		
Yes	1.256	0.202
Job (ref. Students, unemployed, redundant and atypical workers)		
Housewives/retired	18.157	0.000
Employees private sector	12.756	0.000
Employees public sector	12.922	0.000
Self-employed	30.610	0.000
Marital status (ref. Separated people/widowers)		
Not cohabiting dating partners	0.000	0.999
Cohabiting partners	5.628	0.004
Married people (first marriage)	6.892	0.000
People in second marriage/ separated people in a new relationship	3.581	0.008
Educational qualification (ref. elementary, middle, vocational school)		
High school degree	4.232	0.000
University degree	21.886	0.000

Table 1.4. Results of Regression on Relational Characteristics.

	Exp(B)	Significance
Constant	0.016	0.000
Couple satisfaction	1.136	0.012
Co-parenting	1.108	0.042
Secondary social capital	1.078	0.192
Primary social capital	1.104	0.004
Trust in institutions	1.234	0.000

unemployed, redundant and atypical workers. Finally, a medium and a high level of education increases the probability of saving money, in comparison with a low educational level, as well as being married (for the first or second time) or cohabiting, compared with being separated or widowed. The help received from grandparents seems insignificant. Other things being equal, the most significant predictors of the ability to save money appear to be job (in particular, being self-employed), educational qualification (in particular, holding a university degree), marital status (in particular, being married in the first marriage), and geographical area (in particular, residing in the North of Italy).

In the second regression (relational predictors), we used a 'predictive' logistic regression model with dichotomous dependent variables and more continuous independent variables by the method 'Enter' in order to see the odds ratio of all variables considered.

The results highlight that people who have a higher degree of couple satisfaction, co-parenting, primary SC and trust in institutions are more likely to save money than those who score lower on these constructs. Secondary SC appears not to be a significant predictor. The most significant relational predictors are trust in institutions and primary SC.

1.3 Conclusion

The aim of this study was to identify what factors are likely to have the greatest impact in helping families to cope with the economic challenges in Italy. In particular, we focused on the capacity to save money (vs fall into debt) as a marker of the ability to cope with the crisis, analysing whether and how some family *structural* (geographical area; marital status; educational qualification; help received from the grandparents; job; sex; number and age of children; age cohort) and *relational* (couple satisfaction; co-parenting; primary and secondary SC; trust in institutions) characteristics affect this capacity.

Our hypothesis was that the more the family is characterised by stability, commitment, intergenerational solidarity; can count on a solid marital and parental alliance; and belongs to relational networks marked by reciprocity, trust and cooperation, the more it is able to protect against the effects of the crisis.

Results show that from a structural point of view the possibility of making some saving is linked with job, educational qualification and marital status.[10] The

[10]Despite these interesting results, we are aware that the specification of other important independent variables, unfortunately lacking in our survey, could have helped improve our understanding of the ability of households to save money at the end of the month. The most relevant variables in this context could have been income level, the presence of one or more income earners in the household (i.e. dual- or one-earner families), the access to social benefits like unemployment provisions and the presence or absence of debts (mainly mortgage).

first two features confirm data (already in the economic literature and in studies on poverty) regarding the possibility of accessing more stable and profitable job positions. It is interesting, and in line with the hypotheses, to highlight the decisive role of marital status; this result is consistent with studies on marriage and divorce (Amato, 2010; Amato & James, 2010; Waite & Gallagher, 2000).

Relational variables seem to be significant as well, and, in particular, primary SC, trust in institutions and couple satisfaction, dimensions which are both internal and also pertain to the link between the family and the context in which it lives (Rossi, 2011). The result regarding couple satisfaction is also interesting as it shows that it is not only family structure (marital status) which has an impact on economic condition but also the quality of the couple relationship (Donati, 2012a).

Moreover, our results show that being in a family deeply embedded in the social context and with a high level of generalised trust also counts (Rossi, Bonini, & Mazzucchelli, 2011). This is in line with the literature which indicates that family SC is a source of relational, social and economic well-being. Social connections have, in fact, been recognised as critical due to their instrumental power: social connections have a positive impact on health, well-being, job opportunities, financial security and physical safety (Cattell, 2001; Kahneman & Krueger, 2006; Putnam, 1995, 2000).

Cultivating good relationships in the place where one lives may protect against both material and relational poverty which are quite common, especially in urban contexts (Bramanti, 2015). We are facing a new form of social differentiation for families: being embedded or not in competent networks, characterised by reciprocity and cooperation, can be crucial to the quality and the well-being of the family.

Going back to the initial research questions, our data suggest the characteristics that help better facing the crisis – in terms of a higher capacity of making savings – are a family based on a committed and stable bond (marriage or a stable couple relationship), with high levels of couple satisfaction, primary SC and trust in institutions.

In light of this result, additional questions emerge. How can we support the family? What are the family policies that can promote family well-being and enhance the resources that families use to deal with the daily challenges (parenting tasks, professional development, elderly care, etc.)?

In line with some scholars (Campiglio, 2010a, 2010b; Cigoli, 2010; Rossi, 2010), we found that the family can counter the crisis and become a potential recovery factor. For this to happen, it is necessary to invest in the family through policies directed towards the valorisation of human heritage, its development potential and freedom of choice of the generational chain, and to consider the long-term effects of this type of investment, bearing in mind that only family policy can presuppose development policy.

References

Amato, P. R. (2010). Research on divorce: Continuing trends and new developments. *Journal of Marriage and Family*, *72*(3), 650–666.

Amato, P. R., & James, S. (2010). Divorce in Europe and the United States: Commonalities and differences across nations. *Family Science*, *1*(1), 2–13.

Bagnasco, M., Piselli, F., Pizzorno, A., & Trigilia, C. (2001). *Il Capitale sociale. Istruzioni per l'uso*. Bologna: Il Mulino.

Bramanti, D. (2015). Capitale sociale e ambiente amichevole: quali risorse per le famiglie con figli (0-13). *Sociologia e Politiche Sociali*, *18*(2), 130–151.

Campiglio, L. (2010a). Famiglie e figli: verso una macroeconomia del bene comune. In P. Donati (Ed.), *Il costo dei figli. Quale welfare per le famiglie? Rapporto CISF 2009 sulla Famiglia in Italia* (pp. 194–207). Milano: FrancoAngeli.

Campiglio, L. (2010b). La ricchezza (economica) delle famiglie. In E. Scabini & G. Rossi (Eds.), *La ricchezza delle famiglie* (Vol. 24, pp. 57–73). Studi Interdisciplinari sulla famiglia. Milano: Vita & Pensiero.

Cattell, V. (2001). Poor people, poor places, and poor health: the mediating role of social networks and social capital. *Social Science & Medicine*, *52*(10), 1501–1516.

Cigoli, V. (2010). Economia, psicologia, generatività. In E. Scabini & G. Rossi (Eds.), *La ricchezza delle famiglie* (Vol. 24, pp. 149–157). Studi Interdisciplinari sulla famiglia. Milano: Vita & Pensiero.

Cigoli, V., & Scabini, E. (2006). *Family identity, ties, symbols and transitions*. Mahwah, NJ: Lawrence Erlbaum Associates.

Cunha, F., Heckman, J. J., & Schennach, S. (2009). *Estimating the elasticity of intertemporal substitution in the formation of cognitive and non-cognitive skills*. Mimeo.

Cunha, F., & Heckman, J. J. (2009). The economics and psychology of inequality and human development. *Journal of the European Economic Association*, *7*(2–3), 320–364.

Cunha, F., Heckman, J. J., & Schennach, S. M. (2010). Estimating the technology of cognitive and noncognitive skill formation. *Econometrica*, *78*(3), 883–931.

Donati, P. (2007). *L'approccio relazionale al capitale sociale*. Sociologia e politiche sociali.

Donati, P. (Ed.). (2003). *Famiglia e capitale sociale nella società italiana*. Cinisello Balsamo: Edizioni San Paolo.

Donati, P. (Ed.). (2010). *Il costo dei figli. Quale welfare per le famiglie. XI Rapporto CISF sulla famiglia in Italia*. Milano: FrancoAngeli.

Donati, P. (2011). *Relational sociology. A new paradigm for the social sciences*. London; New York, NY: Routledge.

Donati, P. (2012a). *La relazione di coppia oggi – Una sfida per la famiglia, Rapporto Cisf 2011 sulla famiglia in Italia*. Trento: Erickson.

Donati, P. (2012b). *La famiglia come risorsa della società*. Bologna: Il Mulino.

Donati, P. (2013). *La famiglia, il genoma che fa vivere la società*. Soveria Mannelli: Rubbettino.

Donati, P., & Prandini, R. (2007). The family in the light of a new relational theory of primary, secondary and generalized social capital. *International Review of Sociology – Revue Internationale de Sociologie*, *17*(2), 209–223.

Eurostat. (2015). *Smarter, greener, more inclusive? – Indicators to support the Europe 2020 strategy – 2015 edition*, Eurostat: Kirchberg. Retrieved from http://ec.europa.eu/eurostat/documents/3217494/6655013/KS-EZ-14-001-EN-N.pdf/a5452f6e-8190-4f30-8996-41b1306f7367. Accessed on October 6, 2016.

Folgheraiter, F. (2004). Capitale sociale. *Lavoro Sociale*, *4*, 133–140.

Heckman, J. J. (2010). Investire nei nostri giovani. Lezioni dall'economia e dalla psicologia. In E. Scabini & G. Rossi (Eds.), *La ricchezza delle famiglie* (Vol. 24, pp. 17–42). Studi Interdisciplinari sulla famiglia. Milano: Vita & Pensiero.

Heckman, J. J., Humphries, J. E., La Fontaine, P. A., & Rodriguez, P. L. (2012). Taking the easy way out: How the GED testing program induces students to drop out. *Journal of labor economics*, *30*(3), 495–520.

Heckman, J. J., Stixrud, J., & Urzua, S. (2006). The effects of cognitive and noncognitive abilities on labor market outcomes and social behaviour. *Journal of Labor Economics*, *24*(3), 411–482.

Heckman, J. J., & Vytlacil, E. J. (2007). Econometric evaluation of social programs, part I: Causal models, structural models and econometric policy evaluation. *Handbook of Econometrics*, *6*, 4779–4874.

Istituto Nazionale di Statistica. (2015). *La povertà in Italia*, Istituto Nazionale di Statistica: Roma. Retrieved from http://www.istat.it/it/archivio/164869. Accessed on September 30, 2016.

Kahneman, D., & Krueger, A. B. (2006). Developments in the measurement of subjective well-being. *Journal of Economic perspectives*, *20*(1), 3–24.

Lanzetti, C., Lombi, L., & Marzulli, M. (2008). *Metodi qualitativi e quantitativi per la ricerca sociale in sanità*. Milano: FrancoAngeli.

Mazzucchelli, S. (2007). *Formazione alla genitorialità e capitale sociale. Il contributo sociologico alla valutazione*. Milano: Unicopli.

Mazzucchelli, S. (2012). Come la famiglia sostiene il mondo del lavoro. In P. Donati (Ed.), *La famiglia come risorsa della società* (pp. 97–120). Bologna: Il Mulino.

Norton, R. (1983). Measuring marital quality: A critical look at the dependent variable. *Journal of Marriage and Family*, *45*(1), 141–151.

Parise, M., Manzi, C., Donato, S., & Iafrate, R. (2017). Free to love? The role of intrusive parenting for young adult children's romantic relationship quality. *Journal of Prevention & Intervention in the Community*, *45*(3), 187–201.

Prandini, R. (2007). Il capitale sociale familiare in prospettiva relazionale: come definirlo, misurarlo e sussidiarlo. *Sociologia e Politiche Sociali*, *10*(1), 45–67.

Putnam, R. D. (1995). Bowling alone: America's declining social capital. *Journal of Democracy*, *6*(1), 65–78.

Putnam, R. D. (2000). *Bowling alone. The collapse and revival of American community*. New York, NY: Simon & Schuster.

Ranieri, S., Bertoni, A., Pagani, A. F., Donato, S., Rosnati, R., & Iafrate, R. (2016). Coparenting in divorced and intact families and children's psychosocial adjustment. In S. Grant (Ed.), *Divorce: Risk factors, patterns and impact on children's well-being* (pp. 77–88). Hauppauge, NY: Nova Publisher.

Rossi, G. (2010). La famiglia come capitale sociale. In E. Scabini & G. Rossi (Eds.), *La ricchezza delle famiglie* (Vol. 24, pp. 113–130). Studi Interdisciplinari sulla famiglia. Milano: Vita & Pensiero.

Rossi, G. (2011). Legami e percorsi di coppia: le trasformazioni della coniugalità in Italia. In G. Rovati (Ed.), *Uscire dalle crisi – I valori degli italiani alla prova* (pp. 143–179). Milano: Vita & Pensiero.

Rossi, G., Bonini, R., & Mazzucchelli, S. (2011). Family relations as social capital. In R. Jallinoja & E. D. Widmer (Eds.), *Families and kinship in contemporary Europe: Rules and practices of relatedness* (pp. 203–215). Basingstoke: Palgrave Macmillan.

Rovati, G., & Pesenti, L. (2015). *Food poverty, food bank. Aiuti alimentari e inclusione sociale.* Milano: Vita & Pensiero.

Scabini, E., & Rossi, G. (2006). *Le parole della famiglia* (Vol. 21). Studi Interdisciplinari sulla famiglia. Milano: Vita & Pensiero.

Scabini, E., & Rossi, G. (2010). Ricchezza delle famiglie e tempo di crisi. In E. Scabini & G. Rossi (Eds.), *La ricchezza delle famiglie* (Vol. 24, pp. 7–16). Studi Interdisciplinari sulla famiglia. Milano: Vita & Pensiero.

Smith, S. S., & Kulynych, J. (2002). It may be social, but why is it capital? The social construction of social capital and the politics of language. *Politics & Society*, *30*(1), 149–186.

Tronca, L. (2008). La consistenza del capitale sociale, le sue varie forme e la sua incidenza sull'impegno civico. In P. Donati & L. Tronca (Eds.), *Il capitale sociale degli italiani. Le radici familiari, comunitarie ed associative del civismo*. Milano: FrancoAngeli.

Tronca, L. (2012). Appendice metodologica. In P. Donati (Ed.), *La famiglia come risorsa della società* (pp. 327–336). Bologna: Il Mulino.

Turner, J. H. (2000). The formation of social capital. In P. Dasgupta & I. Serageldin (Eds.), *Social capital and multiphase perspectives* (pp. 113–145). Washington, DC: World Bank.

Waite, L., & Gallagher, M. (2000). *The case for marriage: Why married people are happier, healthier, and better off financially*. New York, NY: Doubleday.

Appendix

Table A1. Sample Composition.

		Gender		Age (Years)					Geographical Area		
	Total	M	F	30–35	36–40	41–45	46–50	51–55	North	Centre	South and Isles
Married without children	11.7	12.0	11.3	15.1	9.7	8.8	10.6	14.6	11.2	13.0	11.6
Married with one child	24.8	25.3	24.4	17.8	27.4	28.0	26.8	24.6	25.9	24.5	23.6
Married with children	27.3	25.2	29.4	13.1	21.2	31.7	35.7	38.2	24.2	22.9	34.3
Single parent with one child	2.5	1.3	3.7	2.1	2.6	2.7	2.4	2.7	2.8	2.4	2.0
Single parent with children	1.4	0.3	2.4	0.9	0.7	0.8	2.5	2.3	1.8	1.0	1.1
Cohabiting, without children	13.4	15.2	11.7	23.0	16.1	10.9	8.3	6.7	15.6	15.9	9.0
Cohabiting, with one child	3.3	2.8	3.7	3.1	4.1	4.5	2.4	1.8	3.4	4.0	2.6
Cohabiting, with children	1.8	1.4	2.1	0.4	2.5	2.1	2.2	1.7	1.8	2.2	1.5
Family including other relatives	4.1	4.1	4.2	10.7	4.1	1.7	1.8	1.3	2.9	3.9	6.0
Living alone	9.7	12.4	7.1	13.8	11.6	8.8	7.3	6.0	10.6	10.2	8.2
Total	100.0	100.0	100.0	100.0	100.0	100.0	100.0	100.0	100.0	100.0	100.0
Absolute Value	3522	1,747	1,775	769	731	753	672	597	1,646	694	1,182
How many in the family? (average value)	2.9	2.8	3.0	2.6	2.8	3.0	3.1	3.2	2.8	2.8	3.1

Table A2. Variables and Operationalisation.

Variables	Operationalisation
Sex	Male, female
Age cohort	30–35; 36–40; 41–45; 46–50; 51–55
Number of children	1; 2; 3 or more
Geographical area	North, Centre, South and Isles
Help by grandparents	Yes, no
Marital status	Not cohabiting unmarried partners; cohabiting partners; married at first marriage; remarried or separated in a new relationship; separated/divorced or widowed
Job	Students; unemployed; redundant and atypical workers; housewives/retired; employees in the public sector; employees in the private sector; self-employed
Educational qualification	Low; medium; high
Couple satisfaction	To what extent are you satisfied with your couple relationship? (10-point Likert scale: 1 = not at all; 10 = extremely)
Co-parenting	To what extent are you able to deal with the various educational and caring problems related to the growth of your children in a mutual agreement with your partner? (10-point Likert scale: 1 = not at all; 10 = extremely)
Primary SC ($\alpha = 0.67$)	In my family people are prone to help the other members of the family instead of claiming credits toward them? (10-point Likert scale: 1 = definitely no; 10 = definitely yes)

Table A2. *(Continued)*

Variables	Operationalisation
	In case of urgent need, to what extent can you really count on your close kin? (10-point Likert scale: 1 = not at all; 10 = extremely)
	In general, to what extent in your family do you help each other? (10-point Likert scale: 1 = not at all; 10 = extremely)
Secondary SC (α = 0.78)	Generally, in my family there is a trustworthy attitude toward my neighbours. (10-point Likert scale: 1 = definitely no; 10 = definitely yes)
	In my family there are members who dedicate their time to helping people who do not live in my family. (10-point Likert scale: 1 = definitely no; 10 = definitely yes)
	In my family, there are members who participate in associative activities (social, cultural, religious, political) (10-point Likert scale: 1 = definitely no; 10 = definitely yes)
	How often do you participate as a parent in school activities or in other activities regarding your child (e.g. participating in meetings, knowing sport trainers or educators, knowing the other parents of groups attended by your child)? (10-point Likert scale: 1 = never; 10 = very often)
	How often do you and your close kin listen to people outside your family (e.g. friends or other people) and help them to overcome their problems? (10-point Likert scale: 1 = never; 10 = very often)
	How often do you and your close kin help people outside your family (e.g. friends or other people) to overcome their marital or family problems? (10-point Likert scale: 1 = never; 10 = very often)

	How often do you and your close kin help people outside your family (e.g. friends or other people) to care for their children (helping them to do the homework, hosting them)? (10-point Likert scale: 1 = never; 10 = very often) How often do you and your close kin help people outside your family (e.g. friends or other people) to care for elderly people? (10-point Likert scale: 1 = never; 10 = very often)
Trust in institutions ($\alpha = 0.86$)	To what extent, in your opinion, are these social institutions able to contribute to the development of our country? The church The school and the university The political system Companies and firms Banks The family The judiciary The security force Mass media The public administration (10-point Likert scale: 1 = not at all; 10 = extremely)

Chapter 2

Social Inequality and Intergenerational Solidarity in European Welfare States

Ronny König, Bettina Isengard and Marc Szydlik

2.1 Introduction

Intergenerational support across the entire life course is an important characteristic of parent–child relationships in contemporary societies, especially in times of societal crises and the withdrawal of the welfare state. Despite the consequences of social and demographic changes in recent decades, the relations and bonds between parents and their (adult) children remain impressively strong. Against the backdrop of increasing average life expectancy, children are able to spend more lifetime together with their parents and even their grandparents than ever before. This quantitative extension of shared lifetime together has resulted in a qualitative modification of the relationships between the generations in which families are connected by various forms of solidarity such as strong emotional closeness (affectual solidarity; see, e.g. Bertogg & Szydlik, 2016), contact and shared activities (associational solidarity; see, e.g. König, 2016) and especially transfers of money and time (functional solidarity; see, e.g. Brandt & Deindl, 2013; Deindl & Brandt, 2011; Igel & Szydlik, 2011; Isengard, König, & Szydlik, 2017; Isengard & Szydlik, 2012; König, 2016; Szydlik, 2008, 2016).

As previous research has mainly focused on the consequences of intergenerational solidarity on inequality (e.g. social mobility research), there is a lack of research on the influence of social inequality on families, including intergenerational solidarity and cohesion. Although many studies have intensively analysed individual types of solidarity in the past (see, e.g. Albertini, Kohli, & Vogel, 2007 for money; Deindl & Brandt, 2011 for help; Haberkern & Szydlik, 2010 for care; Igel & Szydlik, 2011 for grandchild care), a joint analysis of different types of functional solidarity against the background of individual, familial and social inequality is still missing.

However, family cohesion and support is important – especially in times of societal and economic crisis. It therefore seems necessary to analyse transfers of money and time, specifically, in the light of social inequality in order to penetrate the private support system among families in general and between generations in particular. Therefore, this contribution addresses this research gap

Families in Economically Hard Times, 31–51

doi:10.1108/978-1-83909-071-420191005

by analysing how social inequality at the individual, familial as well as societal level matters for the extent and distribution of different transfer forms and directions of functional solidarity of adult family generations in Europe.

Our analyses are based on the fifth wave of the Survey of Health, Ageing and Retirement in Europe (SHARE) including 14 European countries: Austria, Belgium, the Czech Republic, Denmark, Estonia, France, Germany, Italy, Luxembourg, the Netherlands, Slovenia, Spain, Sweden and Switzerland. Our sample includes 65,682 adult children from 31,048 parental households (respondents). To analyse the different determinants of solidarity from parents to children as well as from children to parents in view of inequality factors, we have estimated multilevel logistic regressions involving three levels (adult children nested in parental households nested in countries). The dependent variables capture monetary support and time transfers, including practical and administrative help, care as well as grandchild care.

This chapter is organised as follows. First, we give an outline of previous research and its theoretical implications including the hypotheses that we have tested empirically. The subsequent section describes the data, operationalisation of the variables and methods. The empirical results are presented and discussed thereafter. In closing, we provide a short conclusion.

2.2 Theoretical and Empirical Background

Although individual forms of functional solidarity between family members have been a frequent subject of research over the past years, little is known about the influence of social inequality on intergenerational solidarity. Moreover, past research has generally overlooked the complexity of social inequality and has mostly referred to the society level only. This chapter addresses this gap and examines the determinants of family cohesion with regard to social inequality at different levels, namely the individual, family and socio-cultural context.

To explain differences in the degree of familial relationships, we have used a theoretical model designed to explain many aspects of intergenerational relations (see Szydlik, 2008, 2016). In this way, solidarity between generations can be understood as a complex and multi-layered construct composed of six dimensions – namely, associative, affective, consensual, functional, normative and structural solidarity (Bengtson & Roberts, 1991). As our interest here is in the giving and taking of money and time in adult parent–child relationships, we have focused exclusively on the dimension of functional solidarity, which is defined as help in the form of money and time as well as support between family members of two generations.

According to the assumptions of the theoretical framework, intergenerational solidarity in general and functional solidarity in particular can be explained by different structures and at different levels. The givers and receivers of such support can be the (grand)parents or (grand)children. At the micro level, unequal individual opportunities and needs are crucial in explaining functional solidarity. As individuals are embedded in families, their existing family structures are important as well. Therefore, the meso level of unequal conditions within family structures are also thought to have a substantial influence on functional solidarity. Moreover, social inequality at the macro level, such as welfare state expenditures or services and poverty, is likely to substantially influence solidarity patterns between countries. However, family ties and intergenerational solidarity are not solely based upon functional necessities. They can also be understood in terms of reciprocity norms (Kohli, Künemund, Motel, & Szydlik, 2005) and expectations of change (Künemund & Rein, 1999), which crucially affect intergenerational patterns as well.

Previous research on different forms of functional solidarity has shown that family generations are strongly connected and that these ties are particularly strong between parents and (adult) children and grandchildren in most European societies (see, e.g. Attias-Donfut, Ogg, & Wolff, 2005; Cooney & Uhlenberg, 1992; Deindl & Brandt, 2011 on financial and time transfers; Brandt, Haberkern, & Szydlik, 2009; Haberkern & Szydlik, 2010; Igel, Brandt, Haberkern, & Szydlik, 2009 on help and [grandchild] care, and Isengard et al., 2017 for money and space support).

With regard to micro-level influences, previous findings show that individual inequality is an important aspect in explaining intergenerational support patterns. The economic needs of (adult) children are particularly important for parents when exercising intergenerational solidarity: a child's poor economic situation, as indicated by low education, low income and/or unemployment, encourages financial transfers from that child's parents (Brandt & Deindl, 2013; Deindl & Brandt, 2011; Isengard et al., 2017; Kohli, 1999; König, 2016). The picture is the same for time transfers such as instrumental help and (grandchild) care (Brandt & Deindl, 2013; Igel & Szydlik, 2011). Alongside the needs and opportunity structures of the receiving child, individual inequality between parents is also important in explaining different solidarity patterns. For example, Isengard et al. (2017) as well as Schenk, Dykstra, and Maas (2010) found that parents can better afford to give their children financial support the better their own economic position happens to be. This is particularly the case if the parents are still working and/or have higher incomes (see also Aassve, Billari, Mazzuco, & Ongaro, 2002; DaVanzo & Goldscheider, 1990; König, 2016). The same has also been observed for time transfers: parents with better (economic) opportunities and good health are more likely to support their adult children with time (Hank & Buber, 2008; Igel & Szydlik, 2011). Thus, our assumptions lead us to assume that the greater the economic needs of children as well as the opportunities of their parents, the more time and money the parents will give to their adult children (Hypothesis 1).

Yet transfers in the other direction – from adult children to their parents – can also be explained by differences in the need and opportunity structures of the givers and receivers. Although Fokkema, Bekke, and Dykstra (2008) have found that parents are more likely to give money to their adult children than vice versa, transfers can also be observed in the other direction. Furthermore, the probability of receiving money increases over one's life course, whereas the probability of giving decreases. However, there is no clear link that parents with greater economic opportunities receive money from their adult children less often than parents in greater need. In addition, the economic opportunities available to the children seem to be a less important factor in explaining monetary transfers to their parents (Deindl, 2011). Transfers of time, especially in the form of practical help and care, occur more often within parent–child relationships and depend strongly on the need structures of the receiving parents. In these cases, increasing parental age and health-related limitations increase the necessity of such intergenerational help from adult children (see Brandt et al., 2009). On the other hand, previous findings suggest that restricted financial and time resources due to the labour status of the children can have a decisive effect on their opportunities to support their parents (Schmid, 2014). Therefore, we assume that parents with greater needs are more likely to receive time transfers but not money from their adult children and that child's economic- and time-related opportunities play an important role in explaining such transfers (Hypothesis 2).

Beyond micro-level inequalities, (unequal) family structures at the meso level also have a substantial influence on the probability of functional solidarity in both directions. Previous research indicates that the existence of 'competing' or 'supporting' family members, such as siblings and/or partners in the case of children, reduces the likelihood of intergenerational solidarity in general. Living in a partnership, having children of one's own and/or the presence of brothers and/or sisters are likely to reduce financial and time transfers because parents generally want to share available money and time equitably among their children (see König, 2016; Twigg & Grand, 1998 for money; and Igel, 2011 for grandchild care). By the same token, children with siblings can reduce their own responsibility for supporting their parents by themselves (Schmid, 2014). Parents who live in a partnership are also more likely to be able to afford offers of financial assistance (Deindl, 2011; König, 2016) and grandchild care (Igel & Szydlik, 2011) to their children, whereas parents who live alone have a higher potential for economic- and health-related needs and are therefore more likely to receive support from their adult children (see Deindl, 2011; Schmid, 2014). However, the willingness and the possibilities for intergenerational support depend not least on awareness of needs and feasibility of helping. Therefore, in addition to family structures, the spatial and social embeddedness of families can be important in explaining intergenerational solidarity patterns. Frequent contact with each other not only strengthens the family relationship but also provides opportunities to become aware of problems and needs. Here previous research indicates that intergenerational monetary transfers occur more often in parent–child relationships characterised by frequent contact (Deindl, 2011; König, 2016). And it is not just the frequency of contact but also the possibilities for personal assistance that determine intergenerational support. Whereas monetary support increases with intergenerational geographical distance (Deindl, 2011; König, 2016), time-related help such as children caring for their parents or parents caring for their grandchildren normally requires a physical presence and is limited to those relations who live nearby (Igel, 2011; Igel & Szydlik, 2011; Schmid, 2014). Considering this, we can assume that the more competing family members there are as (potential) receivers or the fewer supporting family members there are to (potentially) draw on for assistance, the less money and time will be transferred (Hypothesis 3). We also expect that financial transfers will be provided more often as geographical distance increases, whereas less frequent contact will generally be associated with a decrease in intergenerational solidarity between parents and adult children (Hypothesis 4).

Finally, intergenerational solidarity can be influenced by societal inequality at the macro level, which would explain differences between countries. With regard to solidarity in different European countries, previous research has shown variations that are mainly in line with well-known welfare state regimes (see, e.g. Aidukaite, 2004; Bambra, 2006; Bambra & Eikemo, 2009; Bonoli, 1997; Esping-Andersen, 1990, 1998; Ferrera, 1996). Whereas in the so-called social-democratic welfare regime in Northern European countries, including Denmark and Sweden, welfare state services are quite universalistic and the normative obligations of family members are low, the so-called Mediterranean welfare regime in the south of Europe, including countries such as Italy and Spain, is characterised by a relatively low public service provision and very high family obligations (Matsaganis, Ferrera, Capucha, & Moreno, 2003). An OECD comparison shows that this results in public, family-related support services being very low in these Mediterranean countries, whereas traditional family structures are very strong (see Ferrera, 1997; Sciortino, 2004). In conservative welfare regimes such as in Austria, France and Germany, welfare state services are tightly connected to (prior) labour force participation and are less universalistic. Furthermore, in such societies the family plays an important role owing to the strong influence of the Catholic Church, much like in the Mediterranean part of Europe. According to Deacon (2000), the post-communist or Eastern European welfare regime, such as in the Czech Republic, Estonia or Slovenia, is characterised by the erstwhile central responsibility of the state and a relatively weak role of the family.

In general, differences in the distribution of intergenerational solidarity that are related to welfare regimes can be attributed to the direct impacts of the different kinds of public services and to the indirect impacts of the different extents of income redistribution. On the one hand, direct state assistance in the form of financial transfers to the benefit of families is relevant to the forms of intergenerational solidarity. On the other hand, we can observe an indirect impact of social conditions such as poverty that are strongly connected to welfare state arrangements. In these cases, it can be observed that financial transfers and time-related help are more common but not as intense in the northern part of Europe (for time, see Brandt et al., 2009; Igel & Szydlik, 2011 for money, see Albertini et al., 2007; Lennartsson, 2011). The economic literature tends to justify these relationships by postulating that stronger welfare states replace family services and thus substitute intergenerational solidarity (Cox & Jakubson, 1995). This concept of 'crowding-out' assumes that families only provide support if the respective demand is not satisfied by public arrangements and services (Künemund & Vogel, 2006). However, the 'crowding-in' conceptualisation postulates that public services have the opposite effect on functional solidarity: stronger welfare states and public intervention stimulate intergenerational support (Daatland & Herlofson, 2003; Daatland & Lowenstein, 2005; Künemund & Rein, 1999). In accordance with both theoretical concepts, it can be assumed that the functions provided by family and state interact (Attias-Donfut & Wolff, 2000), where the state provides the framework of more regular support services and the family concentrates on informal and less time-consuming support. By combining the theoretical concepts of substitution and complementation as well as previous findings, we can assume that the more services provided by the welfare state, the lower the probability of regular time transfers and the more monetary support between generations there will be (Hypothesis 5). Moreover, poverty can also have an influence on living conditions, common norms and rules as well as people's feeling of security and thus can be expected to have an influence on intergenerational relations. In this vein, previous findings indicate that living in times of higher poverty goes in line with more frequent contacts between family members but also with increase the potential of intergenerational conflicts (Szydlik, 2016) which finally can lead to more or less functional solidarity within families, depending on transfer type and direction (Hypothesis 6).

2.3 Data and Methods

Our analyses are based on the fifth wave of the Survey of Health, Ageing and Retirement in Europe (SHARE). The data employed were gathered in 2013 and provides standardised information on respondents aged 50 years and older in 14 European countries. The countries included in the survey are Austria, Belgium, the Czech Republic, Denmark, Estonia, France, Germany, Italy, Luxembourg, the Netherlands, Slovenia, Spain, Switzerland and Sweden. The dataset (for details on the fifth wave, see Börsch-Supan, 2017) contains information on a wide range of topics such as demography, income, health, accommodation, education, occupation, behaviour, social support, activities and expectations. The respondents reported information on functional solidarity as well as on individual and familial characteristics on both sides of the relationship only. As our focus relies on adult parent–child relationships, we reshaped the given information provided by the responding parents to each child aged at least 18 years. To determine the influence of social inequality on active family support, we further restricted the sample to those relations in which the adult child does not share the same household with its parents.

The four dependent variables cover the giving and receiving of financial and time (help, care and grandchild care) transfers. *Money* to and from adult and non-coresiding children was determined on the basis of the following questions with the response categories yes (1) and no (0): 'Now please think of the last 12 months. Not counting any shared housing or shared food, have you or your partner given/received any financial or material gift or support to/from any person [...] amounting to 250 euro (in local currency) or more?' If yes: 'To whom did you or your partner provide such financial assistance or gift in the last 12 months?' Or in the case of recipients: 'Who has given you or your partner a gift or assistance in the last 12 months?' In contrast to previous SHARE surveys, the fifth wave did not provide any further information on the transfer amount and reasons. Therefore, our focus fell only on the general situation of whether or not there was a financial transfer from parents to adult children (or vice versa) within the past 12 months.

To capture *time transfers* from adult children we used the following questions: 'Thinking about the last 12 months, has any family member from outside the household, any friend or any neighbour given you or your partner personal care or practical household help?' If yes: 'Which family member from outside the household, friend or neighbour has helped you or your partner most often in the last 12 months?' And: 'In the last 12 months how often altogether have you or your partner received such help from this person? Was it (1) almost daily, (2) almost every week, (3) about every month or (4) less often?' If the responding parent received such a transfer at least weekly from an adult child, we defined it as a regular time transfer.

Regular *grandchild care* as a time transfer provided by the parents to their adult children at least weekly was determined on the basis of the following questions: 'During the last 12 months, have you regularly or occasionally looked after your grandchild(ren) without the presence of the parents?' If yes: 'On average, how often did you look after the child(ren) in the last 12 months? Was it (1) almost daily, (2) almost every week, (3) almost every month or (4) less often?' We focused only on those parent–child relations with at least one living grandchild aged less than six years.

To explain functional solidarity patterns in Europe against the backdrop of social inequality, various explanatory variables at the micro, meso and macro levels were included in the empirical model. Differences at the individual level regarding (economic) opportunities and need structures of the adult children were captured by their *gender* (0 = Daughter, 1 = Son), *age* and *labour force status.* For *age,* we used a combined variable for children and parents with four categories: (a) child younger than 30 and parent younger than 60 years of age; (b) child younger than 30, at least one parent 60+; (c) child 30 years and older, parents younger than 60; and (d) child 30+ and parent 60+. Because of the data structure (child–household dyads), we used the age of the oldest parent. *Labour force status* consists of the following categories: (a) full-time employment, (b) part-time employment, (c) unemployed, (d) in education and (e) others such as homemaker or a person with special needs.

To capture unequal opportunities and needs of parents, we considered their *social class* (on the basis of their educational level and economic situation), their *health conditions* as well as their *ethnic origin. Level of education* was recoded according to the International Standard Classification of Education (ISCED) into (a) low (ISCED 0–2), (b) medium (ISCED 3–4) and (c) high (ISCED 5–6) education and refers to the highest parental degree. For the economic situation of the parental household, we included the information whether at least one parent receive income from *employment* (1) or not (0). Moreover, a subjective *income* measure was used based on the question of whether the household had enough money to make ends meet with a distinction between four categories: (a) with great difficulty, (b) with difficulty, (c) fairly easily and (d) easily. In addition to the total amount of assets (net wealth in euros, controlled for purchasing power parity), our models control for the information on whether the parents own property (1) or not (0) acted as an additional and indirect indicator of household wealth. Along with economic opportunities, individual health also plays an important role in the probability of providing or receiving solidarity. *Parental health* was measured as the number of limitations on the activities of daily living (ADL) and instrumental activities of daily living (IADL). ADL covers, for example, eating, dressing, personal hygiene and walking, whereas IADL includes shopping, preparing meals, housekeeping and dealing with financial matters. For this item, the individual items were tallied and the parent with the greatest number of limitations (ranging from 0 to 13) was selected. Individual inequality is not only closely related to social background but also to ethnic origin. For this reason, we included information on an *immigrant background* of at least one parent (0 = no, 1 = yes).

In addition to individual circumstances, meso-level influences – defined as family structures and the related unequal conditions owing to competing or supporting family members – are also important. To cover each situation, we included the (1) *partnership status of the child,* with 0 = single and 1 = partnered (married or unmarried); (2) *partnership of the parents*, with 0 = couple, 1 = father alone and 2 = mother alone; and (3) *number of siblings*, which refers to the number of siblings from the viewpoint of the children. To measure the influence of the general possibility of personal assistance as well as to capture the relationship of the dyad, we also included the geographical proximity or distance (ranging from same house to more than 500 kilometres away) as well as frequency of contact (ranging from daily to never) as a metric variable.

To capture variations in societal inequality between countries, we considered macro indicators that measure direct welfare state differences as well as the results of indirect welfare state interventions. As a direct measure of welfare state support, we used public *family expenditures* as a percentage of GDP. In this sense, family expenditures represent the provision of benefits and contributions (cash transfers, goods, services) by public institutions to households and individuals including family-related public programmes (e.g. family allowances, maternity and parental leave, early childhood education and care, home help and other cash benefits for families). To assess the indirect effects of redistributive welfare state policies, we considered the *risk of poverty or social exclusion* in each of the 14 countries (after social transfers). The poverty rate is defined as the ratio of the population whose income falls below 60% of the national median equivalised disposable income of the total population. Each of the macro indicators was derived from official sources such as the Eurostat and OECD and refers to the year preceding the interview (2012).

Given non-independence between observations (65,682 non-coresiding adult children nested in 31,048 parental households nested in 14 countries), this hierarchical data structure violates basic regression assumptions and might lead to inaccurate significance values as well as biased standard errors. To analyse the different determinants of functional solidarity at different levels, we estimated multilevel logistic regression models involving the three given levels using the STATA module GLLAMM (Hox, 2002; Rabe-Hesketh & Skrondal, 2008; Snijders & Bosker, 2012). In doing so, we considered the variation not only at the upper country level but also between parental households within countries.

2.4 Empirical Results

2.4.1 Functional Solidarity Patterns in Europe

Although there are country-specific differences, a first glance at functional solidarity for non-coresiding parent–child relationships in Europe shows that, overall, there is intergenerational solidarity between the responding parents and their adult children (see Fig. 2.1 and Fig. 2.2). If we take a more detailed look at transfers from parents aged 50 years or older to their adult children (Fig. 2.1), we can observe that financial transfers are more common in Luxembourg (23%) and with a minimum of 10% in the Northern European countries (Sweden and Denmark) as well as Austria and Germany. By contrast, parents in Southern and Eastern Europe support their adult children to a lesser extent with money. In these cases, especially Spanish (6%) as well as Slovenian (9%) and Estonian (10%) families differ from the European average of 15%. With regard to time transfers from parents to adult children in the form of grandchild care, the results underpin the important role of this form of intergenerational support. Particularly in Belgium, Luxembourg and Italy (42%) as well as Slovenia (41%) grandparents often provide regular care for their young grandchild(ren). Conversely, the rates are relatively low (17–20%) in countries with well-developed childcare facilities such as Sweden and Denmark as well as Estonia and France (20%).

Although intergenerational transfers from parents to adult children occur more often than vice versa, the intergenerational solidarity shown in Europe by adult

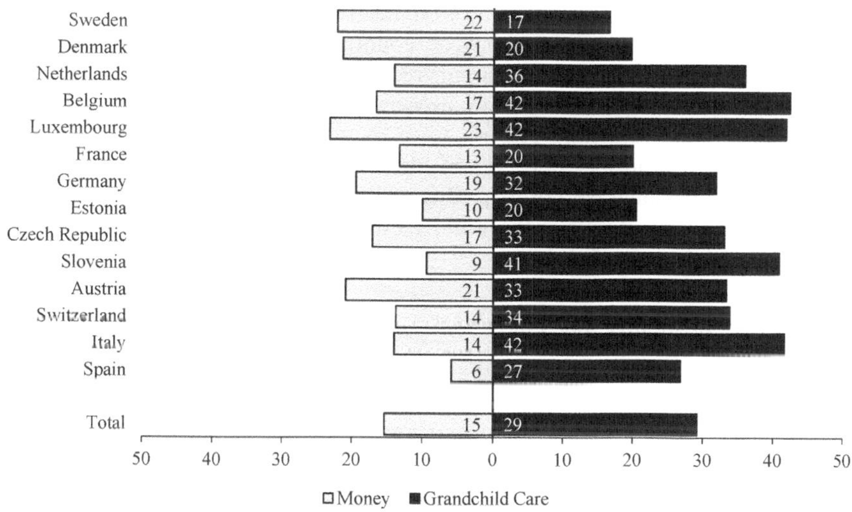

Fig. 2.1. Proportion of Functional Solidarity from Parents to Adult Children in Europe. *Source:* SHARE, wave 5 (2013, release 6.0.0), weighted, 65,682 respondent–child dyads (money) and 12,702 respondent–child dyads (grandchild care), own calculations.

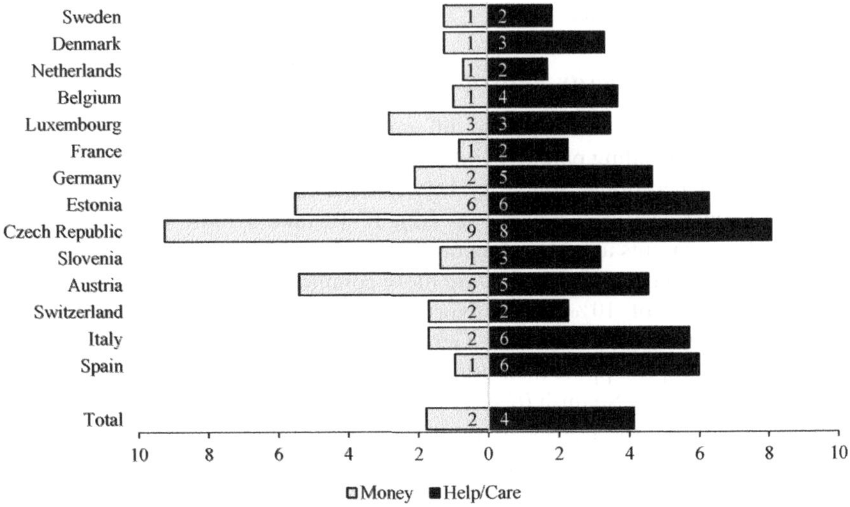

Fig. 2.2. Proportion of Functional Solidarity from Adult Children to Parents in Europe. *Source:* SHARE, wave 5 (2013, release 6.0.0), weighted, 65,682 respondent–child dyads, own calculations.

children towards their parents should not be underestimated. Overall, only 2% of adult children support their parents (aged 50 years or above) with money (see Fig. 2.2). However, the distribution of financial support from the younger to the older generation varies widely between countries. Whereas in most European countries less than 2% of elderly parents receive money from their adult children, the results show a higher occurrence especially in the Czech Republic (9%) followed by Estonia (6%) and Austria (5%). A similar picture emerges for time transfers. Across Europe, only 4% of all adult children support their parents regularly with personal help or care. Once again, the highest transfer rates can be found in the Czech Republic (8%) and Estonia (6%) as well as in Italy, Spain, Germany and Austria (5–6%).

2.4.2 Social Inequality and Functional Solidarity in Europe: Determinants

To determine how various kinds of social inequalities affect different forms and directions of functional solidarity, we estimated multilevel logistic regression models that included micro, meso and macro indicators. To avoid estimation bias, a single regression that controlled for individual and family structures was calculated for each macro indicator separately. Along with different aspects of functional solidarity, we also took top-down as well as bottom-up transfers into account.

The results in Table 2.1 show gender-specific patterns at the micro-level for top-down transfers – which in our case mean support from parents to their adult children – that suggest grandchild care comes more often from her (daughters)

Table 2.1. Social Inequality and Top-down and Bottom-up Solidarity in Europe.

	Top-down: To Adult Children				Bottom-up: From Adult Children			
	Money		Grandchild Care		Money		Help/Care	
	OR	SE	OR	SE	OR	SE	OR	SE
Opportunities and needs of child								
Son	0.99	0.05	0.54***	0.08	1.20*	0.13	0.59**	0.13
Age (child ≤ 30/parent ≤ 60)								
Child ≤ 30/parent 60+	1.16	0.19	1.16	0.22	1.15	0.38	1.35	0.34
Child 30+/parent ≤ 60	0.68***	0.06	1.03***	0.15	1.36	0.37	1.11	0.20
Child 30+/parent 60+	0.53***	0.08	1.25	0.23	1.80*	0.59	1.91***	0.47
Labour force status (full-time)								
Part-time	1.36***	0.12	1.29*	0.20	0.63**	0.15	1.50***	0.19
Unemployed	3.37***	0.59	0.49***	0.08	0.23***	0.10	1.01	0.16
In education	3.35***	0.82	0.71	0.30	0.44**	0.19	1.08	0.30
Other	1.35***	0.13	0.58***	0.10	0.56***	0.07	2.10***	0.46
Opportunities and needs of parents								
Education, maximum (low)								
Medium	1.95***	0.16	1.20*	0.13	1.92***	0.39	0.65***	0.08

Table 2.1. *(Continued)*

	Top-down: To Adult Children				Bottom-up: From Adult Children			
	Money		Grandchild Care		Money		Help/Care	
	OR	**SE**	**OR**	**SE**	**OR**	**SE**	**OR**	**SE**
High	4.42***	0.78	1.51***	0.14	2.53***	0.55	0.59***	0.06
Employed	2.04***	0.25	0.71***	0.09	0.82	0.18	0.51***	0.10
Financial situation (with great difficulty)								
With difficulty	2.13***	0.41	1.46**	0.23	0.73	0.29	1.29	0.30
Fairly easily	4.22***	0.99	1.63***	0.23	0.51	0.26	0.94	0.20
Easily	10.43***	2.72	1.67***	0.26	0.56	0.23	0.88	0.19
Assets	1.35***	0.08	1.08***	0.03	1.05	0.07	0.87	0.10
Home ownership	1.33***	0.15	1.10	0.14	0.87	0.14	0.87	0.12
Limitations (maximum)	0.79***	0.06	0.80***	0.05	1.04	0.13	2.67***	0.14
Migrant	0.71**	0.11	0.92	0.10	1.40***	0.17	0.71*	0.14
Family structures								
Partner (child)	0.60***	0.05	1.05	0.11	1.28*	0.19	1.01	0.07
Partner (parents: couple)								
Father alone	1.47*	0.30	0.16***	0.04	0.97	0.16	5.59***	0.57
Mother alone	1.11	0.12	0.99	0.12	3.21***	0.59	4.90***	0.71
Siblings of child (none)								
1	0.58***	0.07	0.73**	0.12	0.74	0.19	0.54***	0.09
2	0.31***	0.05	0.51***	0.09	0.51**	0.14	0.66***	0.11
3+	0.15***	0.03	0.31***	0.06	0.65	0.32	0.46***	0.11

Geographical distance (close to far)	1.15***	0.05	0.29***	0.03	1.30***	0.09	0.48***	0.02
Contact frequency (daily to never)	0.50***	0.02	0.25***	0.03	0.50***	0.03	0.19***	0.01
Cultural–contextual structures								
Family expenditure	1.14***	0.04	0.84***	0.03	1.97***	0.18	0.83***	0.05
Poverty	1.33***	0.09	1.41***	0.12	0.42***	0.04	0.67***	0.04
Model statistics								
n (children)		65,682		12,702		65,682		65,682
n (households)		31,048		10,086		31,048		31,048
n (countries)		14		14		14		14
ICC (empty model)		0.06		0.04		0.07		0.05
ICC (full model + family expenditure)		0.02		0.06		0.10		0.05
ICC (Full model + Poverty)		0.04		0.11		0.12		0.08
−LL (empty model)		−23,014		−7,377		−6,270		−10,189
−LL (full model + family expenditure)		−21,140		−5,744		−6,131		−7,938
−LL (full model + poverty)		−21,159		−5,760		−6,107		7,941

Source: SHARE, wave 5 (2013, release 6.0.0), Eurostat (2017b) and OECD (2017), multi-level logistic regressions (separate, for each macro indicator), odds ratios (OR), robust standard errors (SE), intraclass correlation (ICC), log likelihood (−LL), all metric variables standardised, coefficients refer to family expenditure as a macro indicator, own calculations. Significance levels: ***$p < 0.01$, **$p < 0.05$, *$p < 0.10$.

parents than from his (sons) parents. For financial transfers, there is no observable gender effect. Our analysis shows that, aside from life cycle–related differences, which are strongly associated with the ages of both parents and children, social inequality demonstrated by the economic needs of adult children plays a particularly important role in explaining parental support. We found that especially children who are unemployed, in education or work only part-time received significantly more monetary support than children employed full-time. However, it does seem that the reconciliation of family and working life, which depends on access to childcare facilities, explains the need for regular parental help to take care of the children. Time restrictions that result from the child's own employment perpetuate the need for informal and regular grandparenting by parents.

The equal or unequal distribution of the opportunity and/or need structures of the parents as givers is important as well. The better their economic situation, as measured by their educational level, income and assets, the more financial and time transfers can be observed. This is not in the same way true for parents owning residential property. Such property ownership enhances only the likelihood of financial but not of time transfers. Moreover, parents who receive income from employment support their children more often financially but are less often able to care for their grandchildren. For the latter one, probably time restrictions due to work commitment hinder their opportunities for regular grandparenting. Parents' need structures is another factor that also plays a role in functional solidarity. As their number of health limitations increases, the extent of grandchild care and financial support decrease significantly. Additionally, children from migrated families, which generally have to face limited economic resources and poverty, receive significantly less often financial but not grandchild care support than children from native families. Overall, the results are consistent with Hypothesis 1, which states that the (economic) needs of children as well as opportunities of parents promote intergenerational support through money and time.

For the other transfer direction – from adult children to parents – the results show partially gender- and age-specific differences. Adult sons support their parents more often with money but less often with time transfers than daughters do. Older parents (aged 60+) are more likely to receive help and care from their children (aged 30+) than younger ones. Furthermore, the (economic) opportunities available to the giving children are particularly significant, whereas the influence of the needs of the receiving parents on assistance is less obvious, especially for financial transfers. Children who are economically better off, as indicated by full-time employment, are able to support their parents more often with money, whereas the economic situation and health status of the parents and thus their need structures have no significant influence. Financial transfers from children to parents can instead be seen against the backdrop of opportunities rather than need; they are much more likely to occur within higher-educated as well as migrated families. For regular time transfers, the results show that time restrictions are significant when helping or caring for elderly parents. the first and foremost, children who work part-time are able to support parents with time transfers as opposed to those who work full-time, are in education or searching for a job. Compared to financial transfers, there are partially reversed class effects for regular time transfers: the better the economic situation of the parents as indicated by their educational level, the less help and care is offered by children. However, the parental financial situation measured by their income and wealth does not affect the situation of receiving help and care from children. Moreover, regular time support is based on the need for solidarity, as greater health limitations – especially after leaving the labour market – significantly promote time transfers from the younger to the older generation. Children born to native parents tend to support them with help and care more often than adult children whose parents migrated. In accordance with Hypothesis 2, it can be stated that parents with greater needs are more likely to receive time but not financial transfers from their adult children. In line with our expectations, the opportunities of the adult children prove to be a factor in explaining this as well.

In addition to individual circumstances, the familial context and the connected inequality at the meso level also play a role in explaining the support behaviour between parents and their adult children in Europe. Children with a partner receive less often financial but not time transfers (grandchild care). By contrast, the partnership status of a parent affects intergenerational functional transfers. Since the results for this variable run partially against expectations, we cannot generalise about the influence of a parent having a partner or not. Previous research points to the benefits of considering the household composition as well as recent events within the family to better understand the influence of a parent living in a relationship on functional solidarity. For this aspect, our results show that fathers who live alone provide less care for their grandchildren but tend to support their children with money more often. In particular, the existence of siblings significantly reduces the probability of a child receiving parental support in both forms of functional solidarity. The geographical distance between the adult children and their parents also determines the kind of intergenerational support. Children who live far away from their parental home are more likely to receive financial transfers, whereas children who live close to their parents benefit more from regular grandchild care. The frequency of contact between parents and their adult children, as a characterisation of the so-called associational solidarity within the relationship, does appear to have a lasting effect on functional solidarity. In this sense, frequent contact increases the likelihood of financial transfers and grandchild care significantly.

But the family structure also has an influence on the kind of support provided in the opposite direction. While the partnership status of the giving child appears to be less important, parents who live as couples are supported by their children less often. In detail, only single mothers were supported financially and mothers as well as fathers without partners were more likely to receive support in the form of time from their adult children. Having more than one child reduced the chance of being supported regularly through help or care by any particular child. And while geographical distance seems to encourage financial support, transfers of time are naturally hindered by less proximity. As for the other transfer direction (i.e. parent to child), intergenerational contact promotes monetary as well as time support. With this in mind, we can show – as assumed in Hypothesis 3 – that more competing family members as well as fewer supporting family members generally reduce intergenerational support in terms of both the form and direction of transfers. We can also confirm Hypothesis 4 because spatial as well as social proximity does seem to be a factor in sustaining intergenerational support.

Finally, societal inequality between countries affects functional solidarity as well. In line with Hypothesis 5, our findings show that the stronger the welfare state, as indicated by more public expenditures for families, the higher the likelihood for financial transfers but the lower the probability for regular time transfers, that means grandparenting as well as help and care. According to these findings, the functions provided by the family and the state interact with regard to intergenerational solidarity. Here, regular assistance in terms of grandparenting or caring for relatives can be seen as a reaction ('crowding-out') to restricted public arrangements, services and transfers for relevant institutions such as childcare facilities and nursing homes. By contrast, the provision of monetary assistance within families follows the concept of 'crowding-in' in which stronger welfare states stimulate intergenerational solidarity. Furthermore, with regard to societal poverty, our findings show different scenarios depending on the transfer direction. For top-down transfers, which are in general more common, the results underline that the stronger the societal inequality as a result of labour market conditions and government interventions, as reflected in higher societal poverty rates, the more often intergenerational transfers – money and time – will be provided from parents to their adult children (Hypothesis 6). By contrast, intergenerational help and care as well as monetary support from the younger generation (bottom-up solidarity) appear to be less often affected by higher societal poverty. As many of such support is associated with expenses and requires sufficient monetary means, a higher risk of societal poverty reduces the probability that adult children are able to support their parents in any way.

On the basis of the empirical results, we can therefore assume that welfare state arrangements matter – directly through cash expenditures and indirectly via the redistributive effects of the tax and transfer systems. In countries with traditionally strong welfare states such as Denmark and Sweden, parents as well as children concentrate on informal and less time-consuming support. Grandchild care in particular is obviously far less necessary in these countries since regular childcare as well as professional care for the elderly is offered by the state. The reverse is true in weak welfare states such as Italy or Spain. In those countries, parents often have to help their own children with grandchild care, and children support their parents with personal care rather than with money. Since the Northern and Western European welfare states intervene more strongly by redistributing income, thereby mitigating the effects of poverty, social inequality is weaker than in other types of welfare regimes. Nevertheless, this picture has to be seen in the context of welfare state arrangements in general as well as of obligations towards the family in particular. In the Czech Republic, for example, we can observe that parents are frequently involved in grandchild care even though societal poverty is comparably low (Eurostat, 2017b). This is due to the fact that public childcare institutions for small children are rare (Eurostat, 2017a).

2.5 Conclusions

Contemporary societies are characterised by demographic ageing and social insecurities. Low fertility rates and increasing life expectancy along with increasing economic inequalities are changing the importance of intergenerational relations. Parents and children spending a greater part of their lifetime together leads to both quantitative and qualitative changes in parent–child relationships. But recent economic crises and the increasing withdrawal of welfare states have also caused families to look inward for assistance. Against this backdrop, family generations are important resources for support. The empirical analyses show that parents and their adult children are strongly connected through direct financial support and by giving time in the form of grandchild care, help and personal care.

The empirical analyses prove that social inequalities at the micro, meso and macro level are crucial in explaining differences in family cohesion in general and intergenerational functional solidarity in particular. Adult children in economic need are more likely to receive support from parents with better economic resources. Children with better economic opportunities are more likely to support their parents with money, whereas parental health complaints generally require more intergenerational personal help and care. Competing family members such as siblings decrease the likelihood of a child receiving parental money and time but allow children with siblings to divide the responsibility of supporting their parents. Societal inequality at the macro level is also highly significant. We can observe that parents as well as children in less familialistic and more generous welfare states predominantly support each other through money. At the same time, regular grandchild care is of less importance when public expenditures focus on important family issues (e.g. the provision of public childcare facilities). A similar picture emerged for further time transfers in form of help and care. Living in difficult and uncertain circumstances such as higher unemployment and an increase risk of poverty can lead to more stress and strain on family members and reduce functional solidarity from children to parents. Simultaneously, our results show that in times of economic and societal crisis especially children have and can rely more on family support. Overall, our results highlight the importance of the family net as a support system especially in times, characterised by increasing insecurities with regard to employment, the unequal distribution of income and wealth as well as the withdrawal of the welfare state.

In summary, this contribution offers insights into the interplay between social inequality structures and intergenerational solidarity. On the basis of the empirical results, we can conclude that (a) individual differences in economic needs and opportunities, (b) scarcity or abundance of family resources and (c) welfare state arrangements and social inequality at the macro level play a crucial role in explaining functional solidarity and cohesion. As a result, inequality in general has an impact on intergenerational solidarity, and unequal conditions lead to cementing existing social inequality in contemporary societies.

Acknowledgements

This paper uses data from SHARE Wave 5 (DOI:10.6103/SHARE.w5.600), see Börsch-Supan et al. (2013) for methodological details. The SHARE data collection has been primarily funded by the European Commission through FP5 (QLK6-CT-2001-00360), FP6 (SHARE-I3: RII-CT-2006-062193, COMPARE: CIT5-CT-2005-028857, SHARELIFE: CIT4-CT-2006-028812) and FP7 (SHARE-PREP: N°211909, SHARE-LEAP: N°227822, SHARE M4: N°261982). Additional funding from the German Ministry of Education and Research, the Max Planck Society for the Advancement of Science, the US National Institute on Aging (U01_AG09740-13S2, P01_AG005842, P01_AG08291, P30_AG12815, R21_AG025169, Y1-AG-4553-01, IAG_BSR06-11, OGHA_04-064, HHSN271201300071C) and from various national funding sources is gratefully acknowledged (see www.share-project.org). For methodological details, see Malter and Börsch-Supan (2015). The data were adjusted for this investigation, and extensive consistency checks were made.

References

Aassve, A., Billari, F. C., Mazzuco, S., & Ongaro, F. (2002). Leaving home: A comparative analysis of ECHP data. *Journal of European Social Policy*, *12*(4), 259–275.

Aidukaite, J. (2004). *The emergence of the post-socialist welfare state: The case of the Baltic states: Estonia, Latvia and Lithuania*. Huddinge: Södertörns högskola.

Albertini, M., Kohli, M., & Vogel, C. (2007). Intergenerational transfers of time and money in European families: Common patterns different regimes? *Journal of European Social Policy*, *17*(4), 319–334. doi:10.1177/0958928707081068

Attias-Donfut, C., Ogg, J., & Wolff, F.-C. (2005). European patterns of intergenerational financial and time transfers. *European Journal of Ageing*, *2*(3), 161–173. doi:10.1007/s10433-005-0008-7

Attias-Donfut, C., & Wolff, F.-C. (2000). The redistributive effects of generational transfers. In S. Arber & C. Attias-Donfut (Eds.), *The myth of generational conflict: The family and state in ageing societies* (pp. 22–46). London: Routledge.

Bambra, C. (2006). Research note: Decommodification and the worlds of welfare revisited. *Journal of European Social Policy*, *16*(1), 73–80. doi:10.1177/0958928706059835

Bambra, C., & Eikemo, T. A. (2009). Welfare state regimes, unemployment and health: A comparative study of the relationship between unemployment and self-reported health in 23 european countries. *Journal of Epidemiology and Community Health*, *63*(2), 92–98. doi:10.1136/jech.2008.077354

Bengtson, V. L., & Roberts, R. E. L. (1991). Intergenerational solidarity in aging families: An example of formal theory construction. *Journal of Marriage and Family*, *53*(4), 856–870. doi:10.2307/352993

Bertogg, A., & Szydlik, M. (2016). Die Enge der Beziehung von jungen Erwachsenen zu ihren Eltern. *Schweizerische Zeitschrift für Soziologie*, *42*(1), 41–59.

Bonoli, G. (1997). Classifying welfare states: A two-dimension approach. *Journal of Social Policy*, *26*(3), 351–372. doi:10.1017/S0047279497005059

Börsch-Supan, A. (2017). *Survey of health, ageing and retirement in Europe (SHARE) Wave 5: Release version: 6.0.0*. SHARE-ERIC. Data set. Retrived from doi: 10.6103/SHARE.w5.600

Börsch-Supan, A., Brandt, M., Hunkler, Ch., Kneip, T., Korbmacher, J., Malter, F., … Zuber, S. (2013). Data resource profile: The survey of health, ageing and retirement in Europe (SHARE). *International Journal of Epidemiology*, *42*(4), 992–1001. doi:10.1093/ije/dyt088

Brandt, M., & Deindl, Ch. (2013). Intergenerational transfers to adult children in Europe: Do social policies matter? *Journal of Marriage and Family*, *75*(1), 235–251. doi:10.1111/j.1741-3737.2012.01028.x

Brandt, M., Haberkern, K., & Szydlik, M. (2009). Intergenerational help and care in Europe. *European Sociological Review*, *25*(5), 585–601. doi:10.1093/esr/jcn076

Cooney, T. M., & Uhlenberg, P. (1992). Support from parents over the life course: The adult child's perspective. *Social Forces*, *71*(1), 63–84. doi:10.1093/sf/71.1.63

Cox, D., & Jakubson, G. (1995). The connection between public transfers and private interfamily transfers. *Journal of Public Economics*, *57*(1), 129–167. doi:10.1016/0047-2727(94)01438-T

Daatland, S. O., & Herlofson, K. (2003). 'Lost solidarity' or 'changed solidarity': A comparative European view of normative family solidarity. *Ageing and Society*, *23*(5), 537–560. doi:10.1017/S0144686X03001272

Daatland, S. O., & Lowenstein, A. (2005). Intergenerational solidarity and the family – Welfare state balance. *European Journal of Ageing*, *2*(3), 174–182. doi: 10.1007/s10433-005-0001-1

DaVanzo, J., & Goldscheider, F. K. (1990). Coming home again: Returns to the parental home of young adults. *Population Studies*, *44*(2), 241–255. doi:10.1080/0032472031000144576

Deacon, B. (2000). Eastern European welfare states: The impact of the politics of globalization. *Journal of European Social Policy*, *10*(2), 146–161.

Deindl, Ch. (2011). *Finanzielle Transfers zwischen Generationen in Europa*. Wiesbaden: VS Verlag für Sozialwissenschaften.

Deindl, Ch., & Brandt, M. (2011). Financial support and practical help between older parents and their middle-aged children in Europe. *Ageing and Society*, *31*(04), 645–662. doi:10.1017/S0144686X10001212

Esping-Andersen, G. (1990). *The three worlds of welfare capitalism*. Cambridge: Polity Press.

Esping-Andersen, G. (1998). *The three worlds of welfare capitalism*. Reprint. Princeton, NJ: Princeton University Press.

Eurostat. (2017a). *Formal childcare by age group and duration – % over the population of each age group – EU-SILC survey: [ilc_caindformal]*. Accessed on September 18, 2017. Retrived from doi:10.6103/SHARE.w5.600

Eurostat. (2017b). *People at risk of poverty or social exclusion by age and sex: [ilc_peps01]*. Accessed on April 18, 2017. Retrived from doi:10.6103/SHARE.w5.600

Ferrera, M. (1996). The 'southern model' of welfare in social Europe. *Journal of European Social Policy*, *6*(1), 17–37. doi:10.1177/095892879600600102

Ferrera, M. (1997). The uncertain future of the Italian welfare state. *West European Politics*, *20*(1), 231–249. doi:10.1080/01402389708425183

Fokkema, T., Bekke, S. T., & Dykstra, P. A. (2008). *Solidarity between parents and their adult children in Europe*. Amsterdam: KNAW Press.

Haberkern, K., & Szydlik, M. (2010). State care provision, societal opinion and children's care of older parents in 11 European countries. *Ageing and Society, 30*(2), 299–323. doi:10.1017/S0144686X09990316

Hank, K., & Buber, I. (2008). Grandparents caring for their grandchildren: Findings from the 2004 survey of health, ageing, and retirement in Europe. *Journal of Family Issues, 30*(1), 53–73. doi:10.1177/0192513X08322627

Hox, J. J. (2002). *Multilevel analysis: Techniques and applications. Quantitative methodology series*. Mahwah, NJ: Lawrence Erlbaum Associates.

Igel, C. (2011). *Großeltern in Europa: Generationensolidarität im Wohlfahrtsstaat*. Wiesbaden: VS Verlag für Sozialwissenschaften.

Igel, C., Brandt, M., Haberkern, K., & Szydlik, M. (2009). Specialization between family and state intergenerational time transfers in Western Europe. *Journal of Comparative Family Studies, 40*(2), 203–226.

Igel, C., & Szydlik, M. (2011). Grandchild care and welfare state arrangements in Europe. *Journal of European Social Policy, 21*(3), 210–224. doi:10.1177/0958928711401766

Isengard, B., König, R., & Szydlik, M. (2017). Money or space? Intergenerational transfers in a comparative perspective. *Housing Studies, 47*(4), 1–23. doi:10.1080/02673037.2017.1365823

Isengard, B., & Szydlik, M. (2012). Living apart (or) together? Coresidence of elderly parents and their adult children in Europe. *Research on Aging, 34*(4), 449–474. doi:10.1177/0164027511428455

Kohli, M. (1999). Private and public transfers between generations: Linking the family and the state. *European Societies, 1*(1), 81–104. doi:10.1080/14616696.1999.10749926

Kohli, M., Künemund, H., Motel, A., & Szydlik, M. (2005). Generationenbeziehungen. In M. Kohli & H. Künemund (Eds.), *Die zweite Lebenshälfte: Gesellschaftliche Lage und Partizipation im Spiegel des Alters-Survey* (pp. 176–211). Wiesbaden: VS Verlag für Sozialwissenschaften.

König, R. (2016). *Bildung, Schicht und Generationensolidarität in Europa*. Wiesbaden: Springer VS.

Künemund, H., & Rein, M. (1999). There is more to receiving than needing: Theoretical arguments and empirical explorations of crowding in and crowding out. *Ageing and Society, 19*(1), 93–121.

Künemund, H., & Vogel, C. (2006). Öffentliche und private Transfers und Unterstützungsleistungen im Alter – 'crowding out' oder 'crowding in'?. *Zeitschrift für Familienforschung, 18*(3), 269–289.

Lennartsson, C. (2011). Need and support: Determinants of intra-familial financial transfers in Sweden. *International Journal of Social Welfare, 20*(1), 66–74. doi:10.1111/j.1468-2397.2009.00715.x

Malter, F., & Börsch-Supan, A. (Eds.). (2015). *SHARE Wave 5: Innovations & methodology*. Munich: MEA, Max Planck Institute for Social Law and Social Policy.

Matsaganis, M., Ferrera, M., Capucha, L., & Moreno, L. (2003). Mending nets in the south: Anti-poverty policies in Greece, Italy, Portugal and Spain. *Social Policy & Admin, 37*(6), 639–655. doi:10.1111/1467-9515.00363

OECD. (2017). *Social expenditure – Aggregated data*. Accessed on April 25, 2017. Retrived from doi:10.6103/SHARE.w5.600

Rabe-Hesketh, S., & Skrondal, A. (2008). *Multilevel and longitudinal modeling using stata*. College Station, TX: Stata Press.

Schenk, N., Dykstra, P. A., & Maas, I. (2010). The role of European welfare states in intergenerational money transfers: A micro-level perspective. *Ageing and Society*, *30*(8), 1315–1342. doi:10.1017/S0144686X10000401

Schmid, T. (2014). *Generation, Geschlecht und Wohlfahrtsstaat: Intergenerationelle Unterstützung in Europa*. Wiesbaden: Springer VS.

Sciortino, G. (2004). Immigration in a Mediterranean welfare state: The Italian experience in comparative perspective. *Journal of Comparative Policy Analysis: Research and Practice*, *6*(2), 111–129. doi:10.1080/1387698042000273442

Snijders, T. A. B., & Bosker, R. J. (2012). *Multilevel analysis: An introduction to basic and advanced multilevel modeling* (2nd ed.). Los Angeles, CA: SAGE Publications.

Szydlik, M. (2008). Intergenerational solidarity and conflict. *Journal of Comparative Family Studies*, *39*(1), 97–114. doi:10.2307/41604202

Szydlik, M. (2016). *Sharing lives – Adult children and parents*. London; New York, NY: Routledge.

Twigg, J., & Grand, A. (1998). Contrasting legal conceptions of family obligation and financial reciprocity in the support of older people: France and England. *Ageing and Society*, *18*(2), 131–146.

Chapter 3

The Influence of Children on Inequality in Employment between Men and Women: The Case of Spain

Diego Dueñas Fernández and Almudena Moreno Mínguez

3.1 Introduction

We have clear empirical proof of the unequal incorporation of men and women in the labour market in Spain and Europe as a whole (Anker, 1998; Comisión Europea, 2009) as the distribution of the two sexes is by no means homogeneous. By 'homogeneous' we do not mean a strictly equal distribution of men and women in different categories of employment, but that there is a majority of occupations or activities that are 'integrated' rather than predominantly masculine or feminine. In the first case the percentages of men and women in a particular occupation or activity are similar to those for employment as a whole, while the second and third are related to occupations where the percentage of men is significantly greater or less than that found in employment overall (with the corresponding differences for women). It has been demonstrated that this is the situation in the Spanish labour market, for both employees and professionals (Cebrián & Moreno, 2018; Iglesias, Llorente, & Dueñas, 2010).

The literature has pointed to various causes to explain the differences between men and women. Firstly, there are the different educational choices they make, degrees related to health sciences being predominantly feminine and technical and engineering courses being masculine (Vázquez & Perera, 2007). This distribution affects the subsequent gender balance when students enter employment.

Secondly, the different preferences of men and women mean that their goals regarding a job are very different (Andringa, Nieuwenhuis, & Van Gerven-Haanpää, 2015; Hakim, 2000; Moreno-Mínguez, Fernández-Martínez, & Carrasco-Campos, 2016; Schwartz & Bilsky, 1990). We thus find a high concentration of women[1] in certain jobs that offer security and job satisfaction, even though they are not highly skilled or well paid (Dueñas, Iglesias, & Llorente, 2014), while they would be

[1]This aspect is described in *Economics and Identity* (Akerlof & Kranton, 2000).

Families in Economically Hard Times, 53–71

doi:10.1108/978-1-83909-071-420191006

Table 3.1. Percentage of Part-time Employment for Men and Women Aged 25 to 49 Years by Number of Children below Six Years, 2017.

	Women			**Men**		
	No children	**1 child < 6 years**	**2 children < 6 years**	**No children**	**1 child < 6 years**	**2 children < 6 years**
Germany	24.5	56.2	72.6	9.9	6.2	5.7
Spain	18.2	25.5	30.4	9.9	5.3	4.1
France	19.2	27.2	37.0	8.2	6.5	6.1
Italy	27.3	36.7	42.7	10.5	5.7	6.1
United Kingdom	16.2	47.0	60.4	6.3	4.8	5.7

Source: Eurostat.

excluded from certain jobs that are predominantly masculine.[2] As a result, the Spanish labour market is characterised by a high degree of segregation (Dueñas, Iglesias, & Llorente, 2013) and salary discrimination (among recent studies that highlight this phenomenon we would refer to those by Dueñas, Iglesias, & Llorente, 2015; Guner, Kaya, & Sánchez, 2014; Murillo & Simón, 2014).

An additional factor that can contribute to the unequal distribution of men and women in the labour market is the point at which they find themselves in the life cycle of the family. For example, using Eurostat data, Table 3.1 shows the divergence between the sexes, in Spain and neighbouring countries, in the percentages of part-time employment as the number of children aged less than six years increases, showing that men and women do not adjust their working hours in the same way when they become parents. Indeed, the differences in the work situation of men and women increase considerably when there are small children in the family. For example, in the case of Spain, in 2017 the 8.3% point difference in part-time employment between men and women who do not have children rose to 36.3% points when there are two children below six years in the home.

Economic and sociological theories have also drawn attention to some factors related to changes in the ideology and culture of gender. It is clear, for example, that substantial changes are taking place in gender roles (Valiente, 2010), leading to the progressive disappearance of the 'male breadwinner model' (Lewis, 2001; Pfau-Effinger, 1998), which is a characteristic of most countries in the south of Europe (Moreno-Mínguez, 2005; Moreno-Mínguez, Ortega-Gaspar, & Gamero-Burón, 2017).

As a catalyst to this trend, economic and family policies have been introduced recently which favour joint responsibility regarding family matters between men and women in Spain, as exemplified by the law introduced on 1 January 2017 on

[2]This aspect is described in A Pollution Theory of Discrimination (Claudia, 2002).

the increase from 13 to 28 days in paternity leave when a child is born, adopted or fostered, and the document presented by the European Commission in April 2017 to review the current legal framework governing paid leave for fathers and mothers when a child is born. In this way, an effort is being made by national and European institutions to combat certain aspects of the Mediterranean approach to welfare, such as the persistence of traditional family structures and the unequal distribution of work in the family between men and women (Ferrera, 1996; Moreno-Mínguez & Crespi, 2016; Naldini & Jurado, 2013; Trifiletti, 1999).

Nevertheless, it would seem that these social, economic and legislative changes are not being fully consolidated in Spanish society, and there are still many families in which a traditional model persists, where women are responsible for looking after small children and their salaries are seen as supplementing men's earnings (Moreno-Mínguez, 2015), while men still have the role of breadwinners.

Studies show that part-time employment is common among women who live with a partner and children than it is among those who do not live with a partner or do not have children (Comisión Europea, 2014; OECD, 2015). This decision is adopted as the best response to families' difficulties in reconciling work and family (Moreno-Mínguez, 2013), bearing in mind the legislative and institutional context which, in Spain at least, effectively conditions the hours women devote to work and the home (Cebrián & Moreno, 2018; Fernández & Sevilla, 2007; Moreno-Mínguez, 2010). Various studies have similarly shown that women reduce their hours of paid employment when there are children in the home, while men do not (Alliaga, 2005).

As an illustration of these conclusions, we would point to the study by Gutiérrez-Domènech (2005a) with data from the International Fertility and Family Survey conducted in a number of EU countries, including Spain, between 1973 and 1993. Among other results, it shows that the greatest drop in the likelihood of continuing to work after becoming a mother occurs in Spain and Germany.

The study by Álvarez-Llorente (2002), using data from the Labour Force Survey between 1987 and 1993, is also indicative, as it shows that the ages of the first and second child are directly related to the likelihood of a woman being in employment. The study by De la Rica and Ferrero (2003) is in line with these findings. Using data from the European Union Household Panel between 1994 and 1998, it concludes that there is a negative correlation between fertility and being in employment.

Gutiérrez-Domènech (2005b), using data from the International Fertility and Family Survey, the Labour Force Survey and the EU Household Panel, also records a significant drop in the proportion of women in paid employment after the birth of their first child. Herrarte, Moral, and Sáez (2012), using data from the Labour Force Survey between 2001 and 2004, also show that the birth of a child significantly increases the likelihood of a woman deciding to give up work.

Finally, in line with the papers mentioned above, the results of the studies by Davia and Legazpe (2012, 2014), using data from the 2006 Fertility, Family and Values Survey, show a high correlation between leaving the employment market when there are children aged under six years, although this is not the case when the youngest child is older than this. They also found that the correlation is at its highest level when the youngest child is two years old.

In the context of this theoretical framework, this study will attempt to analyse how the family and, in particular, children have affected the differing careers of men and women in Spain in the years 2005–2018, a period marked by a serious recession. In order to do this a number of variables will be taken into account as possible determinants of the working hours of both genders, their level of education and personal preferences being of special interest.

3.2 Objectives, Database and Methodology

The main objective of this chapter is to examine and measure the repercussions of the presence of children in the home on the working habits of fathers and mothers. The study divides the population into four groups, all aged 29 to 45: men living with a partner and children (ML), men living with a partner but without children (MNL), women living with a partner and children (WL) and women living with a partner but without children (WNL). The four groups will enable us to verify the differences between working habits determined not only by gender but also by the presence of children in the home.

Fig. 3.1 shows how the four groups have changed in Spain. It can be seen that throughout the period studied the number of men and women who live as couples with children in the home is much greater than the number of those who do not live with children. The proportion of women who live with partners is almost 7.5 percentage points higher on average than the proportion for men. The trend for the four groups shows a slight decrease in the proportion of men and

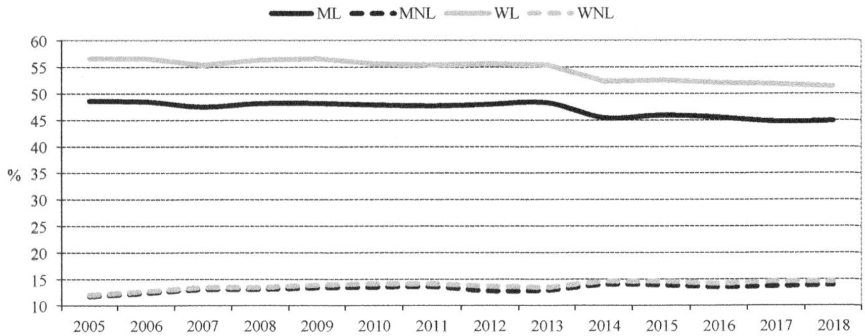

Fig. 3.1. Percentage of Men and Women Aged 25 to 49 Years Who Live as Couples with and without Children. Percentage of Total for Each Sex. Second Quarters: 2005–2018. ML, men living with a partner and children; MNL, men living with a partner but without children; WL, women living with a partner and children; WNL, women living with a partner but without children. *Source:* Labour Force Survey. National Statistics Institute.

women living with children as part of the family and a slight increase in the proportion of those who do not have children.

The database used to track changes in these four groups is the Labour Force Survey provided quarterly by the National Statistics Institute. We have recorded figures for the second quarter of the years 2005–2018 with a view to providing the most up-to-date figures possible and reflecting the employment situation of men and women before, during and after the recession. The data provide extensive information about the personal and employment circumstances of individuals and their family situation (Garrido, Requena, & Toharia, 2000), with the exception of salary variables, and the main tool for dealing with questions related to the labour market, especially if the analysis aims to establish certain relationships between variables linked to employment and socio-economic and demographic factors.

In the Labour Force Survey the fact of being a father or mother living with children and a partner is not recorded directly by the survey, so a series of filters need to be applied to tell us which individuals live with their respective partners and children in a family unit and which do not. The filters use the variable *relpp*, which establishes the relationship each person has with the individual in question, thus enabling us to study the composition of each home unit and determine significant aspects such as the number of children and the age of the youngest child.

Fig. 3.2 shows, for example, how the average size of the family unit has declined because of the fall in the number of children. For both men and women the highest percentages are for families with two children. However, it can also be seen that between 2005 and 2018, there has been an increase in the proportion of

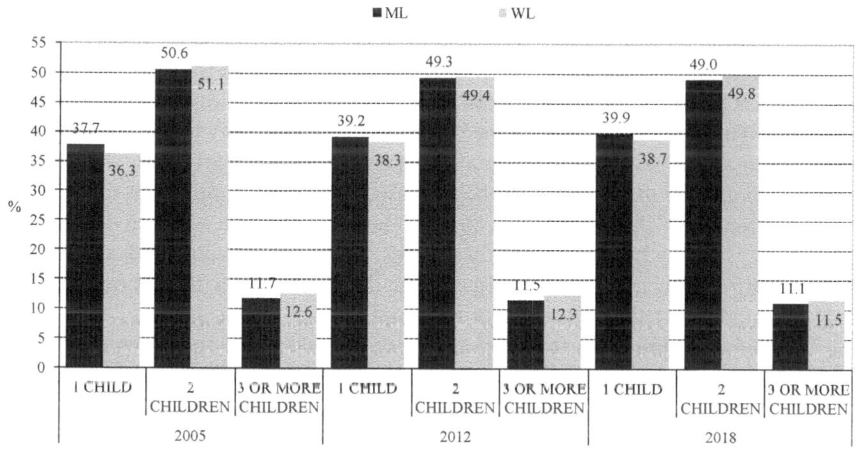

Fig. 3.2. Percentage of Families by Number of Children, Men and Women Aged 25 to 49 Years Who Live as Couples with Children. Percentage of Total for Each Sex. Second Quarters: 2005, 2012 and 2018. ML, men living with a partner and children; WL, women living with a partner and children. *Source:* Labour Force Survey. National Statistics Institute.

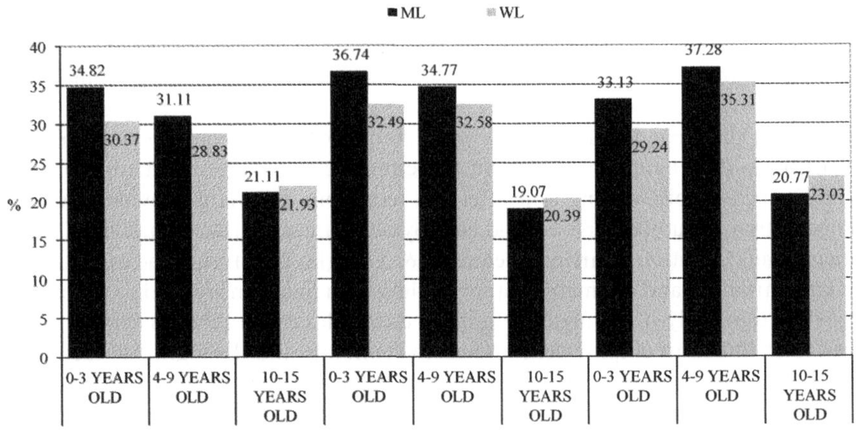

Fig. 3.3. Percentage of Families by Age of Youngest Child; Men and Women Aged 25 to 49 Years Who Live as Couples with Children. Percentage of Total for Each Sex. Second Quarters: 2005, 2012 and 2018. ML, men living with a partner and children; WL, women living with a partner and children. *Source:* Labour Force Survey. National Statistics Institute.

couples who have only one child, while the proportion of those having two, three or more has fallen. Fig. 3.3 also shows the decline in the years 2012–2018 (a period of recession in employment and the economy) in the percentage of families with children aged 0–3 years, which had risen between 2005 and 2012, the end of a period of economic growth.

Both figures reveal a change in the reproductive pattern of mothers and fathers, as there has been a decline in the birth rate. It is likely that behind this change there are underlying features related to the recession in the economy and employment in 2007, such as the increase in male and female unemployment rates, the drop in disposable income in families and the increased reliance of families on the work of women because of the decline of sectors of the economy that were predominantly masculine, such as building.[3] In other words, these figures could indicate a close relationship between family structures and the situation in the labour market, which would affect the behaviour of men and women in the market.

The literature indicates that the relationship could function in two directions, i.e. the type of employment of both sexes may be determined by the presence of children in the home, while the presence of children in the home may be determined by the type of employment men and women have.[4] In this study, however,

[3]One also has to bear in mind the fall in the number of immigrants entering Spain, as these families make a significant contribution to the number of children born.

[4]This two-way relationship has been analysed in connection with the Spanish labour market in various studies, such as those by De La Rica and Ferrero (2003) and Herrarte et al. (2012).

given the options facilitated by the Labour Force Survey, we shall only analyse how the presence of children in the home influences the parents' type of employment. Our working hypothesis would thus be to determine whether the working hours of men and women are different, according to whether they live with children in the family unit, and to verify the existence of a gender bias in many sectors of the labour market.

The authors consider that verifying this hypothesis, i.e. whether the existence of children in the home influences the job preferences of men and women, establishing inter-gender and intra-gender differences, is a matter of considerable importance when social and employment policies are being implemented in this country. For example, if it were confirmed that the working hours of women are different depending on whether they are mothers or not, this would have a bearing on future analyses of women's employment, as it would impose a distinction between those who are mothers and those who are not. It would also make it easier for policy makers to achieve their goals regarding social policies, such as paternity leave, and employment policies, such as those concerning the return to work of women after maternity.

3.3 The Effect of Children. Preferences and Level of Education in the Employment Situation of Men and Women

The first aspect analysed in this study is the type of relationship with work each of the groups defined in the previous section has, considering the existence of a couple and the presence of children. Men with children who live or do not live with a partner have maintained a high level of employment (nearly 90% in 2005 and 2018), although these are the groups that were most affected by job losses and increased unemployment in the recession. Employment levels for these groups fell below 80% and unemployment reached levels close to 20%. For both groups the number of inactive individuals was very low, at less than 4% in the three years analysed.

We find a different situation for women, as their behaviour is not as uniform as that of men. Women living with children have the lowest rate of employment, although the percentage has risen over the years, giving the group a certain immunity to the recession. This increase has led to a sharp reduction in the percentage of women living with children who were inactive, falling from nearly 35% in 2005 to less than 20% in 2018. The transition of this group of women from inactive to working or unemployed reflects what has been referred to in the literature as the 'added worker effect' (Dueñas, Iglesias, & Llorente, 2017), i.e. they are a workforce in reserve until the family needs them to join the labour market, as happened after 2008. These figures suggest that in Spain the recession has stimulated the participation of women living with children in the labour market, contributing to the decline of the 'male breadwinner' model.

The behaviour of women who do not live with children in the home falls between that of men and women living with children. The employment rate for these women is close to 75%, and they have been adversely affected by the

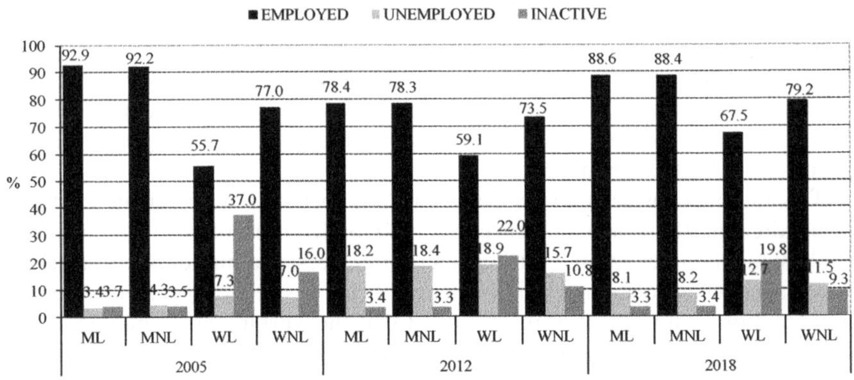

Fig. 3.4. Type of Relationship with Work. Men and Women Aged 25 to 49 Years Living as Couples with and without Children. Percentages of the Total for Each Group. Second Quarters: 2005, 2012 and 2018. ML, men living with a partner and children; MNL, men living with a partner but without children; WL, women living with a partner and children; WNL, women living with a partner but without children. *Source:* Labour Force Survey. National Statistics Institute.

recession, although to a lesser extent than men. In this case the proportion of inactive women has undergone a moderate decrease, falling from about 15% in 2005 to below 10% in 2018.

These initial results point to very significant conclusions. While men living and not living with children display a high degree of uniformity in rates of employment, unemployment and inactivity, the behaviour with regard to work of women living and not living with children is different from that of men and there are differences between groups of women.

In Fig. 3.4, there is also a notable difference between the percentage of inactive men and women living with children. In order to examine this question in greater depth we ask why men and women who do not have jobs and live with children did not look for jobs, i.e. the reason why they continue to be inactive and, in particular, the way in which this decision is influenced by the fact of having family responsibilities such as caring for children or adults who are sick, disabled or elderly, or other family or personal responsibilities.[5] The results of this analysis (Fig. 3.5) show the different roles in work and the family of men and women living with children. For the former, the above reason is of no great importance in the decision to remain inactive, while for the latter it is the main reason. This figure also shows a slight decrease for women at the beginning of the recession, thus reinforcing the figure of the woman as an added worker in the family group.

[5]This information is available in the NBUSCA variable of the Labour Force Survey.

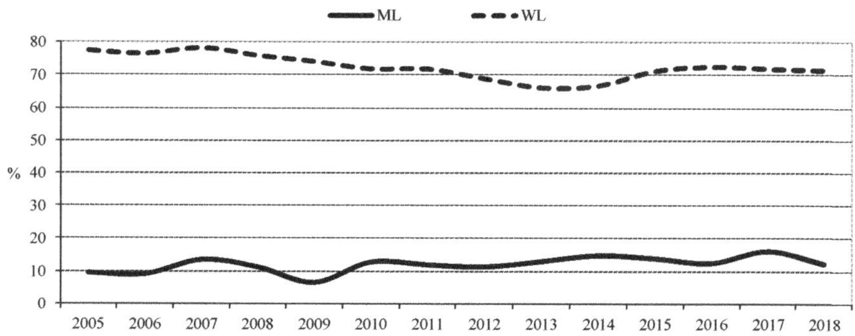

Fig. 3.5. Reasons for Continuing to be Inactive: Care of Children or Adults Who Are Sick, Disabled or Elderly, and Other Personal and Family Responsibilities. Men and Women Aged 25 to 49 Years Who Live as Couples with Children. Percentages of the Total for Each Group. Second Quarters: 2005–2018. ML, men living with a partner and children; WL, women living with a partner and children. *Source:* Labour Force Survey. National Statistics Institute.

So these trends can be examined in greater depth; the analysis includes the possible effect of the variable indicating the level of education on the employment situation of men and women, according to whether they live with children.[6]

The results presented in Fig. 3.6 show a fact of great interest: working women, both those who live with children and those who do not, have a higher level of education than working men in the three years analysed. It can also be seen that unemployed women not living with children have a higher level of education than working men living with children. In the case of inactive women living with children, their level of education is higher than the level of education of inactive men and that of unemployed men living with children, in the three years analysed.

These results have interesting new implications for the case of Spain. Although the literature has highlighted the positive effect that exists between women's level of education and their participation in employment (Crompton & Lyonnette, 2005; Matějů, Smith, Weidnerová, & Anýžová, 2017; Moreno-Mínguez, 2010), these figures would seem to indicate that in the case of women who live with a partner and children the positive effect is less than that in the case of men. This suggests that there are determining family-related factors, such as the approaches of men and women to achieving a satisfactory work–life balance, while the effect

[6]To determine the average level of education of each group of subjects in each year the study used the weighted averages of the values for each level: No schooling (1), Compulsory education (2), Baccalaureate (3), Intermediate vocational training (4), Higher vocational training (5), Professional diploma (6), Degree (7), Doctorate (8).

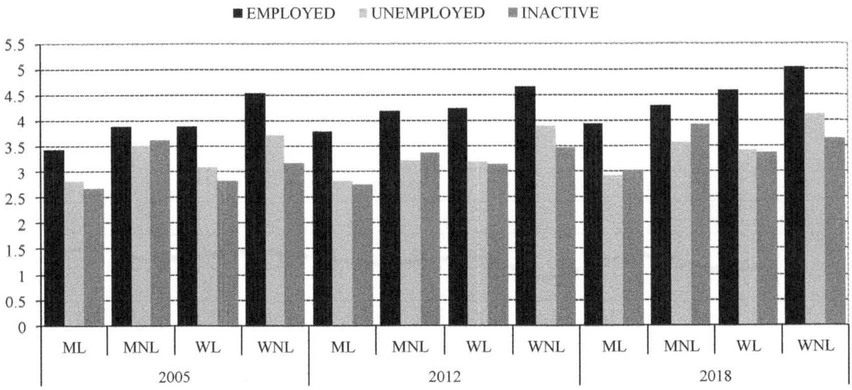

Fig. 3.6. Level of Education in Relation to Work. Men and Women Aged 25 to 49 Years Who Live as Couples with and without Children. Second Quarters: 2005, 2012 and 2018. ML, men living with a partner and children; MNL, men living with a partner but without children; WL, women living with a partner and children; WNL, women living with a partner but without children. *Source:* Labour Force Survey. National Statistics Institute.

of family policies introduced to favour the incorporation of women in the labour market is limited, even when they have intermediate or higher level educational qualifications.

3.4 Family and Type of Employment of Men and Women in the Spanish Labour Market

To analyse the working habits of men and women living and not living with children, Fig. 3.7 shows the average number of hours per week devoted to the main job by each of the four groups. It can be seen that men living with children devote the largest number of hours (42.26 on average) and women living with children the fewest (34.08 on average). The difference between the figures for men and women is not simply a question of gender, as there is a gap between women who live with children and those who do not, the average for the latter group being 37.06 hours. This difference is much smaller in the case of men, as the average number of hours for those who do not live with children is 41.25.

It is also interesting to note from the data in Fig. 3.7 that the recession has not affected the four groups equally in terms of employment. The greatest reduction in hours worked is for men who do not live with children (3.42%), followed by men who live with children (2.21%). The average working hours of women not living with children are down by 1.08%, while, unlike the other three groups, those of women living with children have risen by 0.34%, again showing a relative resistance to the recession, as could be seen in Fig. 3.4.

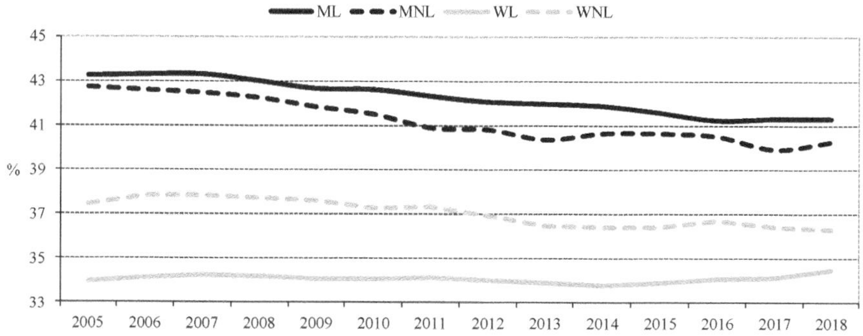

Fig. 3.7. Average Hours per Week Devoted to Main Employment by Men and Women Aged 25 to 49 Years Who Live as Couples with and without Children. Second Quarters: 2005–2016. ML, men living with a partner and children; MNL, men living with a partner but without children; WL, women living with a partner and children; WNL, women living with a partner but without children. *Source:* Labour Force Survey. National Statistics Institute.

To determine whether the working hours shown in Fig. 3.7 reflect the preferences of the groups or whether some would be willing to work fewer hours with the resulting reduction in salary, Fig. 3.8 shows the percentages of those who would be prepared to reduce the number of hours they work while earning less.

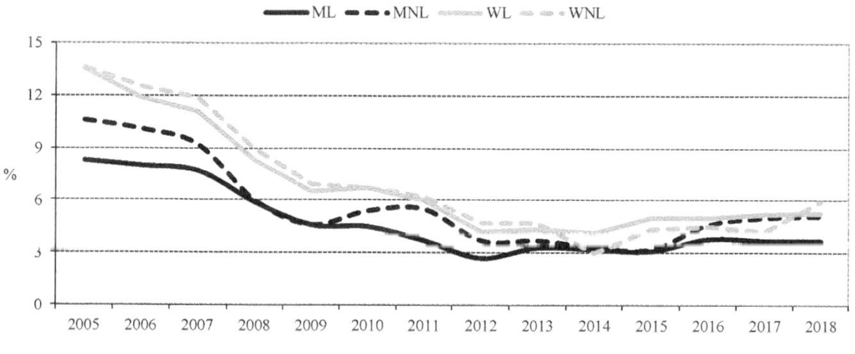

Fig. 3.8. Workers Who Would Like to Work Fewer Hours in Exchange for a Reduction in Salary. Men and Women Aged 25 to 49 Years Who Live as Couples with and without Children. Percentages of the Total for Each Group. Second Quarters: 2005–2016. ML, men living with a partner and children; MNL, men living with a partner but without children; WL, women living with a partner and children; WNL, women living with a partner but without children. *Source:* Labour Force Survey. National Statistics Institute.

If we focus on men and women who live with children in the family unit, we find there is a gap in all the years studied between men and women who want to work fewer hours, possibly because they would like to be more involved in the care of their children. An average of 4.73% of fathers living with children would like to work fewer hours, while the average figure for mothers is 6.94%.

The effects of the recession on the way families organise work is clearly reflected in Fig. 3.8. The numbers of those wanting a reduction in working hours show a decrease, in view of the risk that this decision might increase the likelihood of losing one's job. The figures show a relative concordance between women's preference for working fewer hours in order to look after children and the higher percentage of women who devote fewer hours to their main employment, compared with men.

Fig. 3.9 shows the proportion of part-time workers in each of the four groups. Again we find some of the patterns commented on above. The behaviour of men is uniform, irrespective of whether they live with children. The average percentage for men living with children is 3.36%, and for men not living with children it is 4.82%. Women not only differ from men, but there are differences between the groups of women, according to whether they live with children or not. The average percentage of part-time workers in the first case is 28.49% and in the second case 16.5%. There is thus a considerable gap (25.13 percentage points) between men and women who have children at home.

The reasons why men and women opt for part-time work are shown in Fig. 3.10. In the three years analysed a substantial difference can be observed in the reason 'care of children or sick, disabled or elderly adults', the figure for women living with children being 25 percentage points greater than that for men

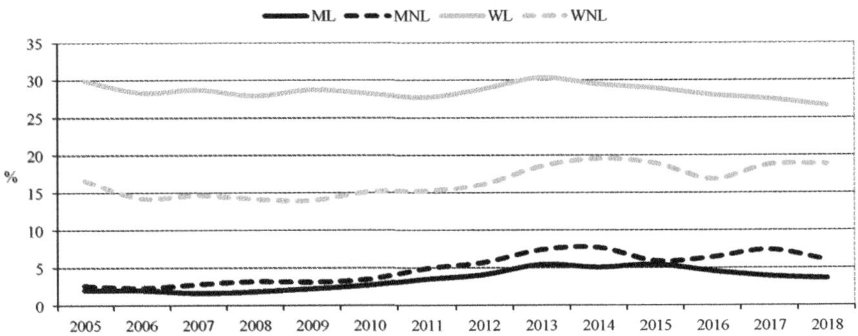

Fig. 3.9. Percentage of Part-time Workers. Men and Women Aged 25 to 49 Years Who Live as Couples with and without Children. Percentages of the Total for Each Group. Second Quarters: 2005–2016. ML, men living with a partner and children; MNL, men living with a partner but without children; WL, women living with a partner and children; WNL, women living with a partner but without children. *Source:* Labour Force Survey. National Statistics Institute.

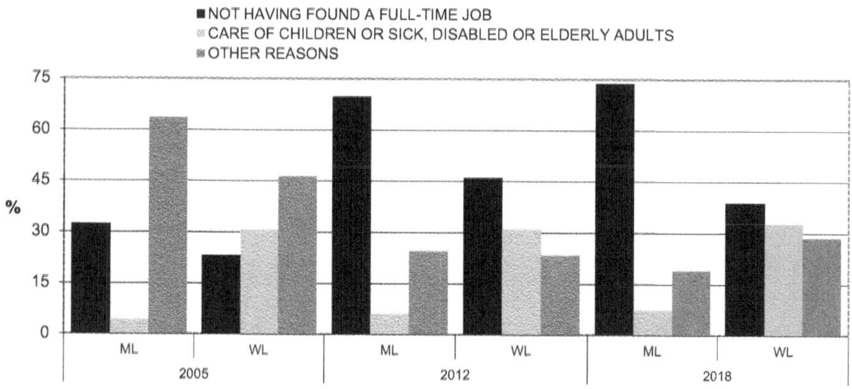

Fig. 3.10. Reason for Having a Part-time Job. Men and Women Aged 25 to 49 Years Who Live as Couples with Children. Percentages of the Total for Each Group. Second Quarters: 2005, 2012 and 2018. *Source:* Labour Force Survey. National Statistics Institute.

living with children. This gap is permanent and independent of the growth or contraction of the labour market and could reflect a greater preference among mothers for part-time work which enables them to achieve a better work–life balance.[7] The recession does not seem to have altered these preferences.

This is not the case with the reason 'not having found a full-time job', more closely linked to changes in the economic cycle, also shown in Fig. 3.10. For both men and women there has been a considerable increase in percentage terms during the recession. This is greater in the case of men living with children, becoming the most important reason to justify having a part-time job.

To conclude our analysis of the differences between the working habits of men and women living or not living with children, we show below the percentage of public sector employees for each group. This sector is considered more family-friendly than the private sector,[8] i.e. it is easier for employees to

[7]The authors would ask the reader to interpret the concept of 'preference' in a broad sense, as it has been shown that there is a substantial 'involuntary' component in the decision to work part-time (Dueñas, Iglesias, & Llorente, 2016). Other studies such as those by Fernández-Kranz and Rodríguez-Planas (2011), and Fernández-Kranz, Lacuesta, and Rodríguez-Planas (2015) point to the existence of a 'penalty for maternity' in view of the large proportion of mothers in part-time employment. The study by Molina and Montuenga (2009) quantifies the penalty in salaries that are 9% lower than those paid to women who are not mothers. We may also note that Tobio (2005) shows that most working mothers consider that the option of working part-time while their children are small is ideal for them.

[8]Pertold-Gebicka, Pertold, and Datta (2016) list a series of studies that consider this to be the case. 'Family-friendly' refers to various practices that make work more flexible: social and employment policies regarding working hours (job sharing, part-time work, flexi-time), paternity leave, workplace location, type of sector (public or private) and financial assistance (child care, paid maternity leave) (Dex & Scheibl, 2001).

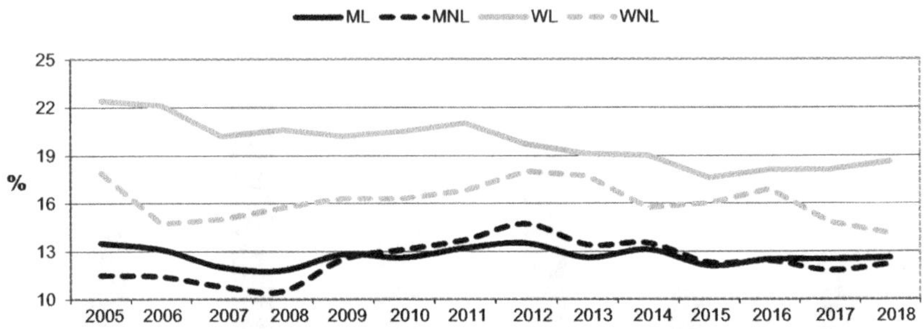

Fig. 3.11. Percentage of Employees in the Public Sector. Men and Women Aged 25 to 49 Years Who Live as Couples with and without Children. Percentages of the Total for Each Group. Second Quarters: 2005–2016. *Source:* Labour Force Survey. National Statistics Institute.

achieve a satisfactory work–life balance. The results shown in Fig. 3.11 confirm the tendencies identified throughout this study. There are very similar average figures for men with and without children (12.71% and 12.41%, respectively), while the average figures for women are higher, especially those who live with children (19.8%, compared with 16.14% for those who do not live with children).

Figs. 3.9–3.11 highlight certain aspects of the situation in the Spanish labour market. Women who live with children have a greater preference than their male counterparts for part-time work or work in the public sector. These two areas, separately or in conjunction, appear to be the strongholds of women who seek an effective way of ensuring a satisfactory work–life balance. This could indicate a degree of failure in the family policies developed to encourage joint responsibility among men and women.

3.5 Conclusions

The results presented here show clearly that the family, and more specifically the presence of children in the home, conditions both the participation of women in the workforce and the type of work they do, even in spite of the correction factor introduced by the recession, which has to some extent favoured women. Although we have abundant empirical evidence of the way in which the family conditions the working life of women in Spain, few studies have looked closely at the family-related effects of the recession on the working profiles of men and women in this country.

First, we would point out that during the recession the size and composition of families in Spain has varied, with a reduction in the number of children in the second decade of the twenty-first century and, consequently, a reduction in the number of children less than three years. We can thus assume the existence of a relationship between the type of family and the economic and employment circumstances in which the family unit lives.

If we compare the four groups analysed, we find that men as a whole have had more uniform working patterns than women, regardless of whether they have children or not. The behaviour of women differs, however, according to whether there are children in the home. Most men work, with very low levels of unemployment and inactivity. The proportion of women who live with children and work is lower, and they are more likely to be inactive. Although they have shown greater resistance to unemployment during the recession, they have moved more often from inactivity to employment and are the only group to have increased the average number of hours worked. However, a majority continue to opt to work part-time and/or in the public sector as a strategy to improve their work–life balance. In women, who do not live with children we find an intermediate pattern between that for men and that for women with children.

These general trends may indicate not only a structural effect related to the labour market but also an effect related to a change in attitude, a break from the patriarchal family model affecting the working practices of women with family responsibilities in response to the devastating effects of the recession on family life and employment. This attitude on the part of women living with children would respond to the 'added worker' effect, their aim being to counteract, or at least relieve, a certain degree of precariousness in the family economy.

Secondly, complementing these general patterns, the authors would like to highlight the conclusions drawn regarding two important variables: level of education and the preferences of men and women. We have found that working women, both those who live with children and those who do not, have a higher level of education than their male counterparts, which is not reflected in the salaries paid to men and women, as shown in numerous studies of gender and pay in the Spanish labour market. And, even more importantly, we also find that inactive women living with children have a higher level of education than unemployed men living with children. In our economy, there are thus inactive individuals who are better qualified than others who are active but cannot find jobs.

A likely explanation of this circumstance is the different reservation wage for men and women who live with children, that for men being lower than that for women. In other words, women living with children need better remuneration than men living with children to give up household responsibilities, including the care of children. In this regard, family, social and economic policies should foster a good work–life balance and responsibility for children that is shared by both sexes, with a view to achieving equal reservation wages for fathers and mothers.

In connection with levels of education, it is also interesting to note that in the case of women living with children there is not such a direct relationship between level of education and participation in the workforce as there is in the case of women without children. The conclusions reached in numerous previous research papers, emphasising the importance of education in the post-patriarchal expectations and values of women and linking the variable to greater participation in work and, as a result, improved financial opportunities for reconciling work and family life, are not reliably evidenced in the Spanish labour market.

Apart from the variable indicating level of education, we should also emphasise the different preferences of men and women living with children concerning various work-related issues. Firstly, women allude to family reasons for remaining inactive, whereas for men these reasons are unimportant. These results show how important family values and the role of the caring wife still are in the attitudes and working habits of women in Spain.

Similarly, when men and women living with children are asked about their reasons for having part-time jobs, a much larger percentage of women than men say that they work part-time for family reasons. It is a strategy for reconciling work and the home that men seem to have discounted *a priori*, both before and during the recession. In the case of men, the reasons for working part-time are associated with the economy (the impossibility of finding a full-time job) rather than the family. The preferences and expectations of women who are mothers have also changed as a result of the recession, as there are fewer who would like to reduce the number of hours they work, possibly because of the repercussions this might have on keeping their jobs and because, in view of the needs of the family, they assume the female role of added worker. In spite of this reduction, there is still a gap between their response and that of men who are fathers. The difference in the respective percentages declined until 2014, although it has risen since then.

These findings illustrate the gender gap in the work-related preferences and behaviour of men and women, the latter being clearly influenced by the family situation, in particular the presence of children in the home. These results point indirectly to a deficient institutional model for family policies that favour the work–life balance on the basis of equality between men and women. Only by developing these policies can we achieve real equality in people's expectations, preferences and behaviour related to work. We have a clear example of how institutional advances have led to progress in the values and behaviour of the post-patriarchal family in northern European countries, where the participation in work of women with young children is among the highest in Europe and where the recession has had least effect on the work situation of parents, in particular, mothers.

Acknowledgements

The authors wish to express their gratitude for the funding received from the Ministry of Economy and Competitiveness through the competitive project LA IMPLICACIÓN PATERNA EN EL CUIDADO DE LOS HIJOS Y EL BIENESTAR INFANTIL EN ESPAÑA (Paternal Involvement in the Care of Children and Infant Welfare in Spain). Reference: CSO2015-69439-R (MINECO/FEDER).

References

Akerlof, G., & Kranton, R. (2000). Economics and identity. *Quarterly Journal of Economics*, *115*(3), 715–753.

Alliaga, C. (2005). *Gender gaps in the reconciliation between work and family life, statistics in Focus 4/2005*. Luxembourg: Eurostat.

Álvarez-Llorente, G. (2002). Decisiones de fecundidad y participación laboral de la mujer en España. *Investigaciones Económicas*, *26*(1), 187–218.

Andringa, W., Nieuwenhuis, R., & Van Gerven-Haanpää, M. M.-L. (2015). Women's working hours: The interplay between gender role attitudes, motherhood, and public childcare support in 23 European countries. *International Journal of Sociology & Social Policy*, *35*(9/10), 582–599.

Anker, R. (1998). *Gender and jobs. Sex segregation of occupations in the world.* Ginebra: International Labour Office.

Cebrián, I., & Moreno, G. (2018). Desigualdades de género en el mercado laboral. *Panorama Social (FUNCAS)*, *27*, 47–63.

Claudia, G. (2002). *A Pollution Theory of Discrimination: Male and Female Differences in Occupations and Earnings*. NBER Working Papers 8985, National Bureau of Economic Research, Inc.

Comisión Europea. (2009). *Gender segregation in the labour market. Root causes, implications and policy responses in the EU.* Luxemburgo: European Commission's Expert Group on Gender and Employment (EGGE).

Comisión Europea. (2014). *Parents at work: Men and women participating in the labour force.* Short statistical report No. 2. Contract Ref. no JUST/2011/GEND/PR/1081/A4. Retrived from https://www.rand.org/content/dam/rand/pubs/research_reports/RR300/RR348/RAND_RR348.pdf. Accessed on April, 2014.

Crompton, R., & Lyonette, C. (2005). The new gender essentialism – Domestic and family 'choices' and their relation to attitudes. *British Journal of Sociology*, *56*(4), 601–624.

Davia, M. A., & Legazpe, N. (2012). Decisiones laborales de las mujeres casadas o cohabitantes en España. *Estudios de Economía Aplicada*, *30*(3), 1–22.

Davia, M. A., & Legazpe, N. (2014). Determinants of employment decisions after the first child birth in Spain. *Journal of Family and Economic Issues*, *35*(2), 214–227.

De la Rica, S., & Ferrero, M. D. (2003). The effect of fertility on labour force participation: The Spanish evidence. *Spanish Economic Review*, *5*, 153–172.

Dex, S., & Scheibl, F. (2001). *SMEs and flexible workings arrangements.* Bristol: Policy Press.

Dueñas, D., Iglesias, C., & Llorente, R. (2013). La segregación laboral en las regiones españolas durante el periodo 1996–2010. *Investigaciones Regionales*, *27*, 91–113.

Dueñas, D., Iglesias, C., & Llorente, R. (2014). Occupational segregation by sex in Spain: Exclusion or confinement? *International Labour Review*, *153*(2), 311–336.

Dueñas, D., Iglesias, C., & Llorente, R. (2015). Is there less gender inequality in the service sector? The gender wage gap in knowledge – Intensive services. *Social Science Information*, *54*(3), 369–393.

Dueñas, D., Iglesias, C., & Llorente, R. (2016). La involuntariedad del empleo a tiempo parcial y la Gran Recesión: un análisis de género en España. *Ekonomiaz*, *90*, 287–319.

Dueñas, D., Iglesias, C., & Llorente, R. (2017). Análisis de las transiciones laborales en España: The (bad) gap is coming back. *Cuadernos de Economía*, *40*, 191–207.

Fernández, C., & Sevilla Sanz, A. (2006). *Social norms and household time allocation.* IESE Business School, SP–SP, Working Paper no. 648.

Fernández-Kranz, D., Lacuesta, A., & Rodríguez-Planas, N. (2015). The motherhood earnings dip: Evidence from administrative records. *Journal of Human Resources*, *48*(1), 169–197.

Fernández-Kranz, D., & Rodríguez-Planas, N. (2011). The part-time pay penalty in a segmented labor market. *Labour Economics*, *18*(5), 591–606.

Ferrera, M. (1996). The southern model of welfare in social Europe. *Journal of European Social Policy*, *1*, 17–37.

Garrido, L., Requena, M., & Toharia, L. (2000). La Encuesta de Población Activa desde la perspectiva de los hogares. *Estadistica Espanola*, *42*, 115–152.

Guner, N., Kaya, E., & Sánchez, V. (2014). Gender gaps in Spain: Policies and outcomes over the last three decades. *SERIES*, *5*, 61–103.

Gutiérrez-Domènech, M. (2005a). Employment after motherhood: A European comparison. *Labour Economics*, *12*, 99–123.

Gutiérrez-Domènech, M. (2005b). Employment transitions after motherhood in Spain. *Labour*, *19*, 123–148.

Hakim, C. (2000). *Work-lifestyle choices in the 21st century: Preference theory*. Oxford: Oxford University Press.

Herrarte, A., Moral, J., & Sáez, F. (2012). The impact of childbirth on Spanish women's decisions to leave the labor market. *Review of Economic of the Household*, *10*, 441–468.

Iglesias, C., Llorente, R., & Dueñas, D. (2010). Diferencias de género en el empleo TIC. *Cuadernos de Economía*, *92*, 105–138.

Lewis, J. (2001). The decline of the male breadwinner model: Implications for work and care. *Social Politics*, *8*, 152–169.

Matějů, P., Smith, M. L., Weidnerová, S., & Anýžová, P. (2017). The role of basic values and education on women's work and family preferences in Europe. *International Journal of Sociology & Social Policy*, *37*(9/10), 494–514.

Molina, A., & Montuenga, V. (2009). The motherhood wage penalty in Spain. *Journal of Family and Economic Issues*, *30*(3), 237–251.

Moreno-Mínguez, A. (2005). Empleo de la mujer y familia en los regímenes de bienestar del sur de Europa en perspectiva comparada. Permanencia del modelo del varón sustentador. *Revista Espanola de Investigaciones Sociologicas*, *112*(1), 131–163.

Moreno-Mínguez, A. (2010). Family and gender roles in Spain from a comparative perspective. *European Societies*, *12*(1), 85–111.

Moreno-Mínguez, A. (2013). Working parents, family and gender in Spain from an European comparative perspective. In A. Moreno-Mínguez (Ed.), *Family well-being: European perspectives* (Vol. 49, pp. 177–201). Social indicators research series. New York, NY: Springer.

Moreno-Mínguez, A. (2015). La ambivalencia ante la corresponsabilidad parental en España: Una cuestión de género. *Revista la Ventana*, *42*, 46–98.

Moreno-Mínguez, A., & Crespi, I. (2016). Gender equality and family changes in the work–family culture in Southern Europe. *International Review of Sociology*, *27*(3), 394–420.

Moreno-Mínguez, A., Fernández-Martínez, L. C., & Carrasco-Campos, A. (2016). Family policy indicators and well-being in Europe from an evolutionary perspective. *Applied Research Quality Life*, *11*, 343–367.

Moreno-Mínguez, A., Ortega-Gaspar, M., & Gamero-Burón, C. (2017). Los modelos familiares en España: reflexionando sobre la ambivalencia familiar desde una aproximación teórica. *Revista Española de Sociología*, *26*(2), 146–167.

Murillo, I., & Simón, H. (2014). La gran recesión y el diferencial salarial por género en España. *Hacienda Publica Espanola*, *208*, 39–76.
Naldini, M., & Jurado, T. (2013). Family and welfare state reorientation in Spain and inertia in Italy from a European perspective. *Population Review*, *52*(1), 43–61.
OECD. (2015). *OECD employment outlook*. Paris: OECD.
Pertold-Gebicka, B., Pertold, F., & Datta, N. (2016). *Employment Adjustments around Childbirth*. IZA Discussion Paper No. 9685.
Pfau-Effinger, B. (1998). Gender cultures and the gender arrangement – A theoretical framework for cross-national gender research. *The European Journal of Social Science Research*, *11*(2), 147–166.
Schwartz, S., & Bilsky, W. (1990). Toward a theory of the universal content and structure of values: Extensions and cross-cultural replications. *Journal of Personality and Social Psychology*, *58*(5), 878–891.
Tobio, C. (2005). *Madres que trabajan. Dilemas y estrategias*. Madrid: Cátedra.
Trifiletti, R. (1999). Southern European welfare regimes and the worsening position of women. *Journal of European Social Policy*, *9*(1), 49–64.
Valiente, C. (2010). The erosion of 'familism' in the Spanish welfare state: Childcare police since 1975. In M. Ajzenstadt & J. Gal (Eds.), *Children, gender and families in Mediterranean welfare states*. London: Springer.
Vázquez, P., & Perera, M. (2007). Un análisis del proceso de feminización de las aulas universitarias. *DT FEDEA*, *27*, 1–23.

Chapter 4

Material Deprivation and Personal Wellbeing of Single Mothers in Lithuania

Aušra Maslauskaitė and Ernesta Platūkytė

4.1 Introduction

Single mothers are one of the most vulnerable groups in society in the good times, but even more so in the bad times following an economic crisis. Generally, single-mother families in many countries are exposed to high risk of poverty, social exclusion and lower overall quality of life (Härkönen, 2017b; Kilkey & Bradshaw, 1999; Maldonado & Nieuwenhuis, 2015). If not targeted by the welfare state policies, these families most likely become sites of accumulated disadvantages, which are transmitted between generations and might strengthen social inequalities (Bernardi & Boertien, 2016; McLanahan & Percheski, 2008). However, single motherhood *per se* is not accountable for the risk of poverty and negative intergenerational outcomes; research proves that not the family structure, but mainly the lack of income and material hardship associated with 'separation penalty' lead to the negative long-term effects for mothers and children (McLanahan & Jacobsen, 2015). Obviously, not all women raising children alone are exposed to the similar degree of disadvantage, since they represent a heterogeneous group in regards to their education and social class standing (Härkönen, 2017b; Rowlingson & McKay, 2005). However, in many countries, the gap in education of single motherhood is large and/or growing, thus the increasing share of single motherhood concentrated at the bottom of educational ladder (Härkönen, 2017a) and exposed to the intensified risk of poverty and disadvantage. The penalty of single motherhood might be substantially mitigated by social policy measures. Generous, comprehensive and universal welfare state decreases the poverty of single-mother families, and the social policy context matters as much or even more for the wellbeing of single women with children than the individual characteristics (Brady & Burroway, 2012).

Although there is a large body of research on single-parent families, the majority of country-specific and comparative analyses focus on developed affluent countries (Brady & Burroway, 2012; Chzhen & Bradshaw, 2012; Kilkey, 2000). So far only a few comparative studies with the focus on single motherhood included several Central European (Härkönen, 2017a; Study on Poverty, 2007) or

Families in Economically Hard Times, 73–98

doi:10.1108/978-1-83909-071-420191007

Baltic countries (Chzhen & Bradshaw, 2012; Van de Velde, Bambra, Van der Bracht, Eikemo, & Bracke, 2014), which in the last two decades underwent comprehensive economic upheaval and social reforms. After 1990 all CEE and the Baltic countries stepped into the path of market capitalism and had a challenge to re-define their inherited social security systems. The transition resulted in the rise of economic and social inequalities, poverty, unemployment and in the rolling back of social protection (Heyns, 2005). After less than two decades, in 2008–2009 all countries experienced a financial–economic crisis, which in the EU hit hardest the three Baltic states (Smith & Swain, 2010). In all three, the crisis was accompanied by the most radical austerity strategy (Sommers, Woolfson, & Juska, 2014), rolling back the social benefits (Kattel & Raudla, 2013), which already before the crisis were very thin if compared to other EU countries (Aidukaite, 2013). However, it needs to be stressed that the financial–economic crisis of 2008–2009 in the Baltics represents only one episode in more than two decades of the sweeping changes in the political economy and this essentially differentiates the region from other affluent democracies. Despite this prolonged 'natural experiment' there is apparent shortage of the thorough academic discussion on the outcomes of the post-socialist developments for such a vulnerable group of society as single-mother families.

The aim of this chapter is to contribute to the field focusing on the Lithuanian case. We assess two components of the quality of life: material deprivation and the personal wellbeing of single mothers. The latter is covered by the analysis of emotional wellbeing, which is indicated by the absence of depressive feelings (DF) and by parenting-related stress. Our study is guided by the argument that single mothers are a heterogeneous group and, consequently, the outcomes of single motherhood are not uniform and therefore, moderated by the socio-economic and structural family-level factors. Considering the country-specific institutional setting, we expect significant disparities by education on all dimensions of life quality and the substantial protective effect of the higher education in regards to the material deprivation and emotional wellbeing of single mothers. Although generally, our main assumptions replicate the one widely apprised in the international scholarship, we nonetheless believe that the study contributes to the field in several ways.

First, in regards to the institutional context, Lithuania as a post-communist country represents an interesting case. Its welfare state is distinct through the combination of the liberal and conservative corporatist regime traits, but also through the extensive social security system and low levels of benefits (Aidukaite, 2013). Some observers conclude that it drifts towards the liberal-marginal regime (Guogis & Koht, 2009). As already mentioned, together with the two other Baltic countries, Lithuania went through the extremely radical liberal economic reforms after 1990 and in this regard significantly differed from the other five CEE countries, which joined the EU in 2004 (Bohle & Greskovits, 2007). The reforms in the Baltics brought the spectacular economic growth, which was manifest until 2008, but also larger social inequalities, less efficient welfare schemes, higher social exclusion. Moreover, after the last financial–economic crisis, Lithuania, differently from Estonia and Latvia, redirected the social security system towards a more targeted model and adopted the least generous support system for families with children (Aidukaite, 2013; Aidukaite, Moskvina & Skuciene, 2016). In this study, we do not directly empirically test the impact of the institutional factors, but rather use the political economy as the contextual explanatory framework, which structures the life quality and the life chances of single-mother families. Second, our study contributes to the field while it assesses the quality of life in a multidimensional manner. The wellbeing is analysed considering simultaneously the material living conditions, emotional wellbeing and parenting-related stress; it thus provides a more complex perspective on the single mothers' life quality. Third, we believe that the research has certain methodological relevance. The material penalty of single motherhood in many studies is measured based on the monetary indicators, such as the poverty risk (Brady & Burroway, 2012; Maldonado & Nieuwenhuis, 2015). However, some argue that nonmonetary indicators more adequately grasp the material conditions (Tomlinson, Walker, & Williams, 2008) because they express the subjective perceptions of resources available and not the arbitrarily assigned thresholds/characteristics. In the presented study, we use novel subjective indicators of material wellbeing, which were developed for the purpose of this study. In addition, the study measures the personal wellbeing including the component of parental-related stress, which was also measured using the multi-item scale invented based on the results of the qualitative study.

The chapter is organised as follows. First, we give a broad overview of the demographic and social policy background of single-mother families in Lithuania. Second, we present the data and methods used in the following analysis. The following sections of the chapter are dedicated to the presentation of the results on the three components of single mothers' wellbeing. Each of the three sections is structured in the following way: it opens with a brief overview of the existing evidence, is followed by the methodological remarks and afterwards presents the results of the empirical analysis. We begin with the material deprivation of single-mother families and uncover the factors contributing to vulnerability. Then the results on the absence of DF and predictors of lower emotional wellbeing are discussed. In the adjunct section, we focus on parental-related stress experienced by single mothers and reveal the protective factors. The chapter concludes with the summary of the main results and the discussion on the outcomes of single motherhood in the weak welfare state context.

4.2 Single Mother Families: Demographic and Social Policy Background

4.2.1 Demographic Trends and Structural Characteristics of Single Mother Families

Single-mother families with underage children are widespread in Lithuanian society; the prevalence of this family type in the country is among the highest in the EU and is similar to Ireland, UK and Nordic countries (Chzhen & Bradshaw, 2012). Single-mother families in Lithuania have a long-standing tradition and could not be linked to the radical socio-economic changes which took place after 1990. They started to proliferate in the late 1960s after the liberalisation of the divorce legislation and grew in heterogeneity in the late 1990s when society progressed towards greater family complexity.

Throughout the twentieth century up till the 1970s single-mother families were formed largely as the outcome of widowhood or non-marital fertility. In the interwar period family life was the subject of religious legislation of the Roman Catholic Church; civil marriage registration was introduced in 1938, though, the civil family law was in full scope introduced only in 1940 (Juozapaitienė, 2011). The non-marital fertility rate, which in the more traditional context indicates the dominant path to single motherhood, was low throughout the whole interwar period and fluctuated at around 5–7% (Maslauskaite, 2014). The non-marital fertility rate remained more or less stable until the beginning of the 1990s with a short-term peak in the years immediately following WWII (Maslauskaite, 2014).

However, the situation was substantially altered at the end of 1965 with the liberalisation of the divorce legislation, which considerably decreased the social, financial and legal barriers of divorce (Maslauskaite & Baublyte, 2012). The reform was followed by a decade of secular growth in the divorce rates. In 1965 the crude divorce rate was 0.9 and a decade later, by 1977, it had reached 3.1 (Demographic Yearbook, 2016). Afterwards the divorce rates stabilised at the same high level placing Lithuania among the divorce leaders in the Soviet Union (Maslauskaite & Baublyte, 2012). They remained at the similarly high level till the recent period with the exception of a few very short-term fluctuations (Marriage and Divorce Statistics, 2016). The reached level places Lithuania among the front runners of divorce in the EU.

It needs to be noted that recently Lithuania also experienced a reversal in the socio-economic composition of divorce. Previously the higher union dissolution risk concentrated in the higher socio-economic status groups; however, currently the divorce risk is more pronounced in the population with lower socio-economical resources, and the trend is particularly evident in urban areas (Maslauskaite, Jasilioniene, Jasilionis, Stankuniene, & Shkolnikov, 2015). The reversal in the socio-economic composition of divorce also reinforces the socio-economic vulnerability of single motherhood.

In addition to the pre-existing paths to single motherhood, cohabitation and childbearing in cohabitation gained in importance after 1990. Cohabitation in Lithuania spread very rapidly in the second half of the 1990s and at the turn of the century it became the dominant path of family formation (Puur, Rahnu, Maslauskaite, Stankuniene, & Zakharov, 2012). However, the transition out of cohabitation into marriage became socially differentiated and as a result, the socio-economically disadvantaged groups manifested significantly lower rates of transition into marriage compared to the more advantageous (Maslauskaite & Baublyte, 2015).

The 2011 Census revealed that 22.5% of all families with children in Lithuania are single-mother families, who live in either independent or complex households (Stankūnienė, Baublytė, & Maslauskaitė, 2016). However, the cross-sectional data did not accurately capture the extent of the phenomenon because single motherhood in many cases represents only a spell in the individuals' family trajectory. Evidence based on the retrospective partnership histories prove that around half (46%) of the Lithuanian women experienced the state of single motherhood at least once in their life course before the age of 50 (Fig. 4.1). Lithuania resembles the trend characteristic to Estonia (49%), France (41%) and the Czech Republic (46%) and together with them represents the most frequent manifestation of single motherhood among the EU countries and is very close to the trend in the US (Andersson, Thompson, & Duntava, 2016).

There is diversity of single mothers in regard to their marital status. Although divorce remains the dominant path into single motherhood (42.6%), almost one-third of single mothers are married, but live without a partner (29.4%) and 19.1% acquire the status never having married (Stankūnienė et al., 2016). A high share of married single mothers potentially could be explained by the very intense out-migration flows. Existing evidence reveals particularly vulnerable socio-economic positions and high dependency on the social protection system of the lower-educated, never-married single mothers. Social benefits are the main source of income for 40% of single women with children and among them particularly disadvantaged are never-married mothers, of whom every second is dependent on the social protection system (Stankūnienė et al., 2016).

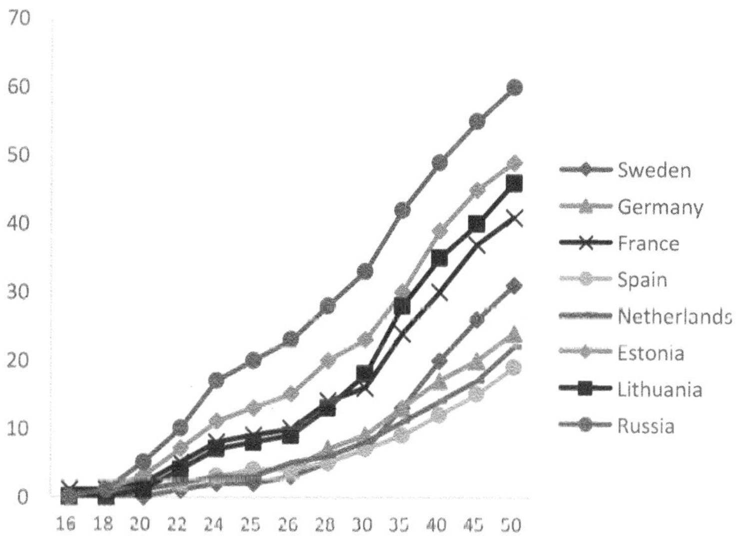

Fig. 4.1. Cumulative Percent ever 'Parent and not in a Union' (Single Mother), Women, Selected European Countries. *Source*: Andersson et al. (2016).

4.2.2 Single Mother Families: Poverty and Social Policy Responses

Single-mother families along with the two-parent families with three or more children are the most deprived households in Lithuania, and their poverty rate is almost twice as high as that for the general population (Income and Living Conditions 2015, 2016). Every second single mother with children lives at the risk of poverty. Overall during the last decade the situation did not change substantially, nonetheless, some dynamics could be distinguished. Single-mother families at-risk-of-poverty rates grew in 2008, the year the economic crisis showed the first signs, afterwards slightly decreased and started to grow again in 2012 (Fig. 4.2). During the last decade it fluctuated within the amplitude of 39–48%.

The role of social policy in buffering the poverty of single-mother families is very limited in the country (Ivaškaitė-Tamošiūnė, 2013). Moreover, differently from other household types, the effect of social transfers is negligible for single-mother families. For example, in 2015 the effect of social transfers on the poverty reduction amounted to 15 percentage points for two-parent families with three or more children, while for single-mother families – only three percentage points (Income and Living Conditions 2015, 2016). Poverty reduction through social transfers was most voluminous in 2009–2011, the years the economic crisis hit the hardest and immediately afterwards, but after 2012 it started to decrease very radically and reached the point where the social transfers have almost no effect on poverty reduction for this type of household. Currently, Lithuania's relative poverty rate for single mothers places the country close to Spain, Portugal,

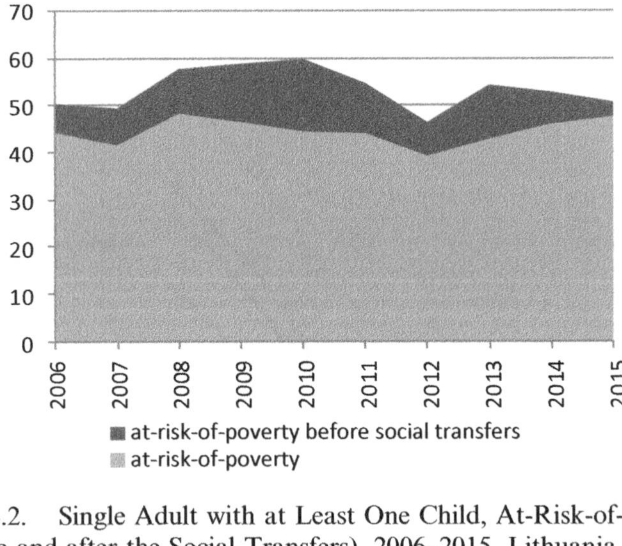

Fig. 4.2. Single Adult with at Least One Child, At-Risk-of-Poverty (before and after the Social Transfers), 2006–2015, Lithuania. *Source*: EU-SILC data. Data collected from annual publications on the results of EU-SILC in Lithuania Income and Living Conditions, 2007, 2008, 2009, 2010, 2011, 2012, 2013, 2013, 2014, 2015, 2016.

Belgium and is somewhat lower than in the EU forerunning countries – the UK, Ireland, Hungary, where the rates reach 60% (Eurostat, 2016).

General developments of the social security system after the economic crisis had an unfavourable effect on the unprivileged groups including single mothers with children. Overall, Lithuania is among the EU countries with the lowest expenditures on the social protection as the share of GDP and in the period after the crisis the expenditures decreased reaching the lowest level of 11.1% (Government Expenditure on Social Protection, 2017). The post-crisis years are characterised by the retrenchment of almost all universal family benefits introduced in the pre-crisis period (2004–2008) and the redirection of the social security system towards a more targeted model (Aidukaite, 2013; Aidukaite et al., 2016). Social assistance for low income or poor families, which in many cases are single-mother families as it was noted above, is based on the means-tested benefits, but to be entitled for the benefits individuals or families have to pass not only the income tests, but also the property and the assets tests. Family support benefits, which include maternity, paternity, parental leave and sickness leave are earnings related and depend on the previous contributions to the Social Insurance Fund. Consequently, persons without previous social insurance contributions are eligible to the family support benefits on the means tested basis. Among the three Baltic countries, Lithuania, according to some scholars (Aidukaite, 2013), represents the least generous support system for families with children.

To sum up the contextual framework, single-mother families are widespread in Lithuania, nearly every fourth family with children is headed by a single mother. The country is among the forerunners in the EU according to the widespread of this family arrangement, which has been in place for more than four decades. However, recent demographic changes in cohabitation and union dissolution substantially altered the socio-economic background of single motherhood. Currently, socio-economically unprivileged women have lower chances to enter marriage after cohabitation, higher risk to bear a child out of marriage and experience higher risk to divorce. Thus, the coupling of family dynamics linked with the instability and inequalities in Lithuania resembles the one reported for such neoliberal welfare states as the US (Perelli-Haris & Lyons-Amos, 2015). Single-mother families are among the most deprived in Lithuania; nearly half of them live in poverty, and the poverty rate is twice as high as for the general population (Income and Living Conditions 2015, 2016). The welfare state plays a very marginal role in mitigating the vulnerability of these families. Moreover, in the post-crisis era the social security system took the direction towards a more targeted model and the overall reduction of the social assistance to the families with children, which sets up the disadvantageous institutional framework for women raising children alone.

4.3 Data and Methods

The results presented in the following sections of the chapter are based on the nationally representative 'Single Mothers and Social Exclusion in Lithuania

Survey' dataset. The survey was conducted in 2014. The unit of information was defined as single mother living without a partner, but with at least one underaged child in the household disregarding of her previous marital status. We surveyed mothers leading an independent household or living together with relatives or other persons. The sample included women who experienced divorce or union dissolution, widowhood or of the status of never having been in partnership. The total size of the sample was 600 respondents. The fieldwork was subcontracted and carried out by the public opinion and market research company Ltd 'Baltic Surveys'. The face-to-face interviews were conducted at the respondents' home. The questionnaire covered the retrospective partnership and fertility histories, child maintenance issues, non-resident father and child contacts, material living conditions, wellbeing of single mother and other issues related to the socio-economic resources of the family. The survey has several advantages compared to the existing datasets (i.e. EU-SILC or Generations and Gender Survey). First, it directly addresses single mothers and thus overcomes the limitations linked to the insufficient number of cases in the general population surveys. Second, the survey covers not only the material living conditions but also other aspects of the wellbeing of single mothers and thus complements the existing data sources. Third, material deprivation is operationalised, placing more emphasis on the component of basic leisure activities and cultural consumption, thus it grasps the deprivation in a more nuanced and country-sensitive manner.

As it was already mentioned, we focus on two components of single mothers' quality of life: material deprivation and personal wellbeing. The last is defined as the absence of negative feelings (depressive symptoms) and the absence of parenting-related stress. The questionnaire included three scales designed to measure each of the corresponding issues.

First, the Adapted Material Deprivation Scale (A-MDS) was used for the measurement of deprivation from goods and services. The A-MDS scale was developed on the basis of the EU MD 17 items scale (Boarini & d'Ercole, 2006; Measuring Material Deprivation in EU, 2012) and it includes items on exclusion from cultural and leisure consumption. This was motivated by the findings of the previously conducted qualitative study with single mothers and findings on the social meanings of a 'decent life' (Maslauskaitė, 2014). The A-MDS measured the self-assessed ability to improve housing conditions (to buy a larger apartment), to maintain adequate level of home heating, to eat meat/fish every other day, to buy new clothes, to buy new furniture, to have at least one week vacation abroad annually, to have at least one week holiday on the Lithuanian beach, to go to the sports club, to have dinner with children in the restaurant/café at least once a month, to go to the cinema, theatre, concert at least once a month.

Second, the Center for Epidemiologic Studies depression scale (CES-D 8) (Radloff, 1977) was employed to measure DF. The scale was previously used in Lithuania implementing the international longitudinal panel 'Generations and Gender Survey' (UNECE, 2005) and thus was validated and adapted for use in the Lithuanian general surveys. It measures some symptoms of depression, which along with others are used to diagnose clinical depression. The scale is self-reported inventory and records seven depression indicating feelings, which might be experienced during the last week; each item is measured on a four-point scale.

Third, the Parenting-Related Stress scale (PRS) was used to measure the tensions which single mothers experience because of being the primary custodian of the child. The PRS scale was developed based on the results of the qualitative study with the single mothers in Lithuania (Maslauskaite, 2014). The scale includes six items, each indicating the different components of the tension linked to the status of single carer and provider in the family. The items are: 'I regret that children grow up without a father', 'I am worried whether I will be able to provide for the education of the children', 'I feel exhausted because of the excess of the family responsibilities', 'I am anxious about falling ill and not being able to take care of my children', 'I hardly make ends meet', 'I have no time for myself'. Each item was measured on the five-point Likert scale.

In the analysis, we included a set of independent variables. The variables reflecting the structural position of single mothers were: education, measured in five categories (incomplete secondary, secondary, vocational, college and university); average monthly incomes per household member, measured in four categories based on income quartiles; place of residence, measured in five categories based on the population size in the settlement. In addition, we included variables on the single mothers' family situation and partnership characteristics. First, we considered the paths towards single motherhood and indicated single mothers who never lived with a partner, divorced, separated after cohabitation and widows. Second, we included the variable on the number of children in the family with three categories: one, two, three and more children. Third, based on the calendar information we calculated the age of the youngest child. Fourth, the variable on the time spent in the state of single motherhood was composed calculating the provided calendar information on the partnership history. In case there were several spells of single motherhood we considered the last one. The detailed information on the adjustment of the variables are provided in each of the following sections. We use the descriptive, one-way mean comparison (ANOVA) and regression analysis, which includes the models based on linear and logistic regression. The main set of control variables is used in each regression model; however, in some cases additional controls are introduced in order to establish the relevant predictors and strengthen explicative power of the models.

4.4 Single Mothers and Material Deprivation

Single motherhood is associated with poverty, which is linked to gender inequalities in the labour market, the gendered nature of care, lack of the spousal incomes and, in addition to it, in the case of divorce, by the loss of the economies of scale benefits (Sørensen, 1994). After union dissolution women are also often encountered by the non-payment of child maintenance by the non-resident father (Nepomnyaschy, 2007) and this in turn also has a negative effect on family resources and increases the risk of poverty. Poverty is multidimensional, thus the lack of financial resources reflects only one side of the vulnerability and precariousness. Material deprivation is the other side of poverty and reflects limited opportunities to consume goods and services that are arbitrarily assigned as a necessary minimum standard for 'decent living' in the society. Material deprivation is also linked to the social exclusion and is often discussed as the objective side of it (Boarini & D'Ercole, 2006). In the following sections we discuss the components of material deprivation experienced by single mothers in Lithuania and also analyse the factors predicting the severity of material deprivation.

Fig. 4.3 displays the descriptive results of the A-MDS, which measures the subjectively assessed opportunities to consume daily goods, leisure and cultural activities. The majority of single mothers in Lithuania are unable to improve housing conditions (96%), to have at least one week vacation abroad (89%), to buy new furniture (86%) (Fig. 4.3). In addition, 72% report the inability to afford the sports club, 56% – to have at least one week holiday on the Lithuania seaside annually, 54% – to have dinner at a restaurant or café with children at least once a month. Half of the single mothers are excluded from the consumption of basic cultural goods and cannot afford the cinema, theatre or concert at least once a month. Every second single mother cannot buy new clothes. Least often reported form of material deprivation is related to the nutrition needs and heating.

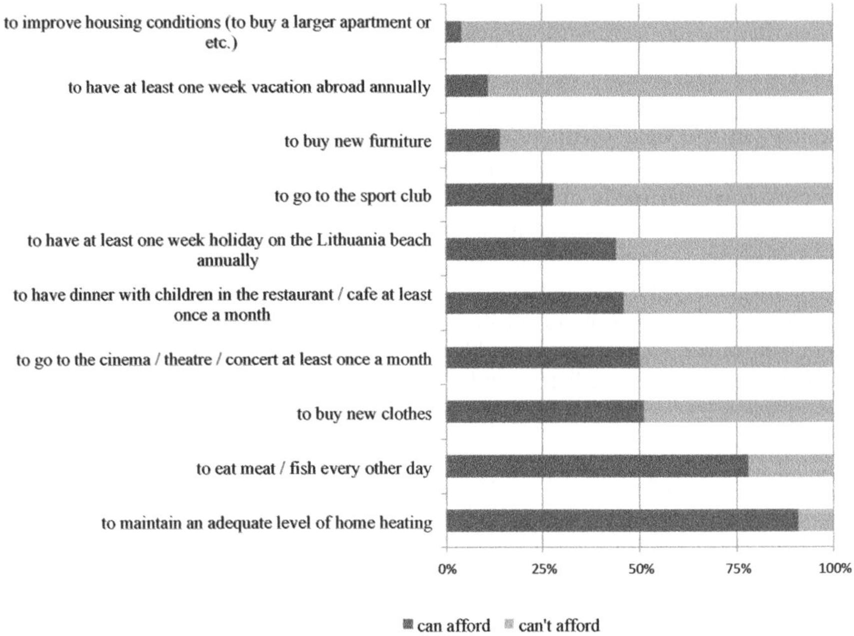

Fig. 4.3. Components of Material Derivation in Single Mother Households (in Percent). *Source*: Single mothers and social exclusion in Lithuania survey.

Consumption of meat and fish every other day is not feasible for 22% of single mothers. Nine percent of single mothers said that they cannot maintain an adequate level of home heating.

For further analysis the Index of Material Deprivation (IMD) has been composed from the A-MDS items. The two items with the one-sided distribution were removed from further analysis. The composite summary measure was created with the minimum value of 1, which indicates the state of no deprivation, and the highest value of 8, which signals the most intense deprivation. Overall, 17% of single mothers reported that they cannot afford any of the listed seven goods or services; an additional 32% declared the inability to afford five to six, consequently, almost half of the women have encountered severe exclusion from the socially acceptable way of life. On the contrary, there are 10% of single mothers who experience no material deprivation.

Single mothers are not a homogenous group and thus are exposed to different degrees of material deprivation depending on their socio-economic positions and structural characteristics of the household. Table 4.1 presents the mean values of IMD for various subgroups and results of the between-group comparison tests.

Material deprivation is negatively associated with the level of education ($r = -0.461$, $p < 0.001$). Highest mean values of IMD are observed for single mothers with incomplete secondary education; they gradually decline in every group of higher level of education and are the lowest for women with university education (Table 4.1). Although the negative association was expected and the result corroborates already reported findings in many previous studies (Brady & Burroway, 2012), one interesting issue is a very large difference in the IMD values between the lowest and the highest educational groups. Comparison between groups proves overall significant differences. The multiple comparison Scheffe tests indicate that university-educated women substantially differ in IMD mean values from all other educational groups, and similar results are for the college educated and groups with incomplete secondary education. There are no statistically significant differences between groups with secondary and vocational education.

Place of residence also markedly differentiates exposure to material deprivation. The largest deprivation is observed for women in rural areas and the lowest for those living in large cities (including the capital city and other large urban areas). The multiple comparison tests indicate significant difference only for rural single mothers; they experience much higher deprivation compared to all other areas of residence.

Household structure and paths to single motherhood are also associated with the level of material deprivation of single mothers. The results show that women living with three or more dependent children are exposed to much higher levels of material deprivation compared to those having only one or two children. The mean values for the last two groups are very close and lower than for single mothers with three or more children. Widows are also more deprived than divorced, separated or never-married women. However, multiple comparison tests prove that there are significant differences only between widows and the two other groups, while never-married single mothers and those who dissolved their unions do not differ in the level of material deprivation.

Table 4.1. Mean Values for Index of Material Deprivation. One-factor Analysis of Variance (ANOVA).

	Mean	SD
Level of education		
Incomplete secondary	6.97	1.7
Secondary	5.67	1.8
Vocational	5.59	2.09
College	4.5	2.3
University	3.25	2.07
F	*38.8****	
Place of residence		
Rural areas	6.0	2.03
Small towns	5.0	2.33
Other urban areas	3.98	2.26
Other two largest cities	4.21	2.29
Capital city	4.42	2.2
F	*14.4****	
Number of children		
One	4.8	2.27
Two	4.9	2.38
Three and more	5.76	2.42
F	*3.29**	
Marital status		
Never had a partner	5.06	2.39
Widow	5.72	2.02
Divorced, separated	4.78	2.34
F	*4.41**	

Note: ***$p < 0.001$; *$p < 0.05$.
Source: Single mothers and social exclusion survey.

In the next step we applied the multiple regression analysis in order to identify factors predicting severity of material deprivation and to eliminate the compositional effects of the individual variables. Table 4.2 depicts the results of the stepwise multiple regression models, in which we controlled for the women's education, place of residence, marital status in the previous partnership, number of children, time elapsed after the union dissolution and age of the mother and the youngest child. The results of the multiple regression analysis to a large extent confirm the descriptive analysis and show that statistically significant factors predicting the severity of material deprivation are women's education, place of

Table 4.2. Standardised Beta Coefficients for Index of Material Deprivation. Linear Regression Models.

	Model 1	Model 2	Model 3
Education	−0.89***	−0.84***	−0.84***
Place of residence		−0.29***	−0.27***
Marital status (widow vs other)			0.97***
R	0.47	0.50	0.52
R Square	0.22	0.25	0.27

Note: (1) Additionally controlled: the youngest child's age, the time of the partnership break up, mothers age, number of children; (2) *** $p < 0.001$.
Source: Single mothers and social exclusion in Lithuania survey.

residence and marital status. All three models prove the inverse association between the level of education and the severity of material deprivation. The effect of residence is statistically significant, but the effect size is not so high. In the case of marital status, the only significant association is observed comparing widows with the other groups of marital status. Surprisingly, other factors linked with the household structure, i.e. number of children and the age of the youngest child, were not significant.

To sum, although the material deprivation of single-mother families is thoroughly examined in the literature, we believe that our results based on the A-MDS brings into perspective significant nuances on the disadvantages of the single-mother families. Inclusion of additional items reveals supplementary sides of single mothers' deprivation and, consequently, exclusion from the socially acceptable way of life, discursively defined as 'normal life'. Besides the deprivation from the improvement of the housing conditions, which is almost universal for Lithuanian single mothers, we observe high deprivation from the consumption of basic leisure and cultural activities. As it was expected, factors contributing to the severity of material deprivation are lower education, rural place of residence and being a widow, as it was proved by the regression analysis. A strong negative effect of education is sound if we consider the contextual factors linked with the welfare state developments in Lithuania. Means-tested welfare model, which was reinforced in the post-crisis period in the country, is counterproductive in assisting single mothers in need, as it has been proved for other countries (Kilkey & Bradshaw, 1999). In such a context, distinct through high commodification, the role of individual resources linked to the education becomes vital in securing the living conditions because the external assistance provided by the state plays only a marginal role.

4.5 Single Mothers' Personal Wellbeing

Single mothers fare worse on many aspects of personal wellbeing. They more frequently report general health problems (Burstrom et al., 2010), experience higher risk of mental or psychiatric disorder (Cairney, Boyle, Offord, & Racine, 2003), states of fear or depression (Rousou, Kouta, Middleton, & Karanikola, 2013), negative thoughts and low self-esteem (Peden, Hall, Rayens, & Grant, 2005). Several hypotheses explain the lower outcomes of personal well-being of single mothers. One highlights the effect of material deprivation and poverty, which leads to long-term chronic stress (Mackenbach et al., 2008), the other points to the long-term stress caused by the burden of responsibilities to raise children alone (Brown & Moran, 1997). In addition, literature suggests that some women are perhaps more vulnerable to stress due to their personality (Cairney et al., 2003). Moreover, individuals differ in their capacities to adjust to the stressful events and to the long-term stress. Amato (2000) suggested the Divorce-Stress-Adjustment perspective and highlighted the role of the protective factors, which act as the 'shock absorbers and weakens the links between divorce-related events and people's experience of stress' (Amato, 2000, p. 1272).

In this section, we examine two components of personal wellbeing. First, we discuss DF, which represent the emotional dimension of personal wellbeing, and investigate factors contributing to the elevated risk of DF. As already discussed, we measure DF with the version of the CES-D 8 Scale (Radloff, 1977; UNECE, 2005). Afterwards, we examine the parenting-related stress, which marks the capabilities of women to cope with the responsibilities of being the single carer and provider in the family.

4.5.1 Depressive Feelings and Associated Factors

In the study, single mothers were asked to assess how often during the last week they had crying spells, felt fearful, felt depressed, felt sad, felt lonely, thought that their life was a failure or felt that even with help they would not be able to get rid of sadness. Generally, on each scale item 10–20% of single mothers in Lithuania reported a very frequent ('often, most or all of the time') manifestation of the symptoms, 35–55% experienced them sometimes and 30–50% reported they almost did not experience them ('seldom or never') (Fig. 4.4). However, there is a wide variation in the frequency of each depressive experience. The most frequently reported are feelings of loneliness, thoughts of life as a failure, feelings of sadness and DF. Around 60% of single mothers experienced them often or sometimes during the week preceding the interview. Least often are the depressive symptoms of crying spells and fear.

In the further step we computed the summary Depression Index (DI), with the minimum value of 0, indicating none of the DF, and the maximum value of 14, which signifies the highest frequency of DF. Based on the theoretical assumptions, we next considered several factors potentially contributing to the reduction of emotional wellbeing and linked to the socio-economic position of single mother (i.e. level of material deprivation (MDI) and education) (Amato, 2000). We also included measurements linked with the mother–child situation such as age of the youngest child. There is evidence that single mothers with young children are particularly vulnerable to depression (Rosman & Yoshikawa, 2001). Time spent in the state of single motherhood could be the next relevant predictor of DF.

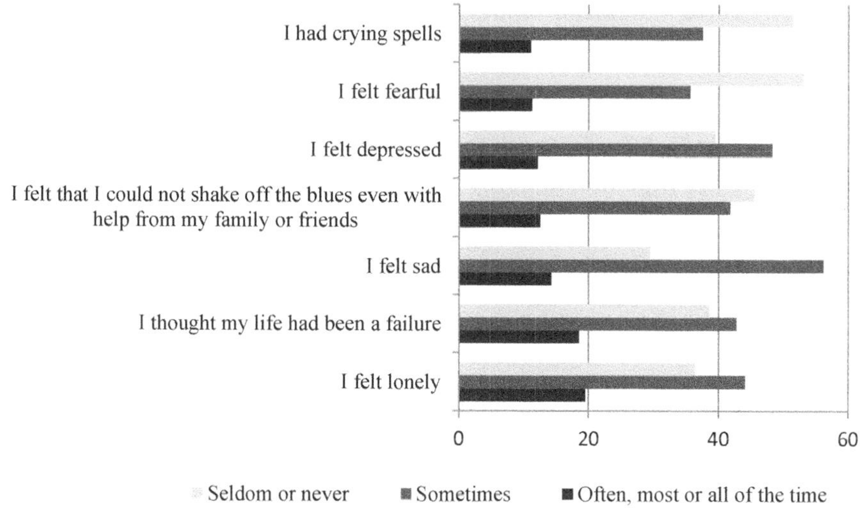

Fig. 4.4. Single Mothers' Psychological Wellbeing, Statements of Shorten Depression Scales (in Percent). *Source*: Single mothers and social exclusion in Lithuania survey.

Previous research suggests that with time people adapt to the stressful events linked to family transitions and return to normal functioning (Amato, 2000). Our analysis also takes into account the paths towards single motherhood, which could also be a significant predictor of the level of DF.

Table 4.3 presents the descriptive results of the DI mean values for various groups. Overall, the analysis indicates significant statistical differences in the mean values of the DI only for the socio-economic factors. The association between the DI and MDI is positive, i.e. more material deprivation is linked to more DF. Similar result is observed for the education: the higher the education, the lower is the level of the DI. Talking of the factors related to household structure, there is some variation of the DI mean values: single mothers with younger children exhibit higher mean values of the DI compared to mothers with older children. However, although the findings point into the expected direction, the differences between groups are not statistically significant. Similar results are for the effect of the path towards and the time spent in the state of single motherhood. Even if there are differences in the mean values, which point to the direction of the association we expected, the differences are not statistically significant.

In the further analysis we applied the multiple linear regression in order to estimate the predictors of the DF. We used all above-discussed variables and, wherever possible, transformed the categorical variables into the interval (time spent in the status of single motherhood and age of the youngest child). One categorical variable, i.e. marital status before single motherhood, was recorded as a dummy variable indicating widowhood versus all other statuses.

Table 4.3. Mean Values for Depression Index. One-factor Analysis of Variance (ANOVA).

	Mean	**SD**
Material deprivation index		
1 (no deprivation)	2.77	3.50
2	2.69	2.59
3	4.36	3.58
4	4.63	3.37
5	4.94	3.58
6	5.65	3.63
7	6.65	3.89
8 (very high deprivation)	7.55	4.31
F	*9.95****	
Level of education		
Incomplete secondary	6.15	4.9
Secondary	6.17	3.7
Vocational	5.36	3.7
College	4.09	3.9
University	4.15	3.5
F	*5.319****	
Age of the youngest child		
Less than 3 years	5.4	4.3
4–6 years	5.5	3.8
7–11 years	4.5	3.7
12–18 years	4.4	3.7
F	*3.37*	
Marital status		
Never had a partner	5.41	3.9
Widow	5.35	3.8
Divorced, separated	4.78	3.8
F	*2.4*	
Time spent in the status of the single motherhood		
Less than 4 years	5.13	3.95
5–9 years	4.62	3.68
10 and more	4.69	3.93
F	*0.71*	

Note: ***$p < 0.001$.

Source: Single mothers and social exclusion in Lithuania survey.

Table 4.4. Standardised Beta Coefficients for Depression Index. Linear Regression Model.

	Standardised Beta Coefficients
Material deprivation	0.38***
Education	n.s
Youngest child age	n.s
Time spent in the single mother state	n.s
Widow vs other	n.s
R	0.48
R Square	0.2

Source: Single mothers and social exclusion in Lithuania survey.

Overall, the results of the regression analysis presented in Table 4.4 corroborate the already discussed descriptive results. The statistically significant predictor of DF experienced by single mothers is the level of material deprivation, if we control for other factors such as education, age of the youngest child and time spent in the state of single motherhood. The association between the two variables is positive, and higher levels of material deprivation predict higher levels of DF in the population of single mothers. This is fully in line with the previous findings (Van de Velde et al., 2014) and supports the idea on the link between depression and long-term stress caused by chronic material disadvantages. Interestingly, that material deprivation was the only significant predictor for the elevated levels of DF. Contrary to our expectations, we did not find any support for the protective effect of education. We anticipated that education is not only the proxy for the economic resources, but also for the stress-coping skills because the higher educated have better communication skills, higher cognitive abilities and thus could better adjust (Wang & Amato, 2000). In addition, our analysis did not support the previous evidence on the effect of the youngest child's age, time spent in the state of single motherhood and path towards the status of single mother on the level of DF.

4.5.2 Parenting-Related Stress

As it was already mentioned, lower personal wellbeing of single mothers could be associated with the long-term stress caused by lone parenting (Pryor & Trinder, 2004). Women raising children alone suffer from the overload of the responsibilities linked with being the single carer and provider; they also in severe ways experience the competing demands of working and family life.

The needs to compensate economic losses linked to single motherhood often require to increase the working time and thus, to decrease time spent on parenting. Obviously, this is reflected in the research findings on parenting outcomes. They suggest that single parents often struggle to monitor and supervise the activities of children (Hetherington & Stanley-Hagen, 2002); they are more inclined to use negative parenting strategies (Braver & Lamb, 2013). Parenting-related stress could also be affected by contextual factors, such as the normative expectations towards the post-divorce parenting, non-resident fathers' involvement in child rearing and also by the legal framework, which could encourage fathers' involvement.

In the following, we discuss the parenting-related stress and contributing socio-economic factors linked with the single mother. As noted above, the measurement is based on the six-item PRS scale developed for the purpose of the study and based on the results of the qualitative study with single mothers in Lithuania (Maslauskaite, 2014).

Fig. 4.5 presents the frequency distribution for each item of the PRS scale. Most frequently reported component is linked to the cognitive dissonance between the normative model of two parents' family and the biographical situation of single mother. A total 63% reported having negative feelings because their children grow in a single-mother family. Against the backdrop of the long tradition of divorce and relatively loose attitudes to it (Maslauskaitė & Baublytė, 2012) we could speculate that this in the first place echoes the sense of loss in the life chances and life quality of the children and not the possible stigmatisation. The majority of women (57%) also expressed concerns regarding their own financial capacities to secure the children's future education. Thus, they negatively assess the current and prospective financial situation, which could have a

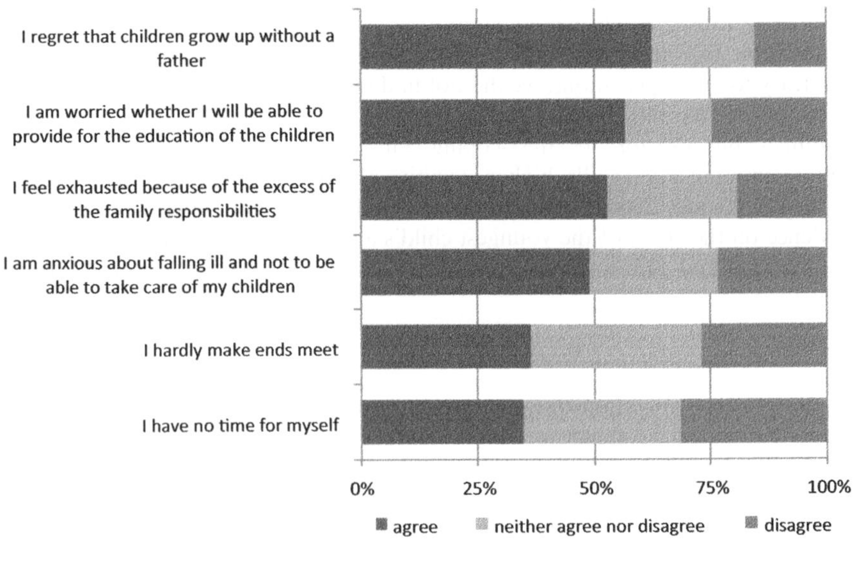

Fig. 4.5. Assessment of the Parenting Stressors (in Percent). *Source*: Single mothers and social exclusion in Lithuania survey.

substantial impact on the educational chances and life prospects of children in the context of the neoliberal educational policies introduced in the country in the post-crisis period. In addition, around every second single mother (53%) suffers negative emotional outcomes linked to being the single carer; thus the excess of care responsibilities for the majority of women is a relevant source of stress. A similar share reported the care-related stress associated with the prospective health risks and their effect on the mothering capabilities. Every second mother felt anxiety to fall ill and not being able to perform as the primary carer. Around one-third of single mothers experience stress because of the limited opportunities to spend some time for their personal needs. Being a single provider for the children also causes additional stress to the mothers, thus almost every third reports the tensions caused by the inability to make ends meet.

What factors contribute to the elevated level of PRS? To answer this, we first developed the compositional variable based on the results of the cluster analysis for the PRS items. Two groups were composed, the first indicates no-experience of the PRS (value 0) and the second – suffering moderate or high PRS (value 1). In the logistic regression analysis, we included several control variables. The existing evidence suggests that poverty is an essential predictor for the emotional well being of single mothers (Van de Velde et al., 2014). Thus, we incorporated into the model the income-based indicator. Four quartile income groups were subtracted. In addition, the control variable measuring mothers' education was included because higher education leads not only to higher financial resources and less overall vulnerability, but also because it indicates higher cognitive abilities and skills to manage parenting stress. We also considered such factors as the place of residence, number of children, age of the youngest child, as well as several life course factors – time spent in the state of single motherhood, last partnership status. All variables were included in the logistic regression model. The odds ratios are presented in the Table 4.5.

The results of the logistic regression prove the strong negative association between the manifestation of the PRS and the financial situation of the single-mother families. Women belonging to the two lowest income quartile groups exhibit around five times higher odds ratio to report the PRS compared to the women from the highest income quartile group. However, there is no statistically significant difference in the PRS manifestation between the two highest income groups. Thus, poverty is a strong predictor for the elevated risk of mothering stress and this finding is in line with the previous results on the outcomes of poor financial conditions on the emotional wellbeing of single mothers (Avison, Ali, & Walter, 2007). Higher level of education has a protective effect on the single mothers' personal wellbeing, while lower education increases the odds to experience the PRS. Lower personal wellbeing is more pronounced for the lowest group of education: women with incomplete secondary education have more than four times higher odds to report the PRS compared to the highest, i.e. university educated, single mothers. The odds ratios for the secondary and vocational education also indicate a higher propensity to experience the PRS compared to the university-educated women. Again, the finding corroborates the existing almost universal evidence on the educational disadvantage and higher exposure to

Table 4.5. Odds Ratios for Parenting-related Stress.

	Exp (B)
Level of education	
University (ref.)	
College	1.6
Vocational	3.42**
Secondary	3.37**
Incomplete secondary	4.52**
Income group	
Highest (291 € >) (ref.)	
High to moderate (221–290 €)	1.8
Moderate to low (161–220 €)	5.1***
Lowest (<160 €)	5.48***
Last partnership status	
Marriage, cohabitation (ref.)	
Never married, without partner	0.28
Widow	7.7***
R	0.25
R square	0.34

Note: (1) additionally controlled for number of children, age of the youngest child, time in the single motherhood status; all predictors are not significant. (2) the model classifies 86% of cases with high parental stress and 59% of no parental stress cases; describes 76% of the total variation. (3) $***p < 0.001$, $**p < 0.05$.

Source: Single mothers and social exclusion in Lithuania survey.

stress, which has been proved at the cross-country level (Van de Velde et al., 2014). An additional significant predictor of the PRS is the path towards single motherhood. Widows experience a substantially higher risk of the PRS compared to divorced or separated mothers. Interestingly, never-partnered single mothers have lower risk to experience the PRS compared to the divorced or separated; however, the finding is not supported by the significance test. Higher exposure of widows to the PRS seems reasonable because individual adjustment to the role of the single mother is marked by a substantial difference compared to divorce. Divorce ends unsatisfactory relationships and is the process which precedes the event of union dissolution, while the death of the partner at a young or middle age is more likely to be a sudden event, which might end a high-quality marital relationship. Moreover, widowhood is among the most crucial stressful life events and as it is well documented it has a very strong impact on health and emotional outcomes (Avison et al., 2007). Contrary to the expectations, we did not find any effect on the PRS of child-related factors (age and number of children) and time spent in single motherhood. We believe that this highlights the essential role of financial and personal resources, the latter linked with the education, in moderating the PRS. If these resources are available, the situational stress linked with the changing demands caused by child's developmental tasks are managed and do not bring tensions into the emotional life of the mother.

4.6 Conclusion

The aim of this chapter was to explore the single mothers' quality of life focusing on the material and subjective dimensions of wellbeing in the context, which is distinct through the marginal role of the welfare state in mitigating the risks associated with single motherhood. The leading argument of the research suggests that single mothers are a heterogeneous group and, consequently, the outcomes of single motherhood are not uniform and therefore moderated by socio economic and structural family-level factors. Considering the country-specific institutional setting, we expected significant disparities by education on all dimensions of life quality and the substantial protective effect of the higher education in regards to the material deprivation and emotional wellbeing of single mothers. Our study is based on the results of the cross-sectional representative survey with women raising children alone. The research contributes to the field, while it adds evidence on the single motherhood disadvantage from Lithuania, an EU country, which represents the transitional society, but also which together with two other Baltic countries was hit the hardest by the 2008–2009 financial–economic crisis (Smith & Swain, 2010) and reacted to the crisis executing the most radical austerity strategy (Sommers et al., 2014). In addition, the study also raises methodological issues on the measurement of the material deprivation and personal wellbeing.

Contextual analysis proves that single-mother families are on high prevalence in Lithuania; the country is among the leaders in the EU (Chzhen & Bradshaw, 2012). The trend had been in place for more than a half of a century, although the socio-economic composition of and paths to single motherhood were substantially altered by the comprehensive societal and demographic changes of the last two decades. Socio-economic vulnerability is positively associated with the chances to move into single motherhood, since marriage, non-marital childbearing and divorce become increasingly socially differentiated (Maslauskaite & Baublyte, 2015; Maslauskaite et al., 2015; Perelli-Harris & Lyons-Amos, 2015, 2016). To a large extent these processes might be associated with the emergence of an extremely radical neoliberal capitalism (Bohle & Greskovits, 2007), which was accompanied by a very thin social protection system. The financial–economic crisis of 2008–2009 conditioned the rolling back of the expenditures on the social protection and the retrenchment of all universal family benefits introduced in pre-crisis period, strengthening the means-targeted model and reduction in the social assistance to families with children (Aidukaite, 2013; Aidukaite et al., 2016). As a result, single-mother families are among the poorest; their poverty rate is twice as high as in the general population (Income and Living Conditions 2015, 2016). Moreover, differently from the other household types they experience almost no reduction in poverty through the social policy measures.

Our analysis reveals the essential role of individual resources in managing the single motherhood disadvantage. Overall, as it has been expected, the life quality is in a substantial way differentiated within the single-mother group and is essentially determined by the material and/or educational resources of women. In talking about the material deprivation, several main findings need to be stressed. First, almost half of single mothers reported severe exclusion from the socially acceptable way of life, which was measured considering the material living conditions and the basic leisure and cultural activities. Second, the gap in the material deprivation by education is large, and this was proved by controlling for various family- and individual-level factors.

The level of personal wellbeing of single mothers, which in this research was measured by the absence of DF and parenting-related stress, is also highly dependent on individual resources. We found that higher levels of material deprivation lead to more severe DF, and this finding is in line with the ones reported previously (Cairney et al., 2003; Cunningham & Knoester, 2007). Our results corroborate the evidence that in the CEE countries, the link between poverty and DF of single mothers is strongest (Van de Velde et al., 2014). However, we could not prove the protective role of education or of other family-related factors for the absence of DF. The second dimension of personal wellbeing – parental-related stress – is also very common among the Lithuanian single mothers. Majority of women are exposed to stress linked with various aspects of being the single carer and provider. Occurrence of stress is strongly related to the financial resources and educational level of the single mother. Poor and lower educated women are more exposed to the long-term stress caused by the burden of parenting responsibilities. We argue that the limited role of the welfare state in buffering the life risks associated with single motherhood could explain the strong effect of the material conditions on the personal wellbeing of single mothers.

On a more general level, our findings suggest that the radical austerity policy, which in the Baltic countries was introduced after the 2008–2009 financial–economic crisis (Sommers et al., 2014), has deepened the vulnerability of the single mothers and particularly those with lower personal resources. We believe that our research highlights an urgent need for adequate social policy measures aimed at reducing the single-mother families' deprivation and lower life quality. Existing evidence based on comparative analysis proves that material hardship is most successfully alleviated by the policies, which combine measures facilitating employment and income transfers through child tax benefits and family allowances (Härkönen, 2017a; Maldonado & Niewenhuis, 2015). Although some argue that income transfers reduce women's participation in the labour market (Thévenon, 2011) and thus increase the welfare dependency of socio-economically vulnerable groups, they, however, help to combat child poverty and thus are a relevant measure of social investment.

References

Aidukaite, J. (2013). Social policy changes in the three Baltic states over the last decade (2000–2012). *Ekonomika*, *3*, 89.

Aidukaite, J., Moskvina, J., & Skuciene, D. (2016). Lithuanian Welfare System in Times of Recent Crisis. In K. Schubert, P. de Villota, & J. Kuhlmann (Eds.), *Challenges to European welfare systems* (pp. 419–441). London: Springer International Publishing.

Amato, P. R. (2000). The consequneces of divorce for adults and children. *Journal of Marriage and Family*, *64*, 1269–1287.

Andersson, G., Thomson, E., & Duntava, A. (2016). *Life-table representations of family dynamics in the 21st century*. Stockhom Research Reports in Demography, *16*. Stockholm University Demography Unit, Stockholm.

Avison, W. R., Ali, J., & Walters, D. (2007). Family structure, stress, and psychological distress: A demonstration of the impact of differential exposure. *Journal of Health and Social Behaviour*, *3*, 301–317.

Bernardi, F., & Boertien, D. (2016). Understanding heterogeneity in the effects of parental separation on educational attainment in Britain: Do children from lower educational backgrounds have less to lose? *European Sociological Review*, *32*(6), 807–819.

Boarini, R., & d'Ercole, M. M. (2006). *Measures of material deprivation in OECD countries*. OECD Social, Employment and Migration Working Papers, *6*. OECD, Paris.

Bohle, D., & Greskovits, B. (2007). Neoliberalism, embedded neoliberalism and neocorporatism: Towards transnational capitalism in Central-Eastern Europe. *West European Politics*, *3*, 443–466.

Brady, D., & Burroway, R. (2012). Targeting, universalism, and single-mother poverty: A multilevel analysis across 18 affluent democracies. *Demography*, *2*, 719–746.

Braver, S. L., & Lamb, M. E. (2013). Marital dissolution. In *Handbook of marriage and the family* (pp. 487–516). New York, NY: Springer.

Brown, G. W., & Moran, P. M. (1997). Single mothers, poverty and depression. *Psychological Medicine*, *27*, 21–33.

Burstrom, B., Whitehead, M., Clayton, S., Fritzell, S., Vannoni, F., & Costa, G. (2010). Health inequalities between lone and couple mothers and policy under different welfare regimes – The example of Italy, Sweden and Britain. *Social Science & Medicine*, *6*, 912–920.

Cairney, J., Boyle, M., Offord, D., & Racine, Y. (2003). Stress, social support and depression in single and married mothers. *Social Psychiatry and Psychiatric Epidemiology*, *35*, 442–449.

Chzhen, Y., & Bradshaw, J. (2012). Lone parents, poverty and policy in the European Union. *Journal of European Social Policy*, *22*(5), 487–506. doi:10.1177/0958928712456578

Cunningham, A. M., & Knoester, C. (2007). Marital status, gender, and parents' psychological well-being. *Sociological Inquiry*, *77*(2), 264–287.

Demographic Yearbook 2015. (2016). Vilnius: Statistics Lithuania.

Eurostat (2016). People at rist of poverty or social exclusion by household type. Retrieved from http://appsso.eurostat.ec.europa.eu/nui/submitViewTableAction.do.

Government Expenditure on Social Protection. (2017). Retreived from http://ec.europa.eu.

Guogis, A., & Koht, H. (2009). Why not the Nordic model of welfare state in Lithuania? Trends in Lithuanian and Norwegian social policies. In J. Aidukaite (Ed.), *Poverty, urbanity and social policy. Central and Eastern Europe in a broader context* (pp. 149–167). New York, NY: Nova Sciences.

Härkönen, J. (2017a). *Diverging destinies in international perspective: Education, single motherhood, and child poverty*. LIS Working Paper Series (No. 713). Luxembourg: Luxembourg Income Study (LIS).

Härkönen, J. (2017b). *Single-mother poverty: How much do educational differences in single motherhood matter?*. LIS Working Paper Series (No. 714). Stockholm: Stockholm University.

Heyns, B. (2005). Emerging inequalities in Central and Eastern Europe. *Annual Review of Sociology*, *31*, 163–197.

Hetherington, E. M., & Stanley-Hagan, M. (2002). Parenting in divorced and remarried families. In *Handbook of parenting, being and becoming a parent* (Vol. 3, pp. 287–316). Mahwah, NJ: Lawrence Erlbaum Associates Publishers.

Income and Living Conditions 2015. (2016). Vilnius: Statistics Lithuania.

Ivaškaitė-Tamošiūnė, V. (2013). *Pajamų perskirstymas formuojantis gerovės kapitalizmui Lietuvoje*. Doctoral dissertation, Vilnius University,Vilnius.

Juozapaitienė, R. (2011). Bažnytinės santuokos registracija Lietuvoje: istorija ir dabartis. *Kultūra ir visuomenė: socialinių tyrimų žurnalas*, *3*, 101–123.

Kattel, R., & Raudla, R. (2013). The Baltic republics and the crisis of 2008–2011. *Europe-Asia Studies*, *3*, 426–449.

Kilkey, M. (2000). *Lone mothers between paid work and care: The policy regime in twenty countries*. Doctoral dissertation, University of York.

Kilkey, M., & Bradshaw, J. (1999). Lone mothers, economic well-being, and policies. In D. Sainsbury (Eds.), *Gender and welfare state regimes* (pp. 147–184). Oxford: Oxford University Press.

Mackenbach, J. P., Stirbu, I., Roskam, A. J. R., Schaap, M. M., Menvielle, G., Leinsalu, M., & Kunst, A. E. (2008). Socioeconomic inequalities in health in 22 European countries. *New England Journal of Medicine*, *23*, 2468–2481.

Maldonado, L. C., & Nieuwenhuis, R. (2015). Family policies and single parent poverty in 18 OECD countries, 1978–2008. *Community, Work & Family*, *18*(4), 395–415.

Marriage and Divorce Statistics. (2016). Retrieved from http://ec.europa.eu/eurostat.

Maslauskaitė, A. (2014). Vienišos motions, vartojimas ir socialinė atskirtis. *Kultūra ir visuomenė*, *2*, 13–37.

Maslauskaitė, A., & Baublytė, M. (2012). *Skyrybų visuomenė*. Vilnius: LSTC.

Maslauskaitė, A., & Baublytė, M. (2015). Gender and re-partnering after divorce in four Central European and Baltic countries. *Sociologický časopis/Czech Sociological Review*, *6*, 1023–1046.

Maslauskaite, A., Jasilioniene, A., Jasilionis, D., Stankuniene, V., & Shkolnikov, V. M. (2015). Socio-economic determinants of divorce in Lithuania: Evidence from register-based census-linked data. *Demographic Research*, *33*, 871–908.

McLanahan, S., & Jacobsen, W. (2015). Diverging destinies revisited. In *Families in an era of increasing inequality* (pp. 3–23). Cham: Springer International Publishing.

McLanahan, S., & Percheski, C. (2008). Family structure and the reproduction of inequalities. *Annual Review of Sociology*, *34*, 257–276.

Measuring Material Deprivation in EU (2012). Luxembourg: Publications Office of the European Union.

Nepomnyaschy, L. (2007). Child support and father-child contact: Testing reciprocal pathways. *Demography*, *44*, 93–112.

Peden, A. R., Rayens, M. K., Hall, L. A., & Grant, E. (2005). Testing an intervention to reduce negative thinking, depressive symptoms, and chronic stressors in low – Income single mothers. *Journal of Nursing Scholarship*, *3*, 268–274.

Perelli-Harris, B., & Lyons-Amos, M. (2015). Changes in partnership patterns across the life course: An examination of 14 countries in Europe and the United States. *Demographic Research*, *33*, 145.

Perelli-Harris, B., & Lyons-Amos, M. (2016). Partnership patterns in the United States and across Europe: The role of education and country context. *Social Forces*, *95*(1), 251–282.

Pryor, J., & Trinder, L. (2004). Children, families, and divorce. In *The Blackwell Companion to the Sociology of Families* (pp. 322–340). Oxford: Blackwell Publishing.

Puur, A., Rahnu, L., Maslauskaite, A., Stankuniene, V., & Zakharov, S. (2012). Transformation of partnership formation in Eastern Europe. The legacy of the past demographic divide. *Journal of Comparative Family Studies*, *1*, 389–417.

Radloff, L. S. (1977). The CES-D scale: A self-report depression scale for research in the general population. *Applied Psychological Measurement*, *3*, 385–401.

Rosman, E. A., & Yoshikawa, H. (2001). Effects of welfare reform on children of adolescent mothers: Moderation by maternal depression, father involvement, and grandmother involvement. *Women & Health*, *3*, 253–290.

Rousou, E., Kouta, C., Middleton, N., & Karanikola, M. (2013). Single mothers' self-assessment of health: A systematic exploration of the literature. *International Nursing Review*, *4*, 425–434.

Rowlingson, K., & McKay, S. (2005). Lone motherhood and socio-economic disadvantage: Insights from quantitative and qualitative evidence. *The Sociological Review*, *1*, 30–49.

Smith, A., & Swain, A. (2010). The global economic crisis, Eastern Europe, and the former Soviet Union: Models of development and the contradictions of internationalization. *Eurasian Geography and Economics*, *1*, 1–34.

Sommers, J., Woolfson, C., & Juska, A. (2014). Austerity as a global prescription and lessons from the neoliberal Baltic experiment. *Economic and Labour Relations Review*, *25*(3), 397–416.

Sørensen, A. (1994). Women's economic risk and the economic position of single mothers. *European Sociological Review*, *2*, 173–188.

Stankūnienė, V., Baublytė, M., & Maslauskaitė, A. (2016). Vienų motinų su vaikais šeimos Lietuvoje: demografinės ir socioekonominės charakteristikos. *Sociologija Mintis ir veiksmas*, *38*(1), 64–85.

Study on Poverty and Social Exclusion among Lone-Parent Households. (2007). European Commission.

Thévenon, O. (2011). Family policies in OECD countries: A comparative analysis. *Population and Development Review*, *37*(1), 57–87.

Tomlinson, M., Walker, R., & Williams, G. (2008). Measuring poverty in Britain as a multidimensional concept, 1991 to 2003. *Journal of Social Policy*, *37*, 597–620.

UNECE. (2005). *Generations and gender programme; survey instruments*. New York, NY/Geneva: United Nations Economic Commission for Europe.

Van de Velde, S., Bambra, C., Van der Bracht, K., Eikemo, T. A., & Bracke, P. (2014). Keeping it in the family: The self-rated health of lone mothers in different European welfare regimes. *Sociology of Health & Illness*, *8*, 1220–1242.

Wang, H., & Amato, P. R. (2000). Predictors of divorce adjustment: Stressors, resources, and definitions. *Journal of Marriage and Family*, *3*, 655–668.

Part II
Families' Strategies against Economic Hardships

Chapter 5

Expectations and Reality of Support Sharing within Personal Networks in Economically Hard Times: The Case of Lithuania

Vida Česnuitytė and Eric D. Widmer

5.1 Introduction

The family was considered for ages as the main and almost the only shelter ensuring protection against threats from external forces, including economic crises (Robila, 2004). Yet, a welfare state developed since the second part of the twentieth century took over part of the family's functions related to social security, protection against financial poverty and material deprivation. Family members obtained an opportunity and greater freedom than ever before to cope with material problems individually without expecting and waiting for support from the family or community (Boh, 1992; Sheppard, 2009; Thornton & Philipov, 2007). The latter circumstances created the conditions for the spread for individualism (Beck & Beck-Gernsheim, 2002), and a diminution of the instrumental role of the family in lives of individuals (Thornton & Philipov, 2007). Such an approach was strongly anchored in the last decade of the past century. Notwithstanding, the later research studies revealed that in situations of material or immaterial vulnerability, priority is mostly given to the family (Pahl & Spencer, 2004). Primary orientation towards family is observed in personal networks unites persons not only from the nuclear and extended families but, also, from beyond.

The issue of the availability of family members to help is of particular importance in economically hard times. It especially concerns youth and members of their families who just started creation of their personal and family networks. Who will provide help in case of need for financial support? Or in need for childcare? Or in case of sudden sickness? On another hand, similar questions are equally important in respect to older persons. At a certain age they start to lose spouses because of their passing away or other reasons, while children already live their own lives, not necessarily in the

Families in Economically Hard Times, 101–127

doi:10.1108/978-1-83909-071-420191009

neighbourhood. That is, for the lives of older people, emptying home nests are inherent while their health presupposes a need for help. Then who will provide help for them? The two mentioned age groups are not unique or the only ones which experience a need for help from the personal network. Adults in other age group also may meet situations in which they need assistance from members of their personal networks, e.g. unemployment, sickness, emotional stress, etc.

Previous research studies already gave answers to most of the questions raised above. However, in the research presented in this chapter we mainly ask: which family practices build personal networks that are ready to share with resources and provide help to each other? Though, the analysis presented is more complex. In order to give a comprehensive image of interplay among support sharing, personal networks and family practices, we analyse threefold research objects: (1) sharing of help and support in the context of problematic situations, (2) personal and family networks in the contexts of sharing of help and support and (3) family practices that create personal networks ready to share with help and support in problematic situations. The aim of the research is to explore interrelations among support sharing, personal networks and family practices in the period of the latest economic crisis and in a short period after it in Lithuania.

In order to achieve the research aim, the following research hypotheses are formulated:

H1. The type of help and support provided directly relate to the problematic situation at hand. That is, in a financially difficult situation financial support is provided, and in emotional stress emotional/psychological support is provided.

H2. Once the institution of the family goes through pluralization, more persons from the extended family and beyond the family are involved actively in the process of help and support provision, despite the problematic situation.

H3. Different family practices create personal networks ready to provide certain type of help and support only.

The test of the hypotheses is based on empirical data of the national representative quantitative survey carried out in Lithuania between November 2011 and January 2012, i.e. few years after the global economic crisis. The sample covers 2000 respondents who represent the habitants of Lithuania, as well, 4 selected for survey birth cohorts: 1950–1955, 1960–1965, 1970–1975 and 1980–1985.

The content of the chapter consists of two main subchapters and a conclusive section. At the end, a list of references is provided. The first subchapter provides a theoretical overview of the issue. In the second subchapter research data and methodology are presented. Further, analysis of empirical data is presented that focus on problematic situations met by the respondents or their families, and on interplay of the types of help and support provided. In the third subchapter, analysis of empirical data in interrelations between help and support is provided and personal networks given. In the fourth subchapter, family practices that build personal networks ready to provide help and support are analysed.

5.2 Theoretical Background

5.2.1 Approaches Towards Informal Support

Informal support is a complex and multidimentional concept. In general, it is interpersonal interaction when persons exchange with material or immaterial resources (Gottlieb, 2000). Several approaches concerning provision of informal support are present. The normative approach concerns the behaviour of individuals' corresponding internalised patterns of behaviour obtained during socialisation (Gottlieb, 2000). According to this approach, provision of support from parents to children, or from adult children to parents is 'normal' (Bengtson, 2001). The economic approach notices the importance of expectations of benefits or returns in the process of support: the support provider often waits or expects directly or in some way to receive benefits in the form of positive interrelations, similar support etc (Becker, 1981). Meanwhile, the altruistic approach states that social support can be provided just for positive emotion or similar feelings (Silverstein et al., 2002).

Support provider and recipient are important actors in the process. Nevertheless, researchers, usually, focus on functions, reasons, motivations, amounts and other features of support provision. Motivations of social support are various, though in any case the process contributes to relief of the situation(s) of involved persons. On the other hand, it was found the trend intrinsic to informal support: expectations often diverge from reality (Gottlieb, 2000).

Concerning the types of informal support provision, there are a lot of various classifications. For example, Gottlieb (2000) proposed a typology with four types: support that helps to solve problems, indirect support, environmental actions and emotional support. Meanwhile, in recent studies another typology is more popular, proposed by Scabini and Lanz (2006): instrumental support, provision with information, companionship, esteem support, emotional support. Similar typology is given by Rowland, Miller, Perlman, Sharon, and Brehm (2007): provision of advice, and material support and emotional support. Regan (2011) extended the latter typologies; in his version typology is appraisal support, informational, instrumental, fellowship support, emotional support. So, though typologies are different they somehow overlap. For example, instrumental support, or emotional support exist in almost all typologies. In practice, researchers in Lithuania, usually, apply types coming from such typologies. For example, in analysis of qualitative data on family networks of social support, Kanopienė (2014) used typology of eight types of social support: emotional support; informational support; financial support; material assistance; rendering of dwelling; instrumental support; care of the older and/or ailing persons; (8) childcare.

For the purpose of our research, four main types of support are explored: services and care, financial support, other material support, and emotional support. Detailed description of its content is provided in Section 5.3.1.

5.2.2 Personal and Family Networks in Support Sharing

Till the end of the twentieth century, the functionalistic perspective in family analysis dominated. The main functions ascribed to the family were to create a material basis for its members, to give emotional care and support, as well as to protect them from external forces (Parsons & Bales, 1955). The nuclear family was analysed mostly as an isolated unit, and was expected that mentioned functions will be implemented by the family and almost exceptionally – inside the family. Numerous studies were conducted on the phenomena (Attias-Donfut & Segalen, 2002; Bengtson, Rosenthal, & Burton, 1995; Finch, 1989, etc.). Meanwhile, the role of personal networks in sharing of support was questionable. From a structural-functionalistic perspective, personal networks are seen mostly as providers of resources to the nuclear family. Even so, more research shows that support is stronger in larger and overlapping personal networks (Widmer, 2004).

Support was often spread among members of the extended family and informal groups. Therefore, at the end of the century, relational perspective gained power in analysis of family and personal networks in sharing of support context. In this perspective, support, usually, is based on personal ties and/or responsibilities. Pahl and Spencer (2004) show that friends and other society members can replace some familial functions like closeness, time for leisure activities, support, etc. Notwithstanding, in the situations of vulnerability, individuals give priority to family members (Pahl & Spencer, 2004; Park & Roberts, 2002). Meanwhile, based on qualitative data on habitants of Lithuania, Kanopienė (2014) found that members of the family of orientation are the main providers of support within networks, while members of the family of procreation are main providers of specific support, e.g. emotional support.

Numerous research studies based on this perspective proved a feminisation of care (Crompton, Lewis, & Lyonette, 2007; Kramer & Thompson, 2002; Stankūnienė & Maslauskaitė, 2009, etc.). It was found that providers of informal support, usually, are mothers, daughters, grandmothers, mothers-in-law, daughters-in-law and other women. Meanwhile, other members of personal and family networks are involved in other types of support, e.g. men often are involved in provision of services, etc.

Informal support, usually, is transferred across the generations. Vertical versus horizontal transfers among generations are usual. Moreover, informal support, usually, is provided from the older to the younger generation (Attias-Donfut, Ogg, & Wolff, 2005; Wall, Aboim, Cunha, & Vasconcelos, 2001). Moreover, care for the parents may increase appreciation of life for adult children (Lowenstein & Daatland, 2006). The concept of intergenerational solidarity (Bengtson, 2001) is most usual in analysis of intergenerational relationships, including informal care and support. The concept is based on the model of relationships between generations that distinguish the following types of solidarity: normative, structural, associational, affectual, consensual, functional. The latter concerns interchange with various types of support between generations. It is mainly based on the following types of support: material, instrumental and emotional. This typology is most suitable for our research, thus adapted in empirical part. Instrumental support in our research corresponds to services and care, the other types applied directly.

5.2.3 Family Practices in Personal Networks Creation

Scabini and Lanz (2006) note that informal support is a didactic phenomenon in which at least two persons are involved. According to Smart (2007), relationships are not just given; for the creation of solid and stable social relationships, traditions, rituals, social actions and other family practices are needed, otherwise these relationships will remain formal or theoretical only. Morgan (1996) suggested the term of family practices that mean activities for creation of interpersonal ties. The term means a set of activities, where individuals can be seen as doing a family, mothering or fathering, etc (Morgan, 2011, pp. 5 9; Smart, 2007). In this way, showing support is possible. Among activities that may be assigned to family practices are joint dinner daily, housework, shopping, leisure activities, sports, gardening, celebration of holidays and all other activities that support direct or indirect interpersonal interaction (Wolin & Bennett, 1984; Hauri, 2011).

Which individuals should be involved in showing support? Everyday routine involves family members, as well as friends and others beyond kinship (Pahl & Spencer, 2004) who can serve as a pool for showing support. According to Morgan (1996), practices and only practices show who counts as a family member, in our research – showing support. For example, research conducted in Lithuania revealed that family practices create networks of caregivers, but in order to involve particular persons into the network of caregivers, different family practices are needed (Česnuitytė, 2012).

5.3 Family Networks and Practices in the Context of Economically Hard Times: Empirical Findings

5.3.1 Research Methodology: Data and Methods

For the test of the research hypotheses, empirical data of the national representative quantitative survey are used. The survey was carried out in Lithuania between November 2011 and January 2012. Empirical data were collected within the research project 'Trajectories of family models and social networks: intergenerational perspective' (code No.VP1-3.1-ŠMM-07-K 01 106) implemented in 2011–2015 by the group of sociologists at Mykolas Romeris University (Vilnius, Lithuania).

The survey was carried out in a few years after the global economic crisis whose peak was in 2008. The crisis gradually calmed down though its effects for the habitants of Lithuania remained significant for a long time. For example, in 2011–2012, unemployment rates in the country were 15.7 %–13.6 % (respectively), i.e. rather high in comparison to 5.9 % in 2008, or 9.8 %–10.6 % in EU-28 in 2011–2012 (Eurostat, 2019e). Risk of poverty in the same years was 33.1 %–32.5 % (respectively). The highest risk of poverty at a time was in the 16–24 year age group (38.4 %–36.7 %), and the age group of 55 years and above (32.5 %–35.9 %) (Eurostat, 2019b). Meanwhile, measures of social security provided by the state to the families and their members were restricted. For example, social protection benefits for family and children were reduced, paid leave for care of infants under the age of 3 years was decreased and so on. As a consequence, as of 2013, the rate of satisfaction with financial situation among the population of Lithuania (16 years and above) was 5.8 in the scale of 10 points, and the rate of overall life satisfaction was 6.7 from 10 points (Eurostat, 2019a). A bit higher was the rate of satisfaction with personal relationships – 8 from 10 points. Even so, 17.4% of the population stated that they cannot afford to get together with friends, family and relatives for a drink or meal at least once a month because of material deprivation (Eurostat, 2019c); 35.1 % of the population cannot afford to regularly participate in a leisure activity (Eurostat, 2019d). In other words, the representative quantitative survey was conducted in the economically hard period for habitants of Lithuania with consequential outcomes in various spheres of personal and family lives.

In total, 2000 respondents were interviewed in the survey. In creation of the sample a multi-stage stratified random method was applied. The sampling criteria were the following: geographic place (10 counties of the country), settlement size (big cities, towns and villages), gender (male, female) and generation. The latter criterion covers persons from four birth cohorts: 1950–1955, 1960–1965, 1970–1975 and 1980–1985. For each of these four birth cohorts, 500 persons were selected in a way that they represent the cohort. Fieldwork was conducted by the public opinion and market research company 'Vilmorus Ltd.'. Survey method was a face-to-face interview at the respondent's home or other place suitable for the respondent.

A standardised questionnaire was used in empirical data collection. The questionnaire consisted of over 100 questions that covered topics on social relations, mutual help and assistance, objective and subjective quality of life, etc. For purposes of this research, a few of the questions selected are detailed as follows.

For the analysis of problems and problematic situations that the respondents and their families experienced, the question *C1 Now, I would like to ask about some events and problems that you might have been through the past year. Of the following list of problems that I'm going to refer to, please tell me all the problems that you have been through (or are going through)* was used. After the formulation of the question, the list of problematic situations follows. In total, it includes 22 items. In the analysis, for the research purposes, all these items were grouped into four main topics: economic problems, health problems, emotional problems and social problems. The group *Economic problems* cover the following problematic situations: long-term unemployment (>9 months) of the respondent, or family member; serious financial difficulties, debts experienced by the respondent or family members; living in a house with poor conditions; emigration of the respondent, family member or close person. The group *Health problems* cover: serious illness or accident experienced by the respondent, family member or close person; death of family member or close person; suicide attempt of a family member or close person; alcoholism or drug addiction of family member or close person; depression of family member or close person; caring for a long period of time for a sick family member or close person; spontaneous abortion (miscarriage) experienced by the respondent, girlfriend or spouse; voluntary abortion experienced by the respondent, girlfriend or spouse. The group *Emotional problems* cover: serious family conflicts; divorce of family members; infidelity of spouse/partner. Finally, the group *Social problems* cover: serious problems with justice respondent, family member or close person; abuse/domestic violence in the family. In the next analysis, four dichotomous variables were used with the measures of 0 = No, not experienced the problem, and 1 = Yes, experienced the problem.

For identification of help and care For identification help and care shared among provided by the members of the personal network to the respondent (further – Ego) and/or from Ego to mentioned members, several questions were used. The question *B3 Next, I am going to read a list of different types of support and help that you may have received or given to those persons. For each statement, please indicate, first, if you have received that type of support or help from any of the persons you mentioned, and second, if you have given that type of support or help to any of them* is the main. Further, it is detailed by the following six questions: *B3.1.A Services and care you received from any of them*; *B3.1.B Services and care you gave to any of them*; *B3.2.A Material support you received from any of them*; *B3.2.B Material support you gave to any of them*; *B3.3.A Financial or patrimonial support you received from any of them*; *B3.3.B Financial or patrimonial support you gave to any of them*. Persons mentioned in the question are members of the personal and family networks of Ego, and related information about them will be provided in this subchapter. Meanwhile, for B3.1.A, B3.1.B, B3.2.A, B3.2.B, B3.3.A and B3.3.B cards with several possible types of help or support were prepared. The respondents were invited to name which of its they received and which provided. Though in the analysis, six dichotomous variables were prepared with measures 0 = No, and 1 = Yes. For B3.1.A, B3.2.A and B3.3.A measure '1' mean the Ego received from members of the personal network, respectively, services and care, material or financial support. For B3.1.B, B3.2.B and B3.3.B measure '1' mean the Ego provided to members of the personal network, respectively, services and care, material or financial support. The content of *Services and Care* cover help with housework, care/assistance in case of sickness, care of pre-school age children, long-term care in case of serious illness, fulfilment of daily orders, performance of small housework tasks, repair of things, transportation, help in finding a job, temporary care of pets, or, finally, comprehensive services and care. The content of *Material support* covers provision of clothing, food, help in purchase furniture and household utensils, help in purchasing a car, temporary accommodation in own home or rent of living space, or even full supply. The content of *Financial support* covers transfer of land by gift or inheritance, real estate (house, apartment, houses, garages and so on.) transfer by gift or inheritance, transfer of land by gift or inheritance, valuable works of art, jewellery, antiques, estate and gift transfer, business partnership proposal or transfer, pecuniary interest-free loan, other financial support or even full board.

For identification of shared *Emotional support*, the question was used: *B2.2 Of these persons mentioned, who gave emotional support to you and to X person? Of these persons mentioned, to whom you and X person give emotional support?* Again, mentioned persons are members of the personal network of Ego, and details on it are provided. Meanwhile, this question was organised in the form of a matrix in which the respondent was invited to make interpersonal exchange of emotional support within the network. In this analysis, we used data on sharing of emotional support between Ego and other members of his/her network only. Two variables were created from the question: B2.2.A for support received by Ego, and B2.2.B for support provided by Ego. Measures of both variables are the following: 0 = No, and 1 = Yes.

One more variable for identification on help and support was used in the analysis. It concerns expectations of Ego for help and support in case of need: *B4 If suddenly a need/problem arises, from whom would you ask help first of all?* Further, the following cases listed: *(a) get ill*; *(b) feel lonely, need for a conversation*; *(c) need for care of young children or other family members*; *(d) need for help in daily burdens*; *(e) need for cash loan*; *(f) need for temporary care of your pet.* The respondents were invited to name members of the personal network from whom they expect to receive help and support in each listed case. Care with possible interrelations (for a detailed description, please refer the next section) was suggested to the respondents in this task.

For identification of the personal network of Ego, open concept of family (Bernardes, 1986, 1999; Levin, 1999; Widmer, 1999) applied. It enables the respondent freely to name members of his/her personal network, despite to which formal unit they depend – the nuclear family, extended families or are beyond any of it. For this reason, the question formulated: *B1 There are some persons that are very important in our life (in a positive and negative sense). Who are those persons that during this last year were important to you?* The respondents were invited to list all those important to him/her (Alters). An additional question *B1.3 How are you and that person related?* made it possible to identify interrelations between Ego and members of his/her network. For the answer to it, the respondents were provided with a card with a list of over 50 possible interrelations. In the analysis, six groups from all these items were created: *Spouse/partner*, *Child(-ren)*, *Parents*, *Siblings*, *Other relatives*, *Non-relatives*. The group *Other relatives* covers possible interrelation within the extended family, including grandparents, grandchildren, aunts, uncles, nephews, nieces, cousins, etc. The group *Non-relatives* covers friends, acquaintances, colleagues, neighbours, roommates, domestic employees, etc. The same process was conducted with answer to the previous question (B4).

For identification of a family network, about each of the named member of the personal network, an additional question was asked: *B1.11 Do you consider this person as your family member?* with measures of 0 = No, and 1 = Yes. Again, the respondent was free to mark that certain member of the personal network as a family member or not, despite to which unit formally he/she may be assigned: the nuclear family, extended family, or are beyond any of it. This way, a family network according to an open concept of family was identified.

In the analysis of personal and family networks, additional variables were created based on the answers to the questions B1.3 and B1.11: size of personal network and size of family network. For both networks, measures applied were: 1 = Narrow network (1–3 members); 2 = Large network (4+ members).

For identification of family practices, the following question was formulated: *C2 Now, I would like to ask you to indicate, for each of the following aspects, to what extent you have invested in each one of them during your life (i.e. spending a lot of time, dedicating a lot of effort and energy, sacrificing other activities if necessary)*. Further, the following cases were listed: (a) *professional activity/work*; (b) *conjugal life*; (c) *children*; (d) *spending time with friends*; (e) *housework*; (f) *family in general (parents, brothers/sisters…)*; (g) *leisure and free time activities*; (h) *civic activities (volunteering, participating in associations, etc.)*; (i) *education and training in general*; (j) *time for yourself*. For the evaluation, the scale with five measures was suggested for the respondents: 1 = A lot; 2 = Quite a bit; 3 = Something; 4 = A little; 5 = Nothing. In the analysis, the measures 'A little' and 'Nothing' gathered into one measure 0 = Not invest; the measures 'A lot', 'Quite a bit' and 'Something' gathered into another measure 1 = Invest.

In the analysis of the quantitative data, the methods of descriptive statistics (frequencies) and multivariate statistical analysis methods (Logistic regression analysis, and Factors analysis) applied. For the data entered, manipulation with variables, and analysis, software package IBM SPSS Statistics 20 was used. The presentation of the research results follow.

5.3.2 Interrelations Between Problematic Situations and Support Types

This section tests hypothesis H1 stating that help and support are directly related to the problematic situation to which certain help and support are provided. After the description of the problematic situations that respondents and/or people of their close environment experienced, the results of the hypothesis test will be presented.

As described in the section on research data and methodology, the respondents were asked to mark which from the listed 22 problematic situations they personally, or their family members or close persons experienced. According to the empirical data, only 43 from the 2000 respondents answered that they and their close ones did not list problematic situations. The rest had experiences of at least one problem. Though the distribution of numbers of experienced problematic situations reveals that, usually, they had experienced between two to eight such situations (Fig. 5.1). The mean number is 6 with standard deviation of 3.9. Moreover, persons from the birth cohorts 1950–1955 and 1960–1965 had experienced in average 7 problematic situations (with SD 3.8 and 4.1, respectively), and persons from the birth cohorts 1970–1975 and 1980–1985 had experienced in average 6 problematic situations (with SD 3.8 and 3.7, respectively). That is, younger cohorts had experienced slightly less problematic situations in comparison to the older respondents.

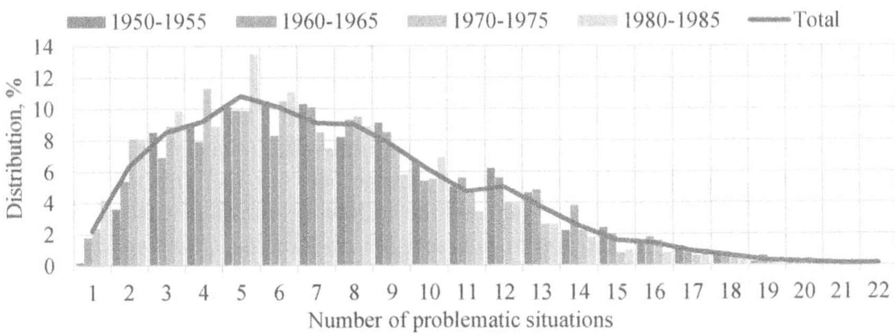

Fig. 5.1. Distribution of Experienced Difficult Situations by Birth Cohort (in Percent). *Source*: Survey data.

Unfortunately, from these quantitative empirical data we cannot know whether several problematic situations were experienced at the same time or in various periods of time by the same persons. Even so, we can state that almost all habitants of Lithuania and/or persons in their close environment were in the situations required for some kind of help or support from outside – other persons or institutions.

What types of problems the respondents, their family members and/or close persons experienced? Less of all respondents were involved in social problems like problems with justice, abuse or domestic violence. According to the empirical data, 80% of the respondents had no experience of such types of problematic situations (Fig. 5.2). Moreover, 15% of the respondents noted experience from two to three such situations. In distribution of situations related with social problems among birth cohort, slight variations were identified. Though these variations are rather small: the highest percentage of the respondents who met social problems are in birth cohorts of 1960–1965 and 1980–1985 (19% and 15%, respectively). The birth cohorts of 1950–1955 and 1970–1975 (14% and 13%, respectively) are in almost the same position. That is, almost all persons, independent of age, have more or less the same (rather low) experience of social problems.

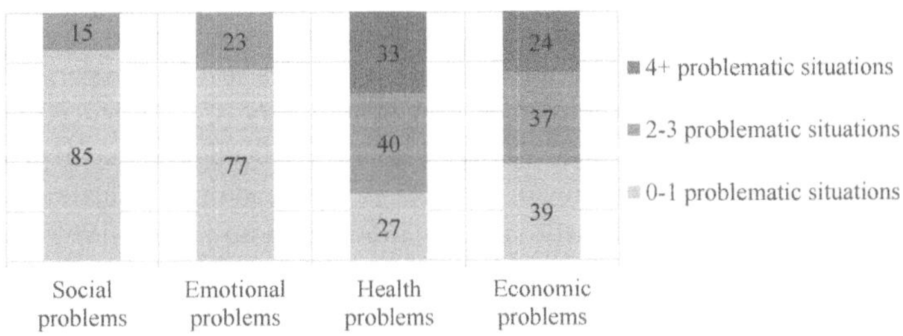

Fig. 5.2. Distribution of Those Who Experienced Problematic Situations by Types of Problems (in Percent). *Source*: Survey data.

Concerning emotional problems, 77% of the respondents stated that they and/or persons from their close environment were not involved in situations related to family conflicts, divorce or infidelity of a family member, or experienced such situations once (Fig. 5.2). Nevertheless, a bit more than one-fifth (23%) respondents had experienced from two to three such situations. Moreover, distribution of emotional problems rather relate to age of the persons (or their birth cohort). According to the survey data, those who experienced 2–3 problematic situations were 23% persons from the birth cohort 1950–1955, 29% from the birth cohort 1960–1965, 24% from the birth cohort 1970–1975 and 16% from the birth cohort 1980–1985. Those who had not experienced emotional problems once were 77% born in 1950–1955, 71% born in 1960–1965, 76% born in 1970–1975 and 84% born in 1980–1985. That is, older persons more often than younger experience situations related to emotional problems. That means, younger persons have higher chances to avoid such problematic situations.

According to the empirical data, health and economic problems are what habitants of Lithuania meet most often. Only 27% of the respondents stated that they and/or persons from their close environment had not experienced difficulties related to health, or they had such situations only once (Fig. 5.2). In total, 40% of the respondents stated experience from two to three problematic situations related with health, and 33% respondents, four or more situations. As a rule, health problems were widespread among older people (in our survey, those born in the birth cohort 1950–1955), and are rather rare in other birth cohorts. According to the survey data, 41% of the respondents born in 1950–1955 experienced four or more problematic situations related to health (in comparison: 1980–1985 – 25%, 1970–1975 – 28% and 1960–1965 – 39%). And only 15% from the oldest birth cohort had no experience related to health or had it once (in comparison: 1980–1985 – 37%, 1970–1975 – 31% and 1960–1965 – 22%). But here it is important to note that all cohorts had almost an equal experience with two to three health problems: the percentages vary between 38 and 44 among cohorts. Such data reveal that all people experience health problems rarely. And health problems like caring for a long period because of a sickness, accident, spontaneous or voluntary abortion (miscarriage), serious illness, alcoholism, drug addiction, depression, suicide attempt, death are rather spread in Lithuania. Moreover, that is not necessarily related to the age of persons.

Finally, 39% of the respondents stated that they and/or persons from their close environment had not experienced economic problems or it happened only once (Fig. 5.2). A total 37% had gone through two to three situations related to long-term unemployment, serious financial difficulties or debts, house with poor conditions, emigration, and 24% went through four or more of such situations. Empirical data, also, reveal that persons from the oldest birth cohorts (born in 1950–1955 and 1960–1965) full into economically difficult situations most often. Meanwhile, persons from the youngest birth cohorts (born in 1970–1975 and 1980–1985) more often avoid such situations. Actually, in the most opportune position are persons born in 1970–1975. That is, economic problems are a bit rare in comparison to health problems, but even so, almost three-fifth of Lithuanians from time to time experience need of financial aid or other material help. Moreover, distribution of these problems highly relate to age of persons.

But how do help and support received by the respondents interrelate with experienced problematic situations? The research results reveal that despite the type of problem experienced, or numbers of experienced problematic situations, support in the form of services and care prevail: around one-third of the respondents noted that they received some kind of services and care in a situation of need. Meanwhile, 20%–22% of the respondents received financial support, 21–23% – material support and 23–25% – emotional support.

In summary, health and economic problems emerge rather often among Lithuanians, meanwhile, social and emotional are less rare. All these problems differently but quite strongly are interconnected with age of persons. In any case, need for help and support is evident for almost everyone from time to time. Services and care is more popular than other types of help. There is no significant differentiation between type of the problem and help provided, at least based on the survey data. That is, the hypothesis H1 is denied.

5.3.3 Personal and Family Networks in Sharing of Support

In this subchapter, interrelation between personal and family networks in sharing of support is analysed. The aim is to test the hypothesis H2 stating that more persons from the extended family and beyond the family are actively involved in the process of help and support provision in younger cohorts than in older cohorts.

According to the survey data, the respondents' personal networks, as well as family networks include from zero to seven important persons. In sum, 2,000 respondents named 6,956 Alters – members of their personal networks. Among them 6,115 were named as family members. In total, 50 respondents stated that their personal networks are completely empty – neither family members nor Alters there are in it. In the personal networks of 110 respondents (or 5.5%) no family members were included. The rest of the 21.2% respondents have personal networks wider than family networks. Size of personal and family networks varies statistically insignificantly. Average size of personal networks is 3.5 persons, and average size of family networks is 3.1 persons. Personal networks of 70% respondents consist of family members only; personal networks of 1.4% respondents consist of non-family family members only. In the personal networks of 10% respondents, family members constitute less than half of the network. In personal networks of 19% respondents, more that half of the network are family members.

But how do personal and family networks function in interpersonal sharing of help and support? Firstly, expectations concerning help providers and supports are analysed. Analysis of empirical data shows that the list of potential providers of assistance is quite large. In average, nine to ten potential (expected) helpers are listed per respondent. The lists extend beyond the nuclear and extended family, encompassing persons with no related kinship bonds, i.e. include friends, neighbours and others. As empirical data reveal, in case of sudden need for services and care, Lithuanians primary expect provision from

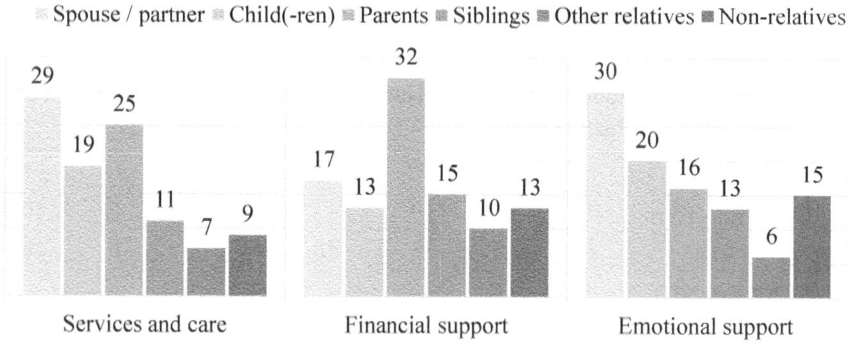

Fig. 5.3. Distribution of Answers on from Whom Respondents Expect Help and Support in Case of Sudden Need or Problem (in Percent). *Source*: Survey data.

their spouse or partner (29%), and parents (25%) (Fig. 5.3). In the same case, less rarely they expect support from non-relatives (9%) and other relatives (7%). In case of sudden need for financial support, Lithuanians expect to receive it, firstly and almost exceptionally, from parents (32%). Assistance from other relatives, children, or non-relatives is expected less rarely (respectively, 10%, 13% and 13%). In cases of loneliness and need for conversation and/or emotional support, habitants, firstly and almost exceptionally, expect assistance from spouse or partner (30%). Least of all, support is expected from other relatives (6%).

In summary, differentiation of orientations towards helpers and support providers in sudden need depends on the need or problem. Moreover, in cases of need for help in services and care, and financial or emotional support, Lithuanians are primary oriented towards a member of the family of procreation – spouse or partner, and members of the family of orientation – parents. Meanwhile, contribution from children and siblings is less rarely expected. Even more rarely is assistance expected from other relatives or non-relatives.

On the other hand, expectations do not necessarily correspond what indeed happened. Therefore, further we ask: from whom Ego receive help and support in reality? And to whom they provide help and support in reality?

The survey data led to state that services and care respondents receive, mostly, from children (34%). The role of parents and spouses/partners here, also, is rather substantial (22% and 19%, respectively) (Table 5.1). Trends in the opposite direction of services and care provision – from Ego to the members of personal networks – are similar: children and parents interact most often (35% and 33%, respectively). Though, share of the respondents who provide services and care to spouses/partners is scarce (2%). Meanwhile, the respondents provide services and care to siblings more often than receive it from them (16% and 13%, respectively). Finally, in all these cases, other relatives and non-relatives are seldom involved.

Table 5.1. Distribution of Answers on Interpersonal Sharing of Help and Support within Personal Network (in Percent).

	Spouse/ Partner	Child (-ren)	Parents	Siblings	Other Relatives	Non-relatives	Total
Services and care							
Ego receives from	19	34	22	13	5	7	100
Ego gives to	2	35	33	16	6	8	100
Financial support							
Ego receives from	2	32	32	17	7	10	100
Ego gives to	2	35	29	17	7	10	100
Material support							
Ego receives from	2	32	33	17	6	10	100
Ego gives to	2	35	30	16	7	10	100
Emotional support							
Ego receives from	24	32	21	12	4	7	100
Ego gives to	23	35	20	12	4	6	100

Source: Survey data.

In cases of financial and material support, alike trends are observed. First is sharing between children and parents, and then sharing with siblings follow. Spouses/partners and other relatives are seldom involved. Here it is important to note the role of non-relatives: they provide financial and material support, as well as receive such types of support more often in comparison to other types of support.

In cases of emotional support, unlike above observed trends, the second important persons after children are spouses/partners (Table 5.1). Parents and siblings follow children and spouses/partners. The role of other kin and non-kin is lowest. Such trends are characteristic as for receiving, and for giving emotional support. In other words, sharing of emotional support is practicing mostly within the family of procreation.

So, sharing of help and support between children and parents is most intrinsic in Lithuania, and help/support provided by spouses/partners and siblings follow the latter. Exceptional trends are specific in cases of financial, material support and emotional support: siblings and non-relatives are involved in these cases more often that in the rest. Non-relatives are involved in sharing of financial, material support more often in comparison to other types of help and support.

The presented results encourage us to take a deeper look into the interrelation between help/support processes and personal and family networks. It is evident that a pool of persons in Ego's personal and family networks is important for the process of sharing care. Persons who have members of the family of procreation in their own personal network have a higher chance to receive services and care, as well as to be involved in sharing of emotional support processes (Table 5.1). Those who have persons beyond the nuclear or extended family in the personal network have a higher chance to be involved in the process of sharing of financial or other material support. That is, such interrelations are closely related to the characteristics of the personal and family networks of Ego. Thus, further we ask: what are the characteristics of available networks and Ego himself that ensure receiving and giving help and support? In order to answer, Logistic regression analysis was conducted whose results are presented in Table 5.2.

The Regression analysis results led to state statistically significantly that the larger the personal network, the higher the chances for Ego to receive from it services and care (Model 1 in Table 5.2), as well as financial and other material support (Models 3 and 5 in Table 5.2). For provision by Ego of financial and material support to members of personal network, analogous trends are intrinsic among Lithuanians (Models 4 and 6 in Table 5.2): the larger the personal network, the higher the chances that Ego will provide help to the members of the personal network. Notwithstanding, the opposite rule is true for emotional support: the narrower the personal network, the more the chances to be involved in sharing of emotional support within the personal network (Models 7 and 8 in Table 5.2). The latter trend encourages to predict that sharing of emotional support is specific in the narrow intimate circles only.

Meantime, interrelations between characteristics of family network and sharing of help and support aren't so evident. It can be statistically significantly stated the narrower the family network, the more possible for Ego to receive services and care within the family network (Model 1 in Table 5.2). For provision of emotional support by Ego to members of family network, an analogous trend is valid: the narrower the family network, the more possible that Ego will give emotional support to other members of his/her family network (Model 8 in Table 5.2). This trend is, probably, again related to the sharing on emotional support within the narrow intimate circle.

The regression analysis statistically significantly revealed interrelations between share of family members within personal network, and sharing of help and support. The more family members are involved in the personal network, the more chances for Ego to receive services and care (Model 1 in Table 5.2). It proves that help in the form of services and care is mostly provided by the members of family, even personal network is rather large. Analogous trends are related to sharing of emotional support: as more family members are involved in the personal network, the more chances for Ego to receive emotional support (Model 7 in Table 5.2), as well as to provide emotional support to the members of his/her network (Model 8 in Table 5.2). Additionally, the opposite but, also, statistically significant trends are identified: as less family members are involved in the personal network, the more possible that Ego will receive financial and material support (Models 3 and 5 in Table 5.2), and will provide services and care (Model 2 in Table 5.2), as well as financial and material support (Models 4 and 6 in Table 5.2) to the members of his/her network.

Table 5.2. Characteristics Related to Interpersonal Sharing of Help and Support within the Personal Network. Results of Logistic Regression Analysis, Exp(B).

	Dependent Variables (0 = No, 1 = Yes)							
	Services and Care		**Financial Support**		**Material Support**		**Emotional Support**	
	Ego Received from	**Ego Gave to**	**Ego Received from**	**Ego Gave to**	**Ego Received from**	**Ego Gave to**	**Ego Received from**	**Ego Gave to**
Independent variables	**Model 1**	**Model 2**	**Model 3**	**Model 4**	**Model 5**	**Model 6**	**Model 7**	**Model 8**
Size of the personal network (1 = narrow network; 2 = large network)	**1.600***	1.019	**1.508*****	**1.757*****	**1.265***	**1.407****	**0.621*****	**0.728***
Size of the family network (1 = narrow network; 2 = large network)	**0.514****	1.197	0.873	0.809	1.104	0.953	0.908	**0.743***
Share of family network within personal network (ref. 0%)								
1–49%	**9.500*****	**1.529*****	**2.326*****	**1.878*****	**2.646*****	**2.546*****	**2.523*****	**3.610*****

50–99%	**13.551*** **	**1.649*** **	**1.807*** **	**1.832*** **	**1.877*** **	**2.013*** **	**3.305*** **	**5.225*** **
100%	**17.203*** **	**1.172** **	1.111	**1.198** **	1.087	**1.248*** **	**3.966*** **	**6.399*** **
Birth cohort (ref. 1950–1955)								
1960–1965	**1.672*** **	**1.191* **	1.105	1.074	1.161*	1.099	0.993	1.112
1970–1975	1.051	**0.753*** **	**0.752*** **	**0.654*** **	**0.745*** **	**0.630*** **	0.933	1.067
1980–1985	1.133	0.927	0.979	**0.798*** **	0.983	**0.789*** **	0.991	**0.771*** **
−2 Log likelihood	3052.539	9389.997	9147.115	9138.328	9098.824	9114.215	8281.674	7030.170
Cox & Snell R Square	0.612	0.036	0.069	0.070	0.075	0.073	0.178	0.313
Nagelkerke R Square	0.816	0.048	0.092	0.093	0.100	0.098	0.237	0.418

Significance levels: ***$p < 0.001$; **$p < 0.01$; *$p < 0.05$.
Source: Survey data.

Considering that creation of their own personal and family networks highly depend on the age of the person, birth cohort of the respondent was included as an additional independent variable in the regression analysis model. The presumption is that the youngest persons (in our research – born in 1980–1985) mostly rely on the family of orientation (parents and siblings) and persons beyond the nuclear or extended family. Meanwhile, the oldest persons (in our research – born in 1950–1955) mostly rely on children and spouses/partners, i.e. members of the family of procreation. And, finally, it can be predicted that persons of middle age (in our research – born in 1960–1965 and 1970–1975) have the largest and most extended networks, and therefore, can rely on members of the nuclear and extended families plus persons beyond the family. There is a higher chance than for those born in 1950–1955 to be involved in sharing of services and care within the personal and family networks (Models 1 and 2 in Table 5.2). For persons born in 1970–1975 there is lower chance in comparison to persons born in 1950–1955 to be involved in sharing of services and care within their own network (Model 2 in Table 5.2). It is also rare for persons born in 1970–1975 than older persons involved in sharing of financial and material support with the members of their own network (Models 3–6 in Table 5.2). Finally, according to survey data, the youngest respondents (born in 1980–1985) are less often involved in provision of financial, material and emotional support to the members of their own network (Models 4, 6 and 8 in Table 5.2).

Finally, extended analysis of interrelation between the personal network and the process of help and support provision led to reject the hypothesis H2: it is not true that more persons from the extended family and beyond the family are involved in help in the younger cohort, even though the family goes through pluralisation.

5.3.4 Interrelations Between Sharing of Help and Family Practices Within Personal Networks

The aim of this section is to test hypothesis H3 stating that different family practices generate personal networks ready to provide certain type of help and support only. In order to build up a personal network that would be ready to share help and care, individuals should be involved in the activities/practices that unite members of the network. In terms of Morgan (1996, 2011), these activities can be called family practices. For identification of such practices, in our research, factor analysis was conducted. Practices like investment into conjugal life, children, family in general, housework, time for yourself, leisure and free-time activities, spending time with friends, education and training in general, professional activity and work, and civic activities are included in the calculations.

Based on the empirical data about services and care received by Ego within the personal network (as selection variable), four factors are identified (Table 5.3). The first factor indicates that Ego who has the network ready to provide services and care is involved in activities like education and training,

Table 5.3. Factors Structuring Personal Investments. Results of Factor Analysis, When Selection Variable – Receiving by Ego Services and Care from the Members of Personal Network.

	Factors			
	Personal Development	**Leisure Activities with Friends**	**Caring about the Family of Procreation**	**Caring about Family in General**
Variances %	*17.36*	*13.61*	*13.14*	*12.08*
Education and training	**0.812**	−0.013	−0.074	0.144
Civic activities	**0.696**	0.061	0.055	−0.062
Time for yourself	**0.667**	0.291	0.002	0.059
Spending time with friends	0.069	**0.783**	−0.070	0.090
Leisure and free-time activities	0.157	**0.760**	0.055	−0.020
Children	−0.026	0.027	**0.791**	0.081
Conjugal life	0.044	−0.056	**0.754**	−0.019
Family in general	0.008	0.105	0.014	**0.742**
Professional activity/work	0.280	−0.170	−0.065	**0.615**
Housework	−0.193	0.195	0.315	**0.485**

Extraction method: Principal component analysis. Rotation method: Varimax with Kaiser normalization.
Source: Survey data.

civic activities, and time for yourself. Civic activities, more detailedly, are related to involvement in volunteering, participating in associations, etc., i.e. in activities that contribute to society, as well as to personal development. Moreover, negative measures on children and housework in this factor show exceptional focus on activities beyond the familial issues. In sum, this group of respondents mainly focuses on personal development; therefore, the factor is named *Personal development*.

The second factor unites the components revealing spending time with friends, leisure and free-time activities. That is, the factor unites persons who mostly spend time outside the family, and focus on personal interests. The latter even strongly is proved by the negative measures on conjugal life, education, training, professional activity and work. Consequently, the factor relatively is named as *Leisure activities with friends*.

The third factor unites the components showing exceptional focus on children and conjugal life, and in part – on housework. Moreover, the factor includes components with negative measures on time for yourself, spending time with friends, education and training, professional activity and work. All these aspects indicate group of persons who almost sacrifice their own interests and activities outside the household on behalf of the family of procreation. Therefore, the factor relatively is named as *Caring about the family of procreation*.

The fourth factor unites the components on investment into family, housework, professional activity and work. The first two components and negative measures on conjugal life reveal focus on family in general, including parents, brothers, sisters, and other members. Concerning the component of professional activity/work can be presupposed that it shows care about earning for ensuring living conditions of the extended family instead of for self-realisation through the professional activity. Focus on the family is even strongly proved by the negative measures on civic activities, leisure and free-time activities. Thus, the factor is relatively named as *Caring about family in general*.

Overall, four groups are identified: Personal development, Leisure activities with friends, Caring about the family of procreation, and Caring about family in general.

Analogous calculations are also conducted for the other types of help and support, i.e. Ego receives financial support, material support, emotional support, and Ego gives services and care, financial support, material support, and emotional support. In almost all these cases, similar results are received: four factors are identified, and they consist of the same groups of family practices. Slight exception is found in case of receiving by Ego emotional support from the personal network. In this case, the factors *Leisure activities with friends* and *Caring about the family of procreation* interchange with their positions. Also, the component on housework becomes even stronger in the factor *Caring about the family of procreation* than in the factor *Caring about family in general*. The latter led to presuppose that the second factor means even stronger involvement in daily practices of the family of procreation. Then the fourth factor means very general attention to family, and, possibly, spending more time in profession activity and work than in family. But, as Morgan (2011) states, even such activity means contribution to family and for its welfare, which is very important in economically hard times.

Finally, in order to test how family practices interrelate with certain types of help and support, logistic regression analysis was conducted. Statistically, regression analysis results significantly reveal that investment into housework, education and training suppose probability to receive sometimes services and care from members of the personal network (Model 1 in Table 5.4). Moreover, no correlation concerning this interrelation and birth cohort of the respondents was found. But from results in the Model 1 it can be designated that identified interrelation is much stronger for personal networks consisting of family members than for personal networks consisting of non-family members. That means that various activities within the household make it for tied ties among family members, who are ready to assist each other.

According to statistically significant regression analysis results, investment into housework and family in general, also, ensure financial support from the personal network (Model 2 in Table 5.4). Meanwhile, investment in children and conjugal life does not necessarily generate personal network from which financial support comes. At the same time, results reveal that the larger the personal network, and it includes non-family members, the more possible it is to receive financial support from it. These finding are weaker for persons from younger birth cohorts (born in 1970–1975 and 1980–1985). That shows that younger persons just build their personal networks. Moreover, already created personal networks, usually are not able to support financially. Meanwhile, older persons who are not focused on a narrow familial network but are open for communication have more chances to build ties with more possibilities to support financially. Analogous trends are found in relation to the possibility to receive material support (Model 3 in Table 5.4).

Finally, regression analysis on emotional support (Model 4 in Table 5.4) shows that spending time with friends, participation in leisure and free-time activities, and investment in family in general create possibilities to receive emotional support from the personal network. On the other hand, regression results in Model 4, also reveal another trend: the narrower the personal network, the more chances to receive emotional support from it. Chances are even larger if the personal network consists of as much as possible from family members. That is, sharing of emotional support mostly going on in narrow, intimate, familial networks who are involved in numerous activities according to their interests.

In summary, results of the analysis presented in the subchapter led to state that family practices create several (at least four) types of personal networks. They all provide various types of help and support. In other words, there is no differentiation or specialisation of activities concerning creation of a specific network that focuses on one or another type of help. Therefore the hypothesis H3 is rejected. On the other hand, types of help are interrelated with certain family practices, and these family practices can involve members from various networks.

Table 5.4. Interrelation between Family Practices and Received by Ego Help and Support within Personal Network. Results of Logistic Regression Analysis, Exp(B).

	Dependent Variables (0 = Not Received, 1 = Received)			
	Services and Care	**Financial Support**	**Material Support**	**Emotional Support**
Independent Variables (0 = Not Invest, 1 = Invest)	**Model 1**	**Model 2**	**Model 3**	**Model 4**
Conjugal life	0.893	**0.455*****	**0.500*****	0.991
Children	1.157	**0.527*****	**0.539*****	0.843
Family in general	1.291	**1.538*****	**1.512****	**1.323***
Housework	**1.784***	**1.511****	**1.557****	1.173
Time for yourself	1.137	1.054	0.983	0.895
Leisure and free-time activities	1.451	1.037	0.988	**1.288****
Spending time with friends	0.720	0.949	1.036	**1.198***
Civic activities	0.827	0.964	1.143	1.025
Education and training	**1.654****	1.055	1.056	1.056
Professional activity/work	1.208	0.980	0.993	0.973

Size of the personal network (1 = narrow network; 2 = large network)	1.086	**1.706*** **	**1.672*** **	**0.516*** **
Share of family network in personal network (ref. 0%)				
1–49%	**5.874*** **	**3.062*** **	**2.671*** **	**1.572* **
50–99%	**5.902*** **	**2.618*** **	**2.135*** **	**2.234*** **
100%	**7.738*** **	**1.589* **	1.357	**2.560*** **
Birth cohort (Ref. 1950–1955)				
1960–1965	0.808	1.066	0.985	0.986
1970–1975	0.834	**0.627*** **	**0.632*** **	0.879
1980–1985	0.814	**0.582*** **	**0.606*** **	0.990
−2 Log likelihood	1596.105	5774.227	5840.304	5311.242
Cox & Snell R Square	0.644	0.097	0.084	0.186
Nagelkerke R Square	0.858	0.130	0.112	0.248

Significance levels: ***$p < 0.001$; **$p < 0.01$; *$p < 0.05$.
Source: Survey data.

5.4 Conclusions

The research presented in the chapter aimed to explore interrelations among support sharing, personal networks and family practices in the face of economically hard times in Lithuania.

Several hypotheses were formulated and tested which helped us to better understand the intricacies of support in personal and family networks. Interestingly, the reception of support did not relate to specific types of problems. In essence, a person having experienced a financial problem has no higher chance of receiving financial support than receiving practical support or emotional support. Support in family and personal networks are not specialized but rather have a generalistic orientation in which various kinds of support may intermingle. This makes the family a rather comprehensive source of support for individuals, although the extent to which this unit is able to address all the basic needs of individuals was not considered in this study.

Support is mostly exchanged between the respondents, their adult children, their siblings and parents. Therefore, the nuclear family of origin (which is sometimes called the "family of orientation") plays a critical role in supportive interactions among network members. As stressed in other publications (Bengston, 2001), the isolation of the family household and the nuclear family defined as a residential unit are rejected by the empirical analysis. Indeed, intergenerational family relationships, as well as sibling relationships between adults, constitute the backbones of solidarity practices occuring in personal networks in Lituania. Far from being obliterated by the pluralization of life courses, such principles of solidarity remain active in the younger generation as well as in the older ones. The differences across generations are indeed rather small and for the most part explainable by the specific life stage in which the younger generation stands at the time of the survey. What truly matters for the provision or reception of support rather are family practices: regular interactions are a major incentive to develop support. This may show the limitation of family support in a time faced by generalized migration, by which such regular interactions might be jeopardized.

Acknowledgements

The author is grateful to the Research Council of Lithuania for funding of the research project 'Trajectories of family models and social networks: intergenerational perspective' (code No.VP1-3.1-ŠMM-07-K-01-106) implemented in 2011–2015 by the group of sociologists at Mykolas Romeris University (Vilnius, Lithuania). The Project funded from the European Social Find, and coordinated by the Research Council of Lithuania under the Global grant measure. Empirical data collected in the Project made it possible to carry out an investigation the results of which presented in this chapter.

References

Attias-Donfut, C., & Segalen, M. (2002). The construction of grandparenthood. *Current Sociology*, *50*(2), 281.

Attias-Donfut, C., Ogg, J., & Wolff, F. C. (2005). European patterns of intergenerational financial and time transfers. *Journal of Ageing*, *2*(3), 161–173.

Beck, U., & Beck-Gernsheim, E. (2002). *Individualization*. London: Sage.

Becker, G. S. (1981). *A treatise on the family*. Cambridge, MA: Harvard University Press.

Bengtson, V. L. (2001). Beyond the nuclear family: The increasing importance of multigenerational bonds. *Journal of Marriage and Family*, *63*(1), 1–16.

Bengtson, V. L., Rosenthal, C. J., & Burton, L. M. (1995). Paradoxes of families and aging. In R. H. Binstock & L. K. George (Eds.), *Handbook of aging and the social sciences* (pp. 253–282). San Diego, CA: Academic Press.

Bernardes, J (1986). Multidimensional developmental pathways: A proposal to facilitate the conceptualisation of a family diversity. *The Sociological Review*, *34*(3), 590–610.

Bernardes, J. (1999). We must not define 'the family'. In B. K. Settles, S. K. Steinmetz, G. W. Peterson & M. B. Sussman (Eds.), *Concepts and definitions of family for the 21st century*. London: Haworth Press.

Boh, K. (1992, February 8–10). Current family structures in Eastern and Central Europe. In *Changing families in changing societies. Proceedings of the International Conference in Brussels* (pp. 28–35). Wiesbaden: Bundesinstitut für Bevölkerungs forschung.

Česnuitytė, V. (2012). Changing family model, social capital and caring: How to reconcile? The case of Lithuania. In *Sociologia e Politiche Sociali* (Vol. 15, pp. 75–104). I. Crespi & G. Rossi (Eds.). *Special issue: Balancing work and family care: European experiences*. Milan: Franco Angeli. Retrieved from https://www.francoangeli.it/Riviste/sommario.aspx?anno=2012&idRivista=66&lingua=it. Accessed on September 30, 2019.

Crompton, R. (2006). *Employment and the family: The reconfiguration of work and family life in contemporary societies*. Cambridge: Cambridge University Press.

Crompton, R., Lewis, S., & Lyonette, C. (Eds.). (2007). *Women, men, work and family in Europe*. Basingstoke: Palgrave Macmillan.

Eurostat. (2019a). Average rating of satisfaction by domain, sex, age and educational attainment level [ilc_pw01]. Retrieved from https://ec.europa.eu/eurostat/data/database. Accessed on July 25, 2019.

Eurostat. (2019b). People at risk of poverty or social exclusion by age and sex [ilc_peps01]. Retrieved from https://ec.europa.eu/eurostat/data/database. Accessed on July 25, 2019.

Eurostat. (2019c). *Persons who cannot afford to get-together with friends or family (relatives) for a drink or meal at least once a month by age, sex and income group [ilc_mdes10a]*. Retrieved from https://ec.europa.eu/eurostat/data/database. Accessed on July 25, 2019.

Eurostat. (2019d). *Persons who cannot afford to regularly participate in a leisure activity by employment status and income quintile*. Retrieved from https://ec.europa.eu/eurostat/data/database. Accessed on July 25, 2019.

Eurostat. (2019e). *Unemployment rates by sex, age and citizenship (%) [lfsa_urgan]* Retrieved from https://ec.europa.eu/eurostat/data/database. Accessed on July 25, 2019.

Finch, J. (1989). *Family obligations and social change*. Cambridge: Polity Press.

Gottlieb, B. (2000). Selecting and planning support intervention. In: Cohen, S., Underwood, L., & Gottlieb, B. (eds) *Social support measurement and intervention.* London: Oxford University Press, 195–220.

Hauri, R. (2011). *Christmas feast, an annual family gathering.* In R. Jallinoja & E. D. Widmer (Eds.) *Families and kinship in contemporary Europe: Rules and practices of relatedness.* Palgrave Macmillan studies in family and intimate life (pp. 45–62). London: Palgrave Macmillan.

Kanopienė, V. (2014). Socialinės paramos apibrėžtis. In V. Česnuitytė, V. Kanopienė, & S. Mikulionienė (Eds.), *Lietuvos šeima: socialinių saitų perspektyva* (138–148). Vilnius: Mykolo Romerio universitetas. Retrieved from http://ebooks.mruni.eu/reader/lietuvos-eima-socialini-sait-perspektyva/286. Accessed on September 30, 2019.

Kramer, B. J., & Thompson, E. H. (2002). *Men as caregivers: Theory, research, and service implications*, pp. 234–249). New York, NY: Springer.

Levin, I. (1999). What Phenomenon is Family? *Marriage & Family Review, 28*(3/4), 93–104.

Lowenstein, A., & Daatland, S. O. (2006). Filial norms and family support in a comparative cross – national context: Evidence from the OASIS study. *Ageing and Society, 26*(2), 203–223.

Morgan, D. H. J. (1996). *Family connections. An introduction to family studies.* Cambridge: Polity Press.

Morgan, D. H. J. (2011). *Rethinking family practices.* Hampshire: Palgrave Macmillan.

Pahl, R. E., & Spencer, L. (2004). Personal communities: Not simply families of 'fate' or 'choice'. *Current Sociology, 52*, 199–221.

Park, A., & Roberts, C. (2002). The ties that bind. In A. Park, J. Curtice, K. Thomson, L. Jarvis, & C. Bromley (Eds.), *British social attitudes: The 19th Report.* London: Sage.

Parsons, T., & Bales, R. F. (Eds.). (1955). *Family socialization and interaction process.* Glencoe: Free Press.

Regan, P. C. (2011). *Close relationships.* New York, NY/London: Routledge, Taylor & Francis Group.

Robila, M. (2004). Families in Eastern Europe: Context, trends and variations. In M. Robila (Ed.), *Families in Eastern Europe. Contemporary perspectives in family research* (Vol. 5, pp. 1–14). San Diego, CA: JAI Press, Emerald Publishing Limited.

Rowland, S., Miller, R. S., Perlman, D., Sharon, S., & Brehm, S. S. (2007). *Intimate relationships.* Boston, MA: McGraw-Hill Higher Education.

Scabini, E., & Lanz, M. (2006). *The transition to adulthood ant family relations. An intergenerational perspective.* Hove/New York, NY: Psychology Press, Taylor & Francis Group.

Sheppard, R. (2009). Gender, marriage, and family in post-industrial society: An international perspective. In J. Powell & J. Hendricks (Eds.), *The welfare state in post-industrial society. A global perspective* (pp. 99–124). London: Springer.

Silverstein, M., Conroy, S. J., Wang, H., Giarrusso, R., & Bengtson, V. L. (2002). Reciprocity in parent-child relations over the adult life course. *Journal of Gerontology: Social Sciences, 57B*(1), S3–S13.

Smart, C. (2007). *Personal life.* Cambridge: Polity Press.

Stankūnienė, V., & Maslauskaitė, A. (Eds.). (2009). *Lietuvos šeima: tarp tradicijos ir naujos realybės*. Vilnius: Socialinių Tyrimų Institutas

Thornton, A., & Philipov, D. (2007). *Developmental idealism and family and demographic change in Central and Eastern Europe*. European Demographic Research Papers, 3. Vienna: Vienna Institute of Demography.

Wall, K., Aboim, S., Cunha, V., & Vasconcelos, P. (2001). Families and informal support networks in Portugal: The reproduction of inequality. *Journal of European Social Policy*, *11*, 213–233.

Widmer, E. D. (2004). Couples and their networks. In Richards, M., Scott, J., & Treas, J. (Eds.), *Blackwell companion to the sociology of families* (pp. 356–373). London: Blackwell.

Widmer, E. D. (1999). Family contexts as cognitive networks: A structural approach of family relationships. *Personal Relationships*, *6*(4), 487–503.

Wolin, S. J., & Bennett, L. A. (1984). Family rituals. *Family Process*, *23*, 401–420.

Chapter 6

Deprivation and Transfers between Three Generations: A Regional Analysis Across Europe

Christian Deindl and Martina Brandt

6.1 Introduction

In times of rising inequality and poverty, the family is one of the most important 'fall back' option for individuals at risk of deprivation. The family provides a safety net throughout life, and intergenerational transfers can be an essential means to prevent material and social deprivation, especially in vulnerable phases of the life course such as youth and old age. Transfers are, however, at the same time a result of the social and material position of individuals and families within different social policy contexts as many studies have shown (e.g. Attias-Donfut, Ogg, & Wolff, 2005; Bonsang, 2007; Brandt & Deindl, 2013; Daatland & Herlofson, 2003). In the following sections we set out to assess the multi-directional links between intergenerational exchange between three generations and deprivation throughout life course and across different societies and regional contexts. Our analysis thus explores some of the potential mechanisms behind the links between social inequality and intergenerational solidarity. This knowledge is an important basis for evidence-based policies which shall preserve intergenerational cohesion and family solidarity in times of population ageing and discussions about the future feasibility of pay-as-you-go-pensions, health insurance schemes and so on – for the old as well as for the young.

Our analyses are based on the fifth wave of the Survey of Health, Ageing and Retirement in Europe (SHARE; Börsch-Supan, 2016; for data and methodological details see Börsch-Supan et al., 2013, and Malter & Börsch-Supan, 2015; for first overview results see Börsch-Supan, Kneip, Litwin, Myck, & Weber, 2015), and include information from over 7,000 households with respondents aged 50 and above and their parents and children from 117 regions across Austria, Belgium, Denmark, the Czech Republic, Estonia, France, Germany, Italy, Luxembourg, the Netherlands, Italy, Slovenia, Spain, Sweden and Switzerland. This is the first study to consider mid-aged Europeans in the 'sandwich' position between older parents and children and include both transfer

Families in Economically Hard Times, 129–144

doi:10.1108/978-1-83909-071-420191010

directions across these three generations (children G3, respondents G2, parents G1) to assess the links between solidarity and social and material deprivation on the respondent as well as in the regional level. We thus follow the call for an environmental perspective on social exclusion in later life (Van Regenmortel et al., 2016) and complement recent research on intergenerational solidarity and transfer patterns in different welfare states by focusing the effects of deprivation risks on different levels.

In the following, we will first give an overview of the theoretical background and empirical studies in the field before introducing our data and methods. We will then present our analyses and conclude by discussing our results as well as limitations and directions for further research.

6.2 Theoretical Background and Empirical Evidence

Parents and children are closely connected across their shared lifetime in numerous ways, living together or close to each other, being in regular contact, caring for each other practically and emotionally, sharing similar values and not least feeling obligated towards each other. These dimensions of 'intergenerational solidarity' were described as 'structural', 'associational', 'functional', 'affectual', 'consensual' and 'normative solidarity' by Bengtson and colleagues (e.g. Bengtson & Roberts, 1991). One common critique, which has been taken up by the authors themselves (Bengtson, Giarrusso, Mabry, & Silversteint, 2002), is that this solidarity-centred view might be naïve as even close relations between family generations can also be characterised by conflict or even ambivalence (Lüscher & Pillemer, 1998). Still, most support in social networks is exchanged between partners and between family generations (Attias-Donfut et al., 2005). As family relations are characterised by interdependency and trust, generalised, long-term reciprocity across the life course and family cycle is enabled insofar transfers do not have to be directly returned in the exact same 'currency' or equivalent value but can be modified and delayed, e.g. when parents support their children practically or financially in earlier years, whereas children take care of their frail parents in later life (Gouldner, 1960; Hollstein, 2005). Others argue that family members intend to improve the situation of the transfer receiver altruistically, without expecting to profit in any (other) way (Monroe, 1994). Studies provided ample evidence for both transfer motives between family members and generations (e.g. Altonji, Hayashi, & Kotlikoff, 1997; Silverstein, Conroy, Wang, Giarrusso, & Bengtson, 2002). Parents and children help each other because they want to and if they can, and this is not limited to situations when there is a specific need for support (Künemund & Rein, 1999) but – especially in the family – due to love and concern for each other (Björnberg & Latta, 2007).

Apart from theses motives, functional solidarity in terms of money, time and space given and received depends on the needs of the potential receiver, the resources and opportunities of the potential giver, as well as the family structures and the socio-cultural and political context they are embedded in (Brandt, 2013). Parents do not only financially and practically support their offspring when the latter is still in education and the family building phase, but also in times of financial distress (due to unemployment, divorce etc.) later on. Deprivation might change exactly that, and the (relative or absolute) lack of resources and higher needs has the potential to change the regular transfer cycle, as demonstrated, for example, by the impressive amount of remittances for parents from children who migrated (Poirine, 2006). More generally, in a three-generational setting, when parents of the middle generation are not able to (financially or practically) support their young offspring and need help themselves, this has important consequences not only for dependent children but also for their own (older) parents and other family members.

Over and above, as shown in several longitudinal studies, solidarity patterns and transfers between family members may not only differ between different socio-economic backgrounds or family structures and change over the family cycle, but also differ between social contexts and public transfer regimes (e.g. Bucx, Van Wel, & Knijn, 2012; Johansson, Sundström, & Hassing, 2003). Summarising the state of cross-national research, we find more sporadic but less intense support between generations in generous welfare states and (different forms of) formal and informal support seem to go hand in hand ('complementarity') (Brandt & Deindl, 2013). We also know that lower welfare state expenditures and services often go along with higher social inequality on the one hand and more individual poverty on the other (for a discussion of different mechanisms see, e.g. Esping-Andersen & Myles, 2012). Such social inequalities at the country level as well as individual poverty risks are likely to alter individual transfer needs and opportunities as well as family transfer patterns and put functional intergenerational solidarity at risk (Deindl & Brandt, 2015; Ellwardt, Peter, Präg, & Steverink, 2014). When family members are not able to support each other in need and are not enabled to do so (or relieved from competing obligations) by generous public policies, this might result in negative spirals with more needs and less resources on the family level and lower exchange – especially in contexts with high social inequality and (already) low social cohesion (Wilkinson & Pickett, 2010). Thus, even if an individual is well-off in a more unequal society, transfers might be diminished due to lower social connectedness and higher social stress (see, e.g. Berkman, Glass, Brissette, & Seeman, 2000).

From what we know about typical influences on intergenerational transfers, we expect that transfers are most often directed to family members in need; if necessary also contrary to the usual patterns (people in mid age support their grown-up children with financial support and help their older parents practically). Such patterns are not least embedded in and linked to regional contexts such as social security (pensions, health and care regimes, social services, etc.), social inequality and wealth. So the helpers from the 'pivot', 'sandwich' or 'middle' generation, 'squeezed' between descendants and parents and balancing obligations for care and work (Grundy & Henretta, 2006; Mooney, Statham, & Simon, 2002; Spitze, Logan, Joseph, & Lee, 1994), might lose their role as supporters for the older and/or the younger in the family and become dependent on intergenerational support instead. They might then also become a burden for their children or older parents who are likely in financial or practical need themselves.

Such situations might then not only be linked to less (mutual) support and but also to an erosion of family solidarity patterns when the (individual and societal) pressure to provide support becomes higher, and the means to do so diminish on both levels. Moreover, giving due to love and concern might be reduced or ceased completely when only scarce resources are available and those have to be directed to the ones most in need. In the following, we will provide cross-national evidence for such links by analysing transfer patterns between respondents, their parents and children and individual social and material deprivation within different social inequality contexts across European regions.

6.3 Data and Methods

In order to analyse intergenerational transfers and socio-economic deprivation across European countries, we base our investigation on data from SHARE Wave 5 respondents aged 50 and above and their older parents and adult children. We restrict our investigation to (financial) respondents with adult children and older parent (s-in-law) in order to investigate transfers in a three-generational setting. Transfers were measured as transfers of time (help with paperwork and household tasks, care, grandchild care) and money (financial gifts of at least 250 Euros) given and/or received between respondents (G2, 50+ including younger partners) and their parents (in-law, G1) and children (G3) within the last year. In the following we will talk about 'parents' when we mean G1, and thus parents and parents-in-law.

In order to measure material deprivation of the respondents we use the new indicators introduced in SHARE wave 5 (Adena, Myck, & Oczkowska, 2015), including the affordability of:

- meat (…[you] do not eat meat, fish or chicken more often [than three times per week] because: you cannot afford to eat it more often)
- fruit (…[you] do not eat fruits or vegetables more often [than three times per week] because: you cannot afford to eat it more often)
- groceries (Can your household afford to regularly buy necessary groceries and household supplies?)
- holidays (Could your household afford to go for a week-long holiday away from home at least once a year?)
- unexpected expenses (Could your household afford to pay an unexpected expense of [country-specific relative poverty line defined at the level of 60% of median monthly equivalised household income] without borrowing any money?)
- clothing (In the last 12 months, to help you keep your living costs down, have you…continued wearing clothing that was worn out because you could not afford replacement?)
- shoes (… continued wearing shoes that were worn out because you could not afford replacement?)
- heating (… put up with feeling cold to save heating costs?)

- glasses (… gone without or not replaced glasses you needed because you could not afford new ones?)
- dentist (… postponed visits to the dentist?)
- doctor (Was there a time in the past 12 months when you needed to see a doctor but could not because of cost?)

The answers to these questions were given by the financial respondent in each household.

Social deprivation was measured according to the suggestion of Myck, Najsztub, and Oczkowska (2015, p. 69) by the indicators:

- Less than one room per person in the household
- Poor reading or writing skills
- Poor computer skills or never used a computer
- Not feeling part of the local area
- Vandalism in the local area
- Local area not clean
- No helpful people in local area
- Difficult access to bank
- Difficult access to grocery shop
- Difficult access to pharmacy
- Waiting too long to see a doctor
- Not attending any course in the past 12 months
- Not taking part in any organisation in the past 12 months
- People cannot be trusted
- Feeling left out of things

Respondents were considered to be socially or materially deprived if they reported at least two problems with social or material deprivation in the descriptive analyses; in the multivariate models deprivation was measured by the logarithm of the number of items mentioned.

Moreover, highest education and household income in country-specific 5% percentiles indicating the relative position of the household and thus comparable across countries were included in the models to measure the socio-economic background of the household (G2). Demographics included the gender composition of household (single male, single female, couple) and the highest age within the household. Family structures were measured by the existence of specific family ties. The relation to parent(s) (G1) and child (ren) (G3) was measured by having at least one child or parent living within 25 km (roughly 15 miles) and at least weekly contact with at least one child or parent. The needs of the latter were operationalised by a poor health status of at least one parent and the employment situation as well as gender of the children (at least one unemployed child; at least one daughter/son).

Social inequality on the regional level was measured by social inequality and general prosperity (Gini and Gross Domestic Product (GDP), retrieved from

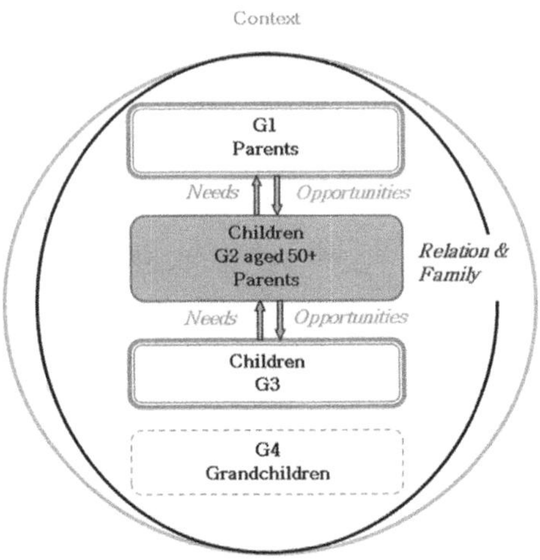

Fig. 6.1. Overview of Transfers Flows and Influences.

OECD (2016)). To control for the fact that observations from different regions are non-independent from each other, we estimated multilevel models (see, e.g. Snijders & Bosker, 1999). In addition to regional characteristics differing considerably within countries (see Table A2) and presumably influencing individuals more directly than the general country context (which is still integral part of the measure by being the backdrop for regional characteristics), there is also a methodological advantage in having a higher number of macro-level observations (see, e.g. Bryan & Jenkins, 2016; Hox, Van de Schoot, & Matthijsse, 2012). Nine regions were excluded from the analysis because they had fewer than five observations.

Fig. 6.1 gives an overview of the analytical setting in terms of the transfer flows between family generations and the influencing factors focused here, and Table A1 describes the basic characteristics of the sample and variables used in order to model this empirically.

Table A2 briefly displays the macro-level information used. Even this general overview shows quite impressively why it is important to measure the regional variation of inequality: there is considerable variation within countries in terms of Gini as well as GDP which shapes the living conditions and objective surroundings and might as well influence subjective evaluations of the respondents.

6.4 Results

A first descriptive overview of the more than 7,000 financial respondents shows that half of the sample households experienced social or material deprivation (two or more items), with almost a third of those reporting a combination of both indicators (16%), and more experiencing only social deprivation (21%) than only material deprivation (12%, Table A1). Even though there was a considerable restriction of resources among half of the respondent households, a lot was given (and received) between these and their children and parents as can be seen in Fig. 6.2. Almost two-thirds gave any kind of support (grandchild care, financial transfers, practical help in this rank order) to their children, and about one-third provided support (mostly practical help or care) to their parents during the last year. As expected and in line with the typical family transfer cycle, the middle generation (G2) received support less likely – in 7% of the cases they received (mostly help or care) transfers from their adult children (G3), and in another almost 7% they received (mainly financial) transfers from older parents (G1) during the last year.

Across all regions we found pronounced links between deprivation and transfers between three generations: more deprivation of the G2 meant less transfers given but (a little more) received within the last year (Fig. 6.3). Children

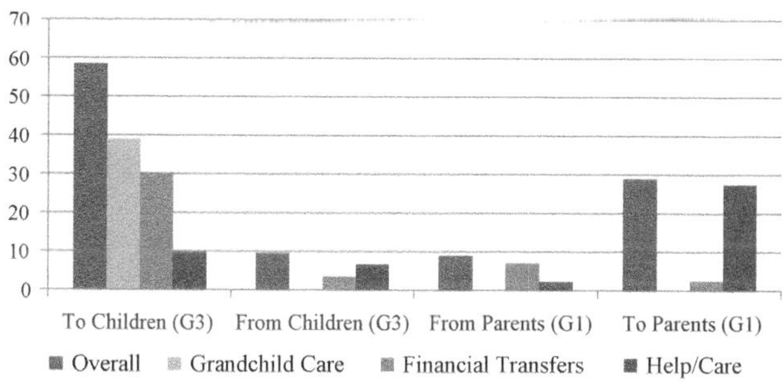

Fig. 6.2. Intergenerational Transfers.
Source: SHARE Wave 5; n = 7,092.

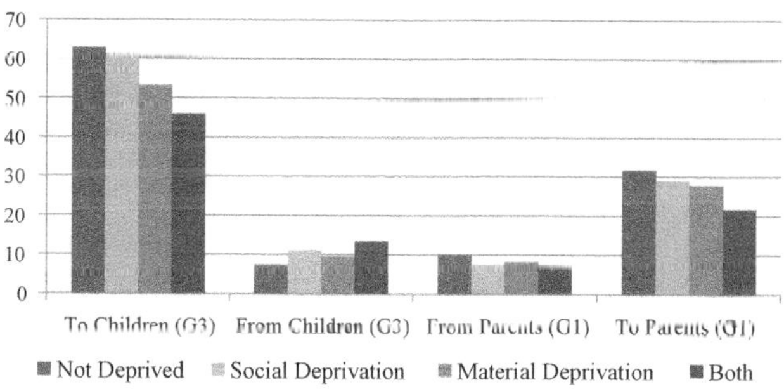

Fig. 6.3. Intergenerational Transfers and Deprivation.
Source: SHARE Wave 5; n = 7,092.

seemed to take over support for the respondents if those were deprived in any way – which was, at least on a descriptive basis, not true for older parents. These correlations do, however, not yet explicitly account for other important socio-economic factors, family structures and regional characteristics as will be done in the following multivariate analyses.

In multilevel models (Table 6.1) we predicted the probability of a transfer in a certain intergenerational direction between G1, G2 and G3 and assessed the influences of social and material deprivation (measured linearly by the logarithm of the number of restrictions mentioned) on the respondent level as well as social inequality on the regional level. When looking at the effects of these deprivation indicators on the respondent (top of Table 6.1) and regional level (bottom of Table 6.1) it becomes very clear that individual and contextual social exclusion and inequality are decisive for family transfer flows, even when controlling for other important influences on the family and regional level. The more deprived respondents were (and the less they had to give), the less they gave to their parents and children. They were, however, more likely to receive transfers from their children. Children thus seemed to react to the higher needs of their socially and/or materially deprived parents – even in their younger years and conversely to the typical family transfer cycle – by supporting their middle-aged parents G2. Over and above, we see a significantly lower likelihood of intergenerational transfers in any direction in regions with higher social inequality as measured by the Gini, irrespective of the general prosperity in a region in terms of the regional GDP.

Educational background and income as further measures for resources and opportunities (implicit deprivation) seemed to be not as decisive as the explicit deprivation measures, but were also linked to a higher likelihood of transfers given to children and/or parents, and the highest educated also received transfers most likely from their parents. Single females were more involved in intergenerational transfers as males and couples who only give more likely to their children but receive less from them. Higher respondent age was linked to significantly less transfers from older parents. Additional models including the (mean) age of parents and children did not provide any additional insights but led to a significant loss of observations and were thus not included here.

Concerning family structures we see that (four) parents alive seemed to be a competing obligation and crowded out transfers to children and vice versa, with more children linked to less transfers to parents. Over and above, having grandchildren was linked to more exchange with children (their parents, respectively), presumably in terms of grandchild care.

(Other) parental characteristics mattered only for transfers between parents and respondents, whereas children's characteristics mattered only for transfers between respondents and the latter. Generally, and as expected, the more contact, the more likely we found transfers. A (low) living distance, however, mattered for parents (due to more practical help and care) but not for children (due to more financial transfers which can bridge distances). Higher needs due to the poor health of a parent were linked to more support from respondents to

Table 6.1. Multilevel Binary Logit Models.

	To Child	From Child	From Parent	To Parent
Respondent households				
Deprived (log (n items))	−0.32**	0.28**	0.03	−0.15**
	(0.046)	(0.074)	(0.075)	(0.050)
Highest education: low	Ref	Ref	Ref	Ref
Medium	0.36**	−0.04	0.05	0.36**
	(0.078)	(0.123)	(0.140)	(0.090)
High	0.38**	0.03	0.50**	0.59**
	(0.085)	(0.137)	(0.145)	(0.097)
Household income	0.04**	−0.01	0.01	0.02**
(5%-ile)	(0.006)	(0.009)	(0.009)	(0.006)
Single male	Ref	Ref	Ref	Ref
Single female	0.60**	0.46**	0.26	0.49**
	(0.104)	(0.160)	(0.163)	(0.115)
Couple	0.32**	−0.28+	−0.24	−0.09
	(0.101)	(0.165)	(0.165)	(0.114)
Highest age	0.00	0.02*	−0.03**	0.01
	(0.005)	(0.008)	(0.010)	(0.006)
Parents				
One parent alive	Ref	Ref	Ref	Ref
Two	−0.03	−0.11	0.32**	−0.04
	(0.065)	(0.109)	(0.103)	(0.071)
Three	−0.20+	−0.37+	0.45**	0.02
	(0.107)	(0.216)	(0.158)	(0.112)
Four	−0.38*	−0.14	0.50+	0.04
	(0.189)	(0.387)	(0.270)	(0.202)
Weekly contact	0.02	−0.10	0.63**	1.53**
	(0.067)	(0.101)	(0.132)	(0.095)
Distance less than 25 km	−0.04	0.02	0.28**	0.80**
	(0.057)	(0.091)	(0.093)	(0.062)
Poor health	0.05	−0.04	−0.12	0.48**
	(0.060)	(0.095)	(0.098)	(0.063)
Children				
Number of children	0.01	0.07	0.01	−0.10**
	(0.032)	(0.047)	(0.051)	(0.035)

Table 6.1. *(Continued)*

	To Child	From Child	From Parent	To Parent
Number of grandchildren	0.35**	0.06**	−0.05+	−0.01
	(0.019)	(0.022)	(0.027)	(0.017)
Weekly contact	0.49**	0.42**	−0.14	0.02
	(0.070)	(0.119)	(0.112)	(0.076)
Distance less than 25 km	−0.02	0.08	−0.17	−0.09
	(0.068)	(0.111)	(0.108)	(0.073)
At least one son	−0.10	0.06	0.09	−0.05
	(0.063)	(0.106)	(0.105)	(0.068)
At least one unemployed	−0.04	−0.39**	−0.00	−0.07
	(0.084)	(0.147)	(0.140)	(0.094)
Regions				
Inequality (Gini)	−0.06**	−0.11**	−0.07**	−0.04*
	(0.016)	(0.033)	(0.025)	(0.020)
Prosperity (GDP)	0.02	−0.05	0.09	0.09
	(0.049)	(0.099)	(0.072)	(0.061)

$^{+}p < 0.10$; $^{*}p < 0.05$; $^{**}p < 0.01$.
Source: SHARE Wave 5, $n = 7{,}092$ respondents, 117 regions.

their parents. The gender composition of children (in terms of having at least one son) was not linked to any differences in intergenerational transfers but the unemployment of a child seemed to be a sign of reduced opportunities for giving to a parent.

6.5 Discussion

The links between social inequality and transfers between middle-aged respondents and their adult children and older parents based on information from 117 European regions showed strong links between individual social and material deprivation, regional social inequality and intergenerational transfer patterns in a three-generational family setting. More deprivation on the individual level is linked to a lower likelihood of intergenerational transfers of time and money to parents and children, and a higher likelihood of transfers by children. Moreover, the likelihood of any intergenerational transfer is significantly lower in regions having more social inequality as measured by the Gini coefficient.

All in all, families provide a safety net, and their members support each other if needed and when they can (cf. Deindl & Brandt, 2015). At the stage of the typical family transfer cycle we focused here, middle-aged parents support their adult offspring (mostly with money and grandchild care) and their older parents with practical hands-on help and care. These patterns seem considerably altered when the middle-aged are materially or socially deprived, and also when the overall level of social inequality in a region is higher. The middle generation then becomes dependent on support from their offspring and turns from being the main giver to being the main receiver. This might be problematic for families not only because these parents lose their typical role in the family but also because they might become a burden for their offspring.

We could only assess deprivation of the respondents themselves, and not explicitly measure deprivation of the children and parents apart from the health and employment indicators used. This could at least partly explain the significant correlation of all kinds of transfers assessed and macro-level inequality irrespective of individual level deprivation in the multivariate models. Unfortunately, there is no indicator for intergenerational mobility or an equivalent measure we could use to control for the links between inequality of the younger and older family generations and general inequality on the macro level. Still, a substantial interpretation of the significant effects of regional social inequality on transfer patterns seems reasonable as the fact that higher inequality goes hand in hand with lower social cohesion has been shown impressively in previous work (e.g. Wilkinson & Pickett, 2010). And it seems to hold for intergenerational relations as well: apart from individual needs and opportunities and family structures, the social environment has an influence on exchange patterns between generations. This might be due to the subjective evaluation of (higher) risk (of becoming poor or developing need) within a more unequal environment and higher overall stress related to such a context over and above actual individual deprivation, which does not only lead to lower overall cohesion but also less transfers between family generations. Future research should not only address this issue by using a multi-actor design including all individual resources but also by modeling the links between (changes in) context and (changes in) individual behaviour from a longitudinal perspective – as soon as the relevant data are available.

Based on our somewhat limited snapshot and in interplay with previous work it seems that families and intergenerational relations are both more vulnerable in regions with higher social inequality. In such settings, individuals suffer not only from a higher likelihood of being materially or socially deprived, but are also less able to rely on the safety net of intergenerational support. Consequently, (functional) solidarity between older parents and older children might be at risk in countries with more economic and social deprivation and inequality on the micro and on the macro level. An effective reduction of social inequalities on all levels might thus be beneficial not only for the individual, but would also promote intergenerational solidarity within families and societies.

Acknowledgements

This chapter uses data from SHARE Waves 1, 2, 3 (SHARELIFE), 4 and 5 (DOIs:10.6103/SHARE.w1.260, 10.6103/SHARE.w2.260, 10.6103/SHARE.w3.100, 10.6103/SHARE.w4.111, 10.6103/SHARE.w5.100), see Börsch-Supan et al. (2013) for methodological details. The SHARE data collection has been primarily funded by the European Commission through FP5 (QLK6-CT-2001-00360), FP6 (SHARE-I3: RII-CT-2006-062193, COMPARE: CIT5-CT-2005-028857, SHARELIFE:CIT4-CT-2006-028812) and FP7 (SHARE-PREP: N°211909, SHARE-LEAP: N°227822, SHARE M4: N°261982). Additional funding from the German Ministry of Education and Research, the US National Institute on Aging (U01_AG09740-13S2, P01_AG005842, P01_AG08291, P30_AG12815, R21_AG025169, Y1-AG-4553-01, IAG_BSR06-11, OGHA_04-064) and from various national funding sources is gratefully acknowledged (see www.share-project.org). We are grateful for the assistance of Markus Kotte, who prepared the information about children for us.

References

Adena, M., Myck, M., & Oczkowska, M. (2015). Material deprivation items in SHARE Wave 5 data: A contribution to a better understanding of differences in material conditions in later life. In A. Börsch-Supan, T. Kneip, H. Litwin, M. Myck, & G. Weber (Eds.), *Ageing in Europe – Supporting policies for an inclusive society* (pp. 25–38). Berlin: De Gruyter.

Altonji, J. G., Hayashi, F., & Kotlikoff, L. J. (1997). Parental altruism and inter vivos transfers: Theory and evidence. *Journal of Political Economy*, *105*(6), 1121–1166.

Attias-Donfut, C., Ogg, J., & Wolff, F.-C. (2005). European patterns of intergenerational financial and time transfers. *European Journal of Ageing*, *2*, 161–173.

Bengtson, V., Giarrusso, R., Mabry, J. B., & Silverstein, M. (2002). Solidarity, conflict, and ambivalence: Complementary or competing perspectives on intergenerational relationships? *Journal of Marriage and Family*, *64*(3), 568–576.

Bengtson, V. L., & Roberts, R. E. L. (1991). Intergenerational solidarity in aging families: An example of formal theory construction. *Journal of Marriage and Family*, *53*, 856–870.

Berkman, L. F., Glass, T., Brissette, I., & Seeman, T. E. (2000). From social integration to health: Durkheim in the new millennium. *Social Science & Medicine*, *51*, 843–857.

Björnberg, U., & Latta, M. (2007). The roles of the family and the welfare state. The relationship between public and private financial support in Sweden. *Current Sociology*, *55*, 415–445.

Börsch-Supan, A. (2016). *Survey of Health, Ageing and Retirement in Europe (SHARE) Wave 5*. Release version: 5.0.0. SHARE-ERIC. Data set, Munich.

Börsch-Supan, A., Brandt, M., Hunkler, C., Kneip, T., Korbmacher, J., Malter, F., … Zuber, S. (2013). Data resource profile: The Survey of Health, Ageing and Retirement in Europe (SHARE). *International Journal of Epidemiology*, *42*, 992–1001.

Börsch-Supan, A., Kneip, T., Litwin, H., Myck, M., & Weber, G. (Eds.). (2015). *Ageing in Europe – Supporting policies for an inclusive society*. Berlin: De Gruyter.

Bonsang, E. (2007). How do middle-aged children allocate time and money transfers to their older parents in Europe? *Empirica*, *34*, 171–188.

Brandt, M. (2013). Intergenerational help and public assistance in Europe. A case of spe-cialization? *European Societies*, *15*(1), 26–56.

Brandt, M., & Deindl, C. (2013). Intergenerational transfers to adult children in Europe: Do social policies matter? *Journal of Marriage and Family*, *75*(1), 235–251.

Bryan, M. L., & Jenkins, S. P. (2016). Multilevel modelling of country effects: A cautionary tale. *European Sociological Review*, *32*, 3–22.

Bucx, F., Van Wel, F., & Knijn, T. (2012). Life course status and exchanges of support between young adults and parents. *Journal of Marriage and Family*, *74*, 101–115.

Daatland, S .O., & Herlofson, K. (2003). Families and welfare states: Substitution or complementarity. In A. Lowenstein & J. Ogg (Eds.), *OASIS: Old age and autonomy – The role of service systems and intergenerational family solidarity. The final report* (pp. 281–305). Haifa: University of Haifa.

Deindl, C., & Brandt, M. (2015). Social exclusion and support between generations In A. Börsch-Supan, T. Kneip, H. Liwin, M. Myck, & G. Weber (Eds.), *Ageing in Europe – Supporting policies for an inclusive society*. Berlin: De Gruyter.

Ellwardt, L., Peter, S., Präg, P., & Steverink, N. (2014). Social contacts of older people in 27 European countries: The role of welfare spending and economic inequality. *European Sociological Review*, *30*, 413–430.

Esping-Andersen, G., & Myles, J. (2012). Economic inequality and the welfare state. In B. Nolan, W. Salverda, & T. M. Smeeding (Eds.), *The Oxford handbook of economic inequality*. Oxford: Oxford University Press.

Gouldner, A. W. (1960). The norm of reciprocity: A preliminary statement. *American Sociological Review*, *25*(2), 161–178.

Grundy, E., & Henretta, J. C. (2006). Between elderly parents and adult children: A new look at the intergenerational care provided by the 'sandwich generation'. *Ageing and Society*, *26*, 707–722.

Hollstein, B. (2005). Reziprozität in familialen Generationenbeziehungen. In F. Adloff, & S. Mau (Eds.), *Vom Geben und Nehmen. Zur Soziologie der Reziprozität* (pp. 187–209). Frankfurt: Campus Verlag.

Hox, J. J., Van de Schoot, R., & Matthijsse, S. (2012). How few countries will do? Comparative survey analysis from a Bayesian perspective. *Survey Research Methods*, *6*, 87–93.

Johansson, L., Sundström, G., & Hassing, L. B. (2003). State provision down, off-spring's up: The reverse substitution of old-age care in Sweden. *Ageing and Society*, *23*, 269–280.

Künemund, H., & Rein, M. (1999). There is more to receiving than needing: Theoretical arguments and empirical explorations of crowding in and crowding out. *Ageing and Society*, *19*, 93–121.

Lüscher, K., & Pillemer, K. (1998). Intergenerational ambivalence: A new approach to the study of parent-child relations in later life. *Journal of Marriage and Family*, *60*(2), 413–425.

Malter, F., & Börsch-Supan, A. (Eds.). (2015). *SHARE wave 5: Innovations & methodology*. Munich: MEA, Max Planck Institute for Social Law and Social Policy.

Mooney, A., Statham, J., & Simon, A. (2002). *The pivot generation. Informal care and work after fifty*. Bristol: Policy Press.

Monroe, K. R. (1994). A fat lady in a corset: Altruism and social theory. *American Journal of Political Science*, *38*(4), 861–893.

Myck, M., Najsztub, M., & Oczkowska, M. (2015). Measuring social deprivation and social exclusion. In A. Börsch-Supan, T. Kneip, H. Litwin, M. Myck, & G. Weber (Eds.), *Ageing in Europe – Supporting policies for an inclusive society* (pp. 67–78). Berlin: De Gruyter.

OECD. (2016). *OECD regional well-being*. Paris: OECD. Retrieved from https://www.oecdregionalwellbeing.org/. Accessed on December 2, 2016.

Poirine, B. (2006). Remittances sent by a growing altruistic diaspora: How do they grow over time? *Asia Pacific Viewpoint*, *47*(1), 93–108.

Silverstein, M., Conroy, S. J., Wang, H., Giarrusso, R., & Bengtson, V. L. (2002). Reciprocity in parent-child relations over the adult life course. *Journal of Gerontology: Social Sciences*, *57B*(1), S3–S13.

Snijders, T. A. B., & Bosker, R. J. (1999). *Multilevel analysis. An introduction to basic and advanced multilevel modeling*. London: SAGE Publications.

Spitze, G., Logan, J. R., Joseph, G., & Lee, E. (1994). Middle generation roles and the well-being of men and women. *Journal of Gerontology: Social Sciences*, *49*, S107–S116.

Van Regenmortel, S., De Donder, L., Dury, S., Semtcoren, A.-S., De Witte, N., & Verte, D. (2016). Social exclusion in later life: A systematic review of the literature. *Population Ageing*, *9*, 315–344.

Wilkinson, R. G., & Pickett, K. (2010). *The spirit level: Why greater equality makes societies stronger*. New York, NY: Bloomsbury Press.

Appendix

Table A1. Sample Characteristics.

	Mean/Percentage
Respondent household	
No deprivation	50.13
Social deprivation	21.26
Material deprivation	12.11
Social and material deprivation	16.50
Highest education: low	19.91
Highest education: medium	43.89
Highest education: high	36.20

Table A1. *(Continued)*

	Mean/Percentage
Household income (ppp)	37,550.76
Single male	9.48
Single female	20.29
Couple	70.23
Highest age	60.08
Parents	
One parent alive	62.96
Two parents alive	26.64
Three parents alive	8.36
Four parents alive	2.04
Contact with at least one parent at least weekly	78.47
Distance to at least one parent less than 25 km	48.67
Poor health of at least one parent	28.91
Children	
Number of children	2.26
Number of grandchildren	1.83
Contact with at least one child at least weekly	79.57
Distance to at least child less than 25 km	77.35
At least one son	75.07
At least one child unemployed	12.49

Source: SHARE Wave 5; n = 7,112.

Table A2. Country Characteristics.

Country	Observations	Level of Disaggregation	Gini Mean	Min–Max	(log)GDP Mean	Min–Max
Sweden	456	1	28.10	28.1	12.88	12.88
Denmark	524	6	24.75	23.4–28.3	10.87	9.94–12.35
Netherlands	342	5	27.84	26.6–30.3	12.25	11.15–13.52
Belgium	705	4	28.38	24.8–35.8	12.05	11.28–12.97
Luxembourg	167	1	28.00	28.0	10.66	10.66
Germany	696	15	28.37	23.6–33.0	12.15	10.70–14.99
Austria	593	10	27.29	22.9–33.7	10.58	8.97–12.76
Switzerland	354	8	28.39	25.6–31.9	11.10	9.77–12.90
France	680	22	28.45	25.3–34.3	11.38	9.89–14.62
Estonia	571	1	33.00	33.0	10.24	10.24
Czech Republic	592	9	25.62	23.7–30.0	10.65	10.08–12.55
Slovenia	294	3	25.07	24.8–25.2	10.47	10.11–10.94
Spain	649	14	31.98	28.7–34.4	11.46	10.13–14.23
Italy	469	18	30.71	26.1–36.9	11.44	9.53–14.54
$n = 14$	$n = 7{,}092$	$n = 117$				

Source: SHARE Wave 5.

Chapter 7

Here to Stay? Intergenerational Spatial Proximity in Europe

Bettina Isengard, Ronny König and Marc Szydlik

7.1 Introduction

In contemporary societies, families are still important institutions in which human beings live. As a consequence of major demographic changes such as increasing life expectancies and declining birthrates, 'family relationships across several generations are becoming increasingly important' (Bengtson, 2001, p. 1). Despite the consequences of demographic changes, the relations and bonds between familial generations remain impressively strong (for an overview, see Szydlik, 2016). Against the background of economic and societal crisis as well as broader socio-political uncertainties, cohesion seems to be still an important characteristic of parent–child relationships. Intergenerational support can be considered in different dimensions (see Bengtson & Roberts, 1991 for details). Alongside aspects of emotional closeness and affection (affective solidarity), the strength of the bond is also indicated by the frequency of contact and shared activities (associative solidarity). Supported by numerous empirical studies, the most striking aspect in contemporary societies seems to be the extent of functional solidarity, which is the giving and taking of money, time and space (for an overview of functional solidarity, see Szydlik, 2016).

Essential preconditions for many types of solidarity are reciprocity norms (Kohli, Künemund, Motel, & Szydlik, 2005), exchange expectations (Künemund & Rein, 1999), existing individual, family, and contextual structures (see, e.g. Szydlik, 2000, p. 85 ff.; 2016) and especially the geographical proximity or distance between generations. In this context, it is only possible to render regular acts of assistance, for which direct contact is essential, when generations live close enough to one another. One exception is financial support, which can easily be transferred across greater distances, or types of assistance that can basically also be given over the phone such as emotional support or assistance with administrative matters.

In this respect, this chapter analyses proximity as well as distances between generations with a particular view to changing patterns. Residential proximity between parents and their adult children can be understood as an important

Families in Economically Hard Times, 145–165

doi:10.1108/978-1-83909-071-420191011

indicator of their availability to provide help and support, especially in times when societies are seeing an increase in their mean ages and welfare states are undergoing changes. Until now, however, research has mainly focused on proximity between generations, co-residence or leaving the parental home while neglecting the interplay of these processes. This study addresses this research gap and investigates the general question of geographical stability and changes within parent–child relationships. It also examines the determinants of spatial mobility, namely, leaving the parental home or an increase or decrease in geographical distance between familial generations. To determine why children move out of the parental home or move closer or farther away, we based our analyses on data drawn from the Survey of Health, Ageing and Retirement in Europe (SHARE), which provides information on respondents aged 50 years and older in various European countries. To investigate intergenerational spatial mobility patterns within adult parent–child relationships in Europe, we have estimated multilevel multinomial regressions based on three levels (17,302 adult children nested in 8,630 parental households nested in 11 countries). Our analyses illustrate the importance of the variability of individual, familial and structural circumstances and their influence on spatial mobility in general and leaving home in particular.

7.2 Background: Theory and Previous Research

Although spatial proximity and co-residence specifically have been frequent subjects of research in the past, little is yet known about the driving forces behind stability and changes in the form of children moving into or out of the parental home as well as of generations moving closer together or farther away from one another in Europe. Previous research has mainly focused on living distances or co-residence patterns, neglecting the fact that the different moving scenarios are strongly connected to each other. Combining those types of spatial mobility opens up new opportunities to understand the complexity of disengagement processes in light of individual, familial and contextual changes. While changes in intergenerational proximity might clearly be a function of moves by either parents or by their children in response to changing circumstances, previous studies on intergenerational relocations (with the exception of first-time move-outs) have mainly focused on moves by parents towards their children and rarely considered the influence of children's moves – and even more rarely both types of moves together (Michielin, Mulder, & Zorlu, 2008). Zhang, Engelman, and Agree (2013) used two waves of the Health and Retirement Study (HRS) and showed that the majority (73%) of senior citizens (aged 69 or older) did not move within the two-year period under observation. However, the follow-up survey revealed that 14% of them had ended up living closer to their children, and most of this increase in proximity resulted from children's moves (two-thirds). The remaining 13% of residential changes were based on other circumstances such as institutionalised moves (e.g. nursing home) or death. Earlier studies by Lin and Rogerson (1995) and Rogerson, Burr, and Lin (1997) reported a residential move within a short period of time for almost a quarter of respondents, and those who lived close to their children showed greater residential stability. This pattern of adult children moving closer to their parents more often than older parents relocating closer to their children has also been confirmed by previous findings (e.g. Michielin, Mulder, & Zorlu, 2008; Rogerson, Burr, & Lin, 1997; Tomassini, Wolf, & Rosina, 2003).

Differences in spatial proximity as a precondition for intergenerational solidarity or co-residence can be explained using Szydlik's theoretical model (2016, p. 20). According to this model and the work of Bengtson and Roberts (1991), intergenerational solidarity can generally be understood as a complex and multi-layered construct composed of six dimensions, namely, associative, affective, consensual, functional, normative and structural solidarity. As this chapter addresses on spatial proximity between generations, we have focused on the structural as well as on the functional dimension. According to the assumptions of the theoretical model, intergenerational spatial proximity can be influenced at the individual level by opportunity and need structures. Whereas the available opportunities contribute to the initial development of relationships and then to their strengthening, the need structures reflect the individual desire for solidarity. In addition to individually based causes, the existing family structures also have a considerable influence on the relationship, as the opportunities depend on a family's circumstances. Furthermore, at the macro level, cultural–contextual structures that vary from region to region or society to society have an impact on the relationship between generations (Szydlik, 2016).

Previous studies have mainly incorporated cross-sectional information on older parents' health status and support needs at the baseline (first interview) without considering potential changes during the course of time. However, the anticipated longevity and its accompanying disabilities might be a key factor in both intended and effectuated moves as it reflects the time horizon associated with a person's expectations towards his or her future health status and potential support needs. Whereas the life-course migration framework has proven useful for understanding the mobility behaviour of the older population, moves are also influenced by considerations related to the financial and psychological costs of relocation and expectations towards future health problems or needs for support. Thus, we propose a life-course framework that explicitly includes an intergenerational perspective and examines older parents' anticipated longevity as a potential explanation for relocation that precedes declines in health or increases in the need for financial, instrumental or other forms of support. In this regard, we explore changes in intergenerational residential proximity by means of analyses that jointly consider moves by parents and their adult children.

Previous studies that have taken into account living distances as well as co-residence and children moving out of the parental home highlight the importance of individual characteristics at the micro level. These characteristics concern the life cycle first and foremost, as family-related relocations such as moving out as well as spatial mobility are considerably determined by age (Lin & Rogerson, 1995). With this in mind, leaving the parental home for the first time can be understood as a milestone in the transition to adulthood and depends strongly on age (see, e.g. Hogan & Astone, 1986; Rosenbaum, 2014, p. 190; White, 1994). According to Bendit and Hein (2003) as well as Leopold, Geissler, and Pink

(2012), this step into autonomy and independence often does not lead too far as children only venture about 10 kilometres on average in their first move. For parental moves, age usually plays a role only in combination with individual health problems (Silverstein, 1995). In this regard, Chen and Wilmoth (2004), as well as Wilmoth (2010) found that diminished health is associated with a closer residential distance to family members (see also Zhang, Engelman, & Agree, 2013). In addition, increasing isolation caused by divorce or the death of a spouse or partner as well as the loss of friends can lead to parents and children (again) moving closer (De Jong Gierveld & Van Tilburg, 1999; Dykstra, Van Tilburg, & De Jong Gierveld, 2005).

Along with age-specific differences, gender plays an important role in explaining differences in proximity or distance patterns between generations. In Europe, daughters move out earlier than sons (Iacovou, 2001), but the picture is less clear for spatial proximity (Billari, Philipov, & Baizán, 2001). Findings for the US have indicated that daughters stay closer to their parents than sons after they have moved out (Lawton, Silverstein, & Bengtson, 1994). In contrast, Pettersson and Malmberg (2009) have shown that in Sweden daughters move farther away from their parental homes than sons. However, Leopold, Geissler, and Pink (2012) have noted that it is worth considering the specific family situation, as daughters move farther away from their parents than sons do, but only if their parents live in a 'couple' household. For the parents, previous studies have indicated that women, especially those of advanced age, are more likely to move closer to their children than their male counterparts (Zhang, Engelman, & Agree, 2013).

In addition, previous studies have also shown that it is mainly children's economic needs that either promote or impede co-residence (e.g. Aassve, Billari, Mazzuco, & Ongaro, 2002; Choi, 2003; Isengard & Szydlik, 2012), and those factors also seem to be important for moves back into the parental household. It has been shown that spatial proximity or distance between generations depends on social status, given that geographical distance increases with status (Bengtson & Harootyan, 1994; Clark & Wolf, 1992; Silverstein, 1995); or as Greenwell and Bengtson (1997, p. 24) have written: 'In conclusion, our results show that social class position and early aspirations affect geographic distance.' Thus, individuals with higher education and socioeconomic status tend to move more often (and farther away) than their counterparts (Kalmijn, 2006; Malmberg & Pettersson, 2007; Michielin & Mulder, 2007; Silverstein, 1995). Previous studies have shown that long-distance moves are mostly prompted by job- and education-related factors (Détang-Dessendre, Piguet, Schmitt, & Rabenoro, 2002; Kulu & Billari, 2004, 2006). In this regard, unemployment and low incomes among children have been suggested to lead to co-residence or to delays in moving out of the parental household (DaVanzo & Goldscheider, 1990; Sweet & Bumpass, 1987) as well as making children more likely to move closer to their parents (Zhang, Engelman, & Agree, 2013). By contrast, changes in family size and housing considerations are major determinants of short-distance residential relocations (Clark & Huang, 2003; Feijten & Mulder, 2010; Withers, 1998).

On the parental side, empirical investigations have indicated that the effects of parents' need structures are more ambiguous (see, e.g. Goldscheider & DaVanzo,

1989; Le Blanc & Wolff, 2006; Lee & Dwyer, 1996). Aquilino (1990, p. 407) has thus shown for the US that it is not parents' dependency that increases co-residence but rather that of their children (see also Ward, Logan, & Spitze, 1992; Ward & Spitze, 1996). Studies for Italy (Tomassini, Wolf, & Rosina, 2003) and the Netherlands (Michielin & Mulder, 2007; Michielin, Mulder, & Zorlu, 2008) have indicated that familial characteristics such as a child's need for housing support are equally or more important than the parents' need for assistance in shaping intergenerational proximity. Family members thus collectively adjust their intergenerational proximity to facilitate mutual support (Michielin, Mulder, & Zorlu, 2008; Zhang, Engelman, & Agree, 2013). In general, previous findings have shown that life changes that bring about an increased need for familial support raise the likelihood of parents moving closer to their children (Rogerson, Burr, & Lin, 1997; Silverstein, 1995; Zhang, Engelman, & Agree, 2013). Opportunities such as the income and assets of the parents have not been found to be primary predictors of parental and child moves (Zhang, Engelman, & Agree, 2013). However, parents have been shown to exert some control over spatial distances. In Italy, for example, parents often assume the role of co-decision-makers owing to poor labour market conditions and tight housing markets (Giannelli & Monfardini, 2003; Glaser & Tomassini, 2000).

Family structures at the meso level also matter. The existence of competing family members or family members who can share the care burden can have a direct impact on living distances, including changes in proximity and co-residence. Entering or being in a relationship, the birth of a child or grandchild, separation or dissolution of relationships through divorce or death – all of these events can have direct effects too. Two opposite trends are apparent for geographical proximity between family generations. Although children frequently leave their parents' home when they enter into a relationship (for Europe, see, e.g. Iacovou, 2001, p. 10), they usually do not move as far away as when they are single (see, e.g. Aquilino, 1990; Glick & Lin, 1986; Lauterbach & Pillemer, 2001 for Germany and the US; Michielin & Mulder, 2007 for the Netherlands, whereas the opposite seems to be true). However, Madigan and Hogan (1991) discovered that single mothers do not live closer to their parents than mothers who cohabitate with the child's father. By contrast, a greater geographical distance appears to exist between widowed fathers and their offspring (Lawton, Silverstein, & Bengtson, 1994). For the Netherlands, Smits (2010) found that adult children rarely live with their coupled parents on the whole, but they are far more likely to do so if they themselves are not married and have children of their own. Here, the existence of grandchildren usually leads to a situation in which generations live closer together (Crimmins & Ingegneri, 1990; Pettersson & Malmberg, 2009; Rogerson, Burr, & Lin, 1997). Other studies found that parents who had experienced marital disruption (divorce) were more likely to move closer to their children or their children were more likely to move closer to them (Zhang, Engelman, & Agree, 2013).

Finally, spatial proximity, co-residence, as well as adult children moving in or out of the parental home can be influenced by cultural–contextual structures at the macro level. These exert effects not only within but also between countries. As most studies have only analysed single countries, relatively little is still known about European differences and similarities in a broader sense. It can be stated that in general the intergenerational proximity is closer in Southern European countries (Hank, 2007) and that in particular co-residence is a far more common living arrangement in the South of Europe compared to Continental and especially Northern Europe (Isengard, König, & Szydlik, 2017; Kiernan, 1999). In addition to cultural influences, differences are also related to welfare state policies and arrangements as well as labour market conditions. Welfare benefits have direct effects on poverty and inequality as well as on (regional) unemployment, and thus on the necessity of moving or utilising the family as a support network.

According to this relationship, in countries where family-related benefits are relatively weak, the family should be more important as a support network than in countries with extensive benefits and well-developed social systems (for welfare states in more detail, see Esping-Andersen (1990) as well as modifications by Leibfried (1992), and Keune (2009)). In this vein, a comparison by the Organisation for Economic Co-operation and Development (OECD) has shown that public, family-related support services are very low in countries where traditional family structures are very strong (see the work by Ferrera, 1996; Sciortino, 2004). However, Giuliano (2007) has attributed such differences to cultural divergences that are expressed in a different self-image of the family. Overall, previous research using European data has found that an increase in societal wealth – as measured by the development of country-specific GDP over time – reduces the likelihood that adult children will leave their parental home. At the same time, an increase in social expenditures in general and family expenditures in particular gives children the ability to move out of their parents' home. Economic uncertainties as indicated by an increase in (youth) unemployment do not significantly affect spatial mobility but do tend to extend periods of intergenerational co-residence (König, 2016).

7.3 Data and Methods

Our analyses are based on the Survey of Health, Ageing and Retirement (SHARE), which provides standardised information on respondents aged 50 years and older in various European countries. The dataset employed in this study was gathered in the first (2004/2005) and second (2006/2007) wave (for details on the first and second wave, see Börsch-Supan, 2017a, 2017b) and contains information on a wide range of topics such as demography, income, health, accommodation, education, occupation, behaviour, social support, activities and expectations.

To capture dynamics in geographical distance within parent–child relationships, namely, adult children moving into and out of the parental home as well as changes in residential distance for non-co-residing parent–child relationships, we used a two-wave panel design in which each respondent participated in both SHARE waves including 11 countries (Austria, Belgium, Denmark, France, Germany, Greece, Italy, the Netherlands, Spain, Sweden and Switzerland).

As our focus relies on adult parent–child relationships, we further reshaped the given information provided by the responding parents to each child who was aged at least 18 years in the first wave. As only SHARE respondents and their households can be uniquely identified across waves, we constructed a key variable for each child based on a combination of their gender, year of birth and parent's identification number. For twins and multiples, we extended this information with additional individual characteristics, which do not change over the waves.

Transferring the situation of individual, familial and contextual changes into a statistical model demands that the data structure meets specific requirements. On the one hand, a longitudinal design is necessary to cover interpersonal changes over time. On the other hand, the construction of the dynamic behaviour must be based on a uniform definition (questioning) in each wave, and variables covering individual, familial and contextual structures have to be available in sufficient cases over the entire period. These requirements were ensured by the existing two-wave panel design and statistically embedded in a change score or first difference model. This method is based on the elimination of interpersonal similarities between two waves and focuses on the dynamics, which allows one to neutralise the transformation effect of the explanatory variables on the development (Giesselmann & Windzio, 2012). To estimate changes for a person (within variance), each variable (dependent and independent) needs to be subtracted by the chronologically previous eigenvalue. In line with the usually short observation period between two waves (in our case, 11 - 42 months with a mean of 28 months), the degree of change and therefore explanatory variance is restricted but cannot be equated with a weakness of the model (Allison, 2009; Johnson, 2005). Conversely, time-constant variables (e.g. gender, cohort) were included in their original form. The interpretation of the effects is based on their interaction with the factor time. The advantage of this design is the fact that it can, like all panel-analytical methods, expose causal effects of an event on a dependent variable. In addition, time-constant heterogeneities are also controlled for without their direct observation, and measurement errors are compensated by the model, which ultimately minimises estimation errors and distortions (Giesselmann & Windzio, 2012).

The dependent variable was determined by the residential distance between the parental household and the adult child for each interview on the basis of the following question and multiple-choice answers: Where does [child name] live? (1) In the same household, (2) in the same building, (3) less than 1 kilometre away, (4) between 1 and 5 kilometres away, (5) between 5 and 25 kilometres away, (6) between 25 and 100 kilometres away, (7) between 100 and 500 kilometres away, or (8) more than 500 kilometres away (in another country). The combination of the individual situation for each child and each interview allows to identify whether or not there was a change in their residential distance over time as well as the kind of change. Here, those parents and adult children who were co-residing at baseline but not during the follow-up were characterised as having moved out, whereas the opposite situation (having moved in) was given if the adult child co-resided in the second interview but did not in the first one. For those dyads who did not share the same household at the time of both interviews, the information on the residential distance for both surveys capture a situation in which the distance either changed or did not over time. The dependent variable is therefore based on the change score for the residential distance from both interviews and is differentiated according to its direction: (1) no change, (2) moving out, (3) moving in, (4) moving closer and (5) moving farther away.

To explain such patterns in Europe against the background of change, various explanatory variables at the micro, meso and macro levels were included in the empirical model. In spite of a short examination period, the possibility of temporary and opposing dynamics was taken into account. Time-variant variables were measured as the difference between the eigenvalues at both times of measurement, whereas categorical variables were dichotomised according to the state of change. With regard to the individual situation of the child at the micro level, a change of personal and economic needs was captured. The models include situations in which a child's partnership began or ended over time. Changes in a child's own family were captured by information about whether or not there had been a birth between the two interviews. The labour force status consists of the situations in which the child became employed, unemployed or began further education.

For the parental situation, similar information with regard to their partnership status like parent in a new partnership or the loss of a parental partner was chosen. For the economic situation of the parental household, a subjective income measure was used based on a question about whether the household had enough money to make ends meet and answers that fell into four graduated categories (ranging from 'with great difficulty' to 'easily'). On the basis of the information from both interviews, our analysis determined whether or not there was an income change and in those cases the specific direction (worse or better). A similar procedure was chosen to address parental health, which was measured as the number of limitations on the activities of daily living (ADL) and instrumental activities of daily living (IADL). For this item, the individual items were added together, and the parent with the most limitations at baseline was selected. This allowed us to identify whether there was a change in individual health and the direction (better or worse) over time. As a change in geographical distances within parent-child relationships might not result only from a child relocating, we further controlled for changes in where the parents resided. On the basis of the given information by the respondents as well as the interviewers, we determined if there had been a change in the regional background in terms of the community sizes of the respondents' living area (big city, suburbs or outskirts, large town, small town, and village or rural area). Although this leaves the possibility of a relocation within the same area or to a new area of the same community size, the questionnaire does not explicitly ask about whether the respondent had moved. Thus, we further defined a parental relocation according to a territorial change based on the Nomenclature of Territorial Units for Statistics (NUTS) classification. Drawing on the individual NUTS region of each respondent during both interviews, we were able to identify a relocation even if the size of the community did not change (e.g. moving from one small town to another in a different NUTS region).

To explain differences within countries and over time at the macro level, our analyses considered indicators that capture variations in structural differences and societal inequality between European countries. In addition to the gross domestic product per capita (GDP, adjusted for purchasing power), we used social and family expenditures as a percentage of GDP as a direct measure of welfare state support. Furthermore, we considered the country-specific youth unemployment rate, which represents the number of unemployed persons aged 15–24 years as a percentage of the labour force (the total number of people employed and unemployed in this age group). The macro indicators refer to the year preceding each interview. They were drawn from official sources (for details, see Eurostat, 2017; OECD, 2017a, 2017b) and have been entered into the models as the delta of both values.

Finally, our analyses controlled for a set of constant terms. These included the cohort and gender of the adult child as well as the social class of the parents. Although the latter variable might change over time, we have assumed that education as a proxy for cultural, economic, and social capital would not change individual behaviour over such a short period. The level of education was recoded according to the International Standard Classification of Education (ISCED) as low (ISCED 0–2), medium (ISCED 3–4), and high (ISCED 5–6) and refers to the most advanced parental degree at baseline.

Given non-independence between observations (adult children nested in parental households nested in different countries), this hierarchical data structure violates basic regression assumptions and might lead to inaccurate significance values as well as biased standard errors. To analyse the influence of changes in the determinants at the individual, familial and contextual level on leaving home or relocation, we estimated multilevel multinomial logit models (Hox, 2002; Rabe-Hesketh, & Skrondal, 2008; Snijders & Bosker, 2012) involving three levels. In this way, we were able to account for the variation not only at the upper country level but also between parental households. In addition to the fixed or released parameters at the individual and family levels, these analyses included the context variables separately to avoid estimation biases that stem from multiple macro-level indicators (Maas & Hox, 2005). All non-dichotomous variables were standardised to enable comparisons between the effects of the determinants at the micro (individual), meso (family) and macro (context) levels. With the exception of the dependent variables, all of these variables have a mean value of 0 and a standard deviation of 1.

7.4 Empirical Results

7.4.1 Intergenerational Spatial Proximity and Distance in Europe over Time

Although there are differences in intergenerational spatial proximity, a preliminary glance suggests that, overall, there have been no major shifts in the average distances between parents and their adult children between the two observation points (see Fig. 7.1). Our analysis indicates that approximately one out of every two adult children does not live in the same household or building

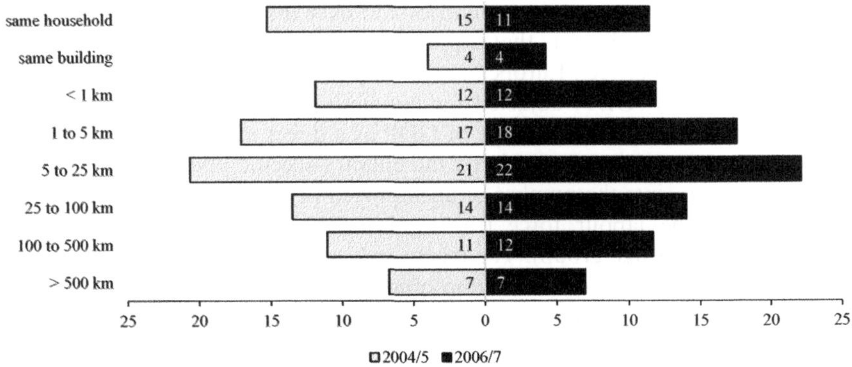

Fig. 7.1. Intergenerational Geographical Distance in Europe (in Percent). *Source*: SHARE waves 1 (2004/5), and 2 (2006/7), release 6.0.0, 17,484 respondent–child dyads. Our own calculations.

with their parents but does live in the immediate vicinity at a maximum of 25 kilometres. Whereas co-residence seems to follow age- and life-course-specific patterns of adult children and decreased between the two observation periods (from 15% to 11%), near co-residence (defined as living in the same building but in separate households) remained constant at 4%. Moreover, the proportion of parent–child relationships characterised by a general greater geographical distance generally remained stable. Approximately 14% of adult children live within a radius of 25–100 kilometres from their parental home. A further 11 or 12% live at least 100 kilometres away, and further 7% live more than 500 kilometres away or even abroad. Taken together approximately two-thirds of older Europeans (50+) live nearby their adult children, that means the generations lives not more than 25 kilometres away from each other.

Despite these seemingly stable distances, further detailed analysis (see Fig. 7.2) clearly indicates changes in residential situations and distances for individual parent–child relationships in the European countries. In general, the overall proportion of young adults who left their parents' homes during this period of two waves is higher (about 32%) than those who returned (1%). Although moving back into the parental home is comparatively rare in Europe, Spanish children tend to return more often back (4%) to their parents compared to other European countries. By contrast, almost 80% of formerly co-residing children in Denmark and 63% in Sweden left their parental home in the period between the two survey waves, whereas this appears to have been the case for only 11% of adult children in Greece followed by 26% in Italy and 31% in Spain, respectively. Therefore, we can sum up, that spatial changes in general between two waves of observation occurs more often in the Northern and Western part of Europe, whereas the residential mobility especially in the Southern part of Europe is less obvious.

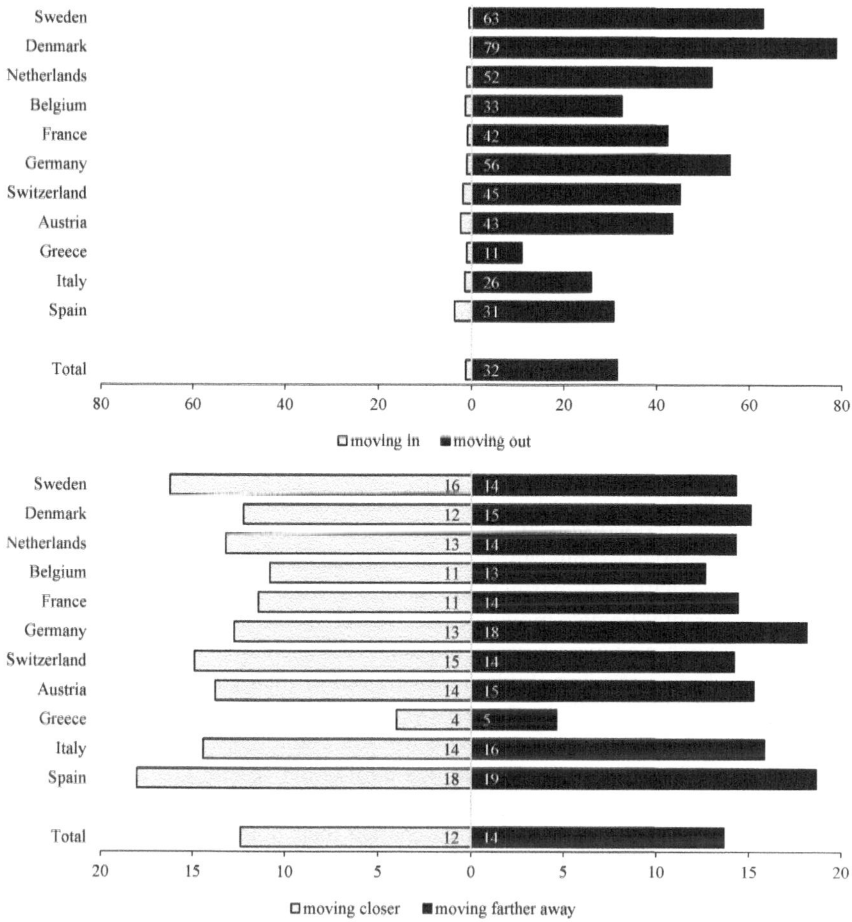

Fig. 7.2. Changes in Intergenerational Geographical Distance (in Percent). *Source*: SHARE waves 1 (2004/5), and 2 (2006/7), release 6.0.0, 17,484 respondent–child dyads. Our own calculations.

In addition to intergenerational moves into and out of the parental home, further relocations among non-co-residing parents and children are not uncommon. Whereas the proportion of parents and children who increased the geographical distance between themselves and those who moved closer together is quite similar in all included countries, in general terms spatial mobility varies highly across Europe. In this context, the distance between parents and adult children changed (farther away or closer) for at least one-third in Spain (37%) followed by Germany (31%), Sweden (30%) and Italy (30%). By contrast, only 9% of the Greek parents reported being a greater or shorter distance away from their adult children at the time of the follow-up survey.

7.4.2 Intergenerational Spatial Proximity and Distances in Europe: Determinants

To determine which circumstances affect spatial mobility in European families, we estimated multilevel multinomial regression models and took change scores of micro-, meso-, and macro-level indicators into account. Given the marginal number of instances of adult children moving back into the parental home (only 1.2% overall), we excluded such situations from our multivariate setting. Thus, the dependent variable identifies whether there was a change in geographical distance over time or not (0), and if so, the nature of such change, which is defined as moving out (1), moving closer (2), and moving farther away (3).

Table 7.1 summarises the results of the multi-level multinomial logit regressions that predict different changes in parent–child proximity relative to the reference category of no change between baseline and follow-up. In general, our analysis first clarifies whether individual changes in needs or opportunities as well as changing family contexts have an impact on spatial proximity between generations. As far as child relocations are concerned, changes in partnership status would seem to have a significant impact. Whereas leaving the parental home is only connected with new partnerships and not with breakups, for relocations outside the parental home – moving closer as well as moving farther away – both types of partnership changes have an impact. Having children appears to decrease the likelihood of co-residing children moving out of their parental home because they – usually lacking the help of a partner – can rely on their parents' experience and assistance in raising children. Births for adult children who are already non-co-residing appear to promote relocations both closer to and farther away from their parents. Here, the necessity for more space to fit the changed family size seems to be decisive that those children change their housing situation. Furthermore, we can also observe that changes in children's labour force status also have an impact on their residential mobility. Becoming employed requires or allows them to move out of the parental home but also encourages relocations that can increase or decrease the distance between them and their parents. By contrast, adult children who become unemployed or begin a further education and probably face greater financial restrictions are not significantly more likely to move out or to relocate.

Changes in the life of children's parents with regard to their own partnership, economic situation and physical health also influence intergenerational geographic mobility. Parental partnerships that have ended – perhaps owing to the death of one parent – appear to encourage children to move out of the parental home while not encouraging non-co-residing generations to move closer together or farther away. For parental economic opportunities, the results underpin the notion that the geographical distances decrease with a deterioration of the financial situation of the parents indicating that either parents moved to a better affordable home near their children or that their children moved closer to provide financial, practical or emotional support. For a change in parents' health conditions over time, which is an indicator of their need

Table 7.1. Changes in Intergenerational Geographical Distance in Europe: Determinants.

	Moving Out		Moving Closer		Moving Farther Away	
Base: No Change	**RRR**	**SE**	**RRR**	**SE**	**RRR**	**SE**
Micro and meso level						
Child:						
Partnership						
New	12.93***	4.72	2.09***	0.35	2.65***	0.42
Ended	0.64	0.22	1.66***	0.23	1.60***	0.19
Child born	0.52***	0.13	1.45**	0.23	1.43***	0.18
Became employed	1.58***	0.25	1.26*	0.17	1.24***	0.10
Became unemployed	1.18	0.34	1.22	0.19	1.32	0.30
Began education	1.51	0.41	1.20	0.27	0.97	0.18
Parents:						
Partnership						
New	1.09	0.62	1.10	0.49	1.48	0.45
Ended	2.44**	0.93	1.28	0.30	1.18	0.36
Financial situation						
Worse	1.16	0.13	1.12**	0.07	1.08	0.06
Better	1.18	0.17	1.07	0.09	1.15	0.13
Health conditions						
Worse	0.81*	0.10	1.02	0.07	1.08	0.08
Better	0.94	0.10	1.00	0.07	1.07	0.09
Relocation	1.06	0.09	1.06	0.08	1.15	0.11
Macro level						
Months between interviews	1.15**	0.08	0.92*	0.05	0.95	0.04
Δ – GDP	0.76**	0.10	0.95**	0.02	0.89***	0.02
Δ – Social expenditure	1.01	0.13	0.64***	0.03	0.67***	0.03
Δ – Family expenditure	0.97	0.12	1.01	0.03	0.92***	0.02
Δ – Youth unemployment	0.82**	0.08	1.15**	0.08	1.09**	0.04
Constant terms						
Year of birth (Child)	4.90***	1.12	0.90**	0.06	0.97	0.07
Son (Child)	1.25***	0.07	0.99	0.05	0.96	0.04
Social class (Parents), Ref.: Low						
Middle	0.59***	0.08	0.88**	0.05	0.95	0.04
High	0.53***	0.07	0.90	0.07	0.91	0.07

Table 7.1. *(Continued)*

	Moving Out		Moving Closer		Moving Farther Away	
Base: No Change	**RRR**	**SE**	**RRR**	**SE**	**RRR**	**SE**
n (Children)	17,302					
n (Parents)	8,630					
n (Countries)	11					

Source: SHARE waves 1 (2004/5), and 2 (2006/7), release 6.0.0, Eurostat (2017), OECD (2017a, 2017b), multi-level multinomial logistic regressions (separate for each macro indicator), reference for varying variables: no change, relative risk ratios (RRR), coefficients refer to the GDP as a macro indicator, robust standard errors (SE); all metric variables standardised. Our own calculations. Significance levels: $***p < 0.01$; $**p < 0.05$; $*p < 0.10$.

structure, the results show that an increase in physical limitations – measured by ADL and IADL – hinders moving outs but does not promote non-co-residing children moving closer. Here, it seems that co-residing children extent their stay at home to support their needy parent in daily routines. Furthermore, our results show that a change in intergenerational geographical distance in European families is mainly attributable to children's relocations and not to those of their elderly parents. This is all the more astonishing as almost 28% of the responding parents changed their place of living between baseline and follow-up which – as our results show – did not lead to an increase or decrease of their geographical distance to their children.

With regard to contextual influences, we can observe that time plays an important role in spatial mobility. The longer the period between baseline and follow-up, the more likely adult children leave their parental home. Although the indications are reverse for non-co-residing relations, we can assume that a longer observation period would lead to some kind of movement (moving closer as well as farther away). In addition, cultural–contextual structures matter for spatial mobility in Europe. In countries with better economic development between baseline and follow-up measured by the delta of the GDP over the two periods – adult children moved less often or even left the parental home. Due to better living conditions the necessity to move (farther away) can be reduced on one side, while on the other side in countries who perform better from an economic point of view, the individual need for expanding the inhabitation in the parental home is less pronounced. However, an increase in public social expenditures (e.g. for social support and housing) does not affect moving outs but decreases spatial mobility for non-co-residing relationships. Although the effects for relocations, which decrease the geographical distance are not significant, the same patterns seem to be true for family expenditures in particular. Finally, social insecurity as measured by an increase in the youth unemployment rate seems to affect moves that decrease but also increase the geographical distance between parents and their adult children. This might be because adult children have to actively seek for open vacancies that involve relocations. By contrast, increased labour market insecurities decrease the likelihood that adult children leave the parental home and thus rely longer on parental resources and help.

As for the constant structure of our model, the results also allow us to identify specific movements through socio-demographic characteristics and social background. Whereas the younger adult children who co-reside tend to leave their parental homes, further relocations which reduce the geographical distance to their parents are more relevant in later adulthood – for example, after completing further education, gaining professional experience or starting their own family. Furthermore, the results highlight that leaving the parental home appears to be more relevant for sons, who generally co-reside for a longer period of time, than for daughters. However, further spatial mobility patterns do not seem to differ according to their gender. Finally, co-residing children from higher social classes are less likely to move out of the parental home, probably because they are waiting to complete their education.

7.5 Conclusions

Relationships between generations have been very stable – despite demographic changes in contemporary societies they can be characterised by lifelong solidarity (Szydlik, 2000). Against the demographic background of increased life expectancy in conjunction with lower fertility rates (grand)parents and (grand)children spend a longer period of their lives together and even under one roof (Grünheid & Scharein, 2011; Lauterbach, 1995). Although co-residence seems to be opposed to the 'family cycle' concept in which, as a general rule, children leave their parental home when they start their own families, extended periods of education and delayed family formation leads to adult children often remaining in the parental household for a longer period of time. And even if they do leave the nest, they stay close to the parental home.

In this context, this study of intergenerational spatial proximity in European countries is not only of scientific interest but is also relevant to social policies since geographic proximity is a necessary prerequisite for many forms of time support such as assistance in the household, nursing, or grandchild care. Especially in times of economic crisis familial support and cohesion is an important safety net Therefore, spatial proximity is an important aspect of residential mobility decisions can be determined by (financial) hardship as a strategy to catch insecurities which are not covered by state interventions.

Our empirical analysis shows that changes in residential mobility are influenced by micro-, meso-, and macro-level indicators. Adult children who start a new relationship are more likely to leave the parental household or relocate in a way that changes their proximity to the parental household than children who undergo no changes in their partnership status. Having a child increases adult children's probability of remaining in the parental home or changing their proximity to it if they have already moved out. The need for additional space or the desire for an environment more favourable to raising children seems to be major determinants of families deciding to change their residence. A change in labour force status often leads to children moving out of their parental home as well as changes in spatial mobility.

Although changes in child's life conditions are the primary factors affecting the geographical distance between generations, on the basis of our analysis, we can state that changes in parents' living circumstances affect spatial proximity as well. For example, changes in parental health conditions or variations in their partnership status also have an influence on whether co-residing children move out or remain in the parental home.

Finally, contextual structures have an impact on why children either move out of the parental home or have to relocate more often. Overall, a greater uncertainty in the labour market leads to a situation in which generations rely on each other more and thus children have to extent their stay at home. On the other side, children who already left their parents are increasingly faced with an unsecure situation in which they have to move to find a job. By contrast, in economically stronger welfare states with higher public spending, adult children have to move less frequently due to fewer insecurities and a more well-developed social security net.

To summarise, our contribution offers insight into the interplay between changing living conditions on the one hand and residential decisions on the other. Our empirical results lead us to conclude that individual changes according to the life cycle (family formation processes) as well as changes in the economic situation play a crucial role in intergenerational spatial proximity. But societal uncertainties during (economic) crises also matter. Next to individual experiences of poverty and other hardships such as unemployment or precarious employment, co-residence as direct form of solidarity and spatial mobility are also influenced by poverty and income inequality at the societal level. Increasing insecurities and unemployment rates promotes the necessity to change the living place. For this reason, family cohesion in general and intergenerational support in particular have become [more] important characteristics of contemporary family relationships. Not least in an era of economic crisis and the withdrawal of the welfare state, parents and children are taking [greater] responsibility for each other and standing by one another.

Acknowledgements

This chapter uses data from SHARE Waves 1 and 2 (DOIs: 10.6103/SHARE.w1.600, 10.6103/SHARE.w2.600), see Börsch-Supan et al. (2013) for methodological details. The SHARE data collection has been primarily funded by the European Commission through FP5 (QLK6-CT-2001-00360), FP6 (SHARE-I3: RII-CT-2006-062193, COMPARE: CIT5-CT-2005-028857, SHARELIFE: CIT4-CT-2006-028812) and FP7 (SHARE-PREP: N°211909, SHARE-LEAP: N°227822, SHARE M4: N°261982). Additional funding from the German Ministry of Education and Research, the Max Planck Society for the Advancement of Science, the US National Institute on Aging (U01_AG09740-13S2, P01_AG005842,

P01_AG08291, P30_AG12815, R21_AG025169, Y1-AG-4553-01, IAG_BSR06-11, OGHA_04-064, HHSN271201300071C) and from various national funding sources is gratefully acknowledged (see www.share-project.org).

References

Aassve, A., Billari, F. C., Mazzuco, S., & Ongaro, F. (2002). Leaving home: A comparative analysis of ECHP data. *Journal of European Social Policy*, *12*(4), 259–275.

Allison, P. D. (2009). *Fixed effects regression models 160*. Los Angeles, CA: Sage.

Aquilino, W. S. (1990). The likelihood of parent-adult child co-residence: Effects of family structure and parental characteristics. *Journal of Marriage and Family*, *52*(2), 405–419. doi:10.2307/353035

Bendit, R., & Hein, K. (2003). Jugendliche in Europa auf dem Weg in die Selbstständigkeit. *DJI Bulletin*, *63*, 4–7.

Bengtson, V. L. (2001). Beyond the nuclear family: The increasing importance of multigenerational bonds. *Journal of Marriage and Family*, *63*(1), 1–16. doi:10.1111/j.1741-3737.2001.00001.x

Bengtson, V. L., & Harootyan, R. A. (1994). *Intergenerational linkages: Hidden connections in American society*. New York, NY: Springer.

Bengtson, V. L., & Roberts, R. E. L. (1991). Intergenerational solidarity in aging families: An example of formal theory construction. *Journal of Marriage and Family*, *53*(4), 856–870. doi:10.2307/352993

Billari, F. C., Philipov, D., & Baizán, P. (2001). Leaving home in Europe: The experience of Cohorts born around 1960. *International Journal of Population Geography*, *7*(5), 339–356.

Börsch-Supan, A. (2017a). Survey of Health, Ageing and Retirement in Europe (SHARE) Wave 1: Release version: 6.0.0): SHARE-ERIC. Data set. doi: 10.6103/SHARE.w1.600

Börsch-Supan, A. (2017b). "Survey of Health, Ageing and Retirement in Europe (SHARE) Wave 2: Release version: 6.0.0." SHARE-ERIC. Data set. doi: 10.6103/SHARE.w2.600

Börsch-Supan, A., Brandt, M., Hunkler, C., Kneip, T., Korbmacher, J., Malter, F., … Zuber, S. (2013). Data resource profile: The Survey of Health, Ageing and Retirement in Europe (SHARE). *International Journal of Epidemiology*, *42*(4), 992–1001. doi:10.1093/ije/dyt088

Chen, P.-C., & Wilmoth, J. M. (2004). The effects of residential mobility on ADL and IADL limitations among the very old living in the community. *Journals of Gerontology Series B: Psychological Sciences and Social Sciences*, *59*(3), S164–S172. doi:10.1093/geronb/59.3.S164

Choi, N. (2003). Co-residence between unmarried aging parents and their adult children: who moved in with whom and why? *Research on Aging*, *25*(4), 384–404. doi:10.1177/0164027503025004003

Clark, R. L., & Wolf, D. A. (1992). Proximity of children and elderly migration. In A. Rogers, W. H. Frey, P. Rees, A. Speare, & A. Warnes (Eds.), *Elderly migration and population redistribution: A comparative study* (pp. 77–96). London: Belhaven Press.

Clark, W. A. V., & Huang, Y. (2003). The life course and residential mobility in British housing markets. *Environment and Planning A*, *35*(2), 323–339.

Crimmins, E. M., & Ingegneri, D. G. (1990). Interaction and living arrangements of older parents and their children: Past trends, present determinants, future implications. *Research on Aging*, *12*(1), 3–35.

DaVanzo, J., & Goldscheider, F. K. (1990). Coming home again: Returns to the parental home of young adults. *Population Studies*, *44*(2), 241–55. doi:10.1080/0032472031000144576

De Jong Gierveld, J., & Van Tilburg, T. G. (1999). Living arrangements of older adults in the Netherlands and Italy: Co-residence values and behaviour and their consequences to loneliness. *Journal of Cross-Cultural Gerontology*, *14*(1), 1–24.

Détang-Dessendre, C., Piguet, V., Schmitt, B., & Rabenoro, M. (2002). Life cycle variability in the microeconomic determinants of urban-rural migration. *Population*, *57*(1), 31–56. doi:10.2307/3246626

Dykstra, P. A., Van Tilburg, T. G., & De Jong Gierveld, J. (2005). Changes in older adult loneliness: Results from a seven-year longitudinal study. *Research on Aging*, *27*(6), 725–47. doi:10.1177/0164027505279712

Esping-Andersen, G. (1990). *The three worlds of welfare capitalism*. Cambridge: Polity Press.

Eurostat. (2017). *GDP per Capita in PPS: tec00114*. Retrieved from http://ec.europa.eu/eurostat/tgm/table.do?tab=table&init=1&language=en&pcode=tec00114&plugin=1. Accessed on July 02, 2017.

Feijten, P., & Mulder, C. H. (2010). The timing of household events and housing events in the Netherlands: A longitudinal perspective. *Housing Studies*, *17*(5), 773–792. doi:10.1080/0267303022000009808

Ferrera, M. (1996). The 'Southern model' of welfare in social Europe. *Journal of European Social Policy*, *6*(1), 17–37. doi:10.1177/095892879600600102

Giannelli, G. C., & Monfardini, C. (2003). Joint decisions on household membership and human capital accumulation of youths. The role of expected earnings and local markets. *Journal of Population Economics*, *16*(2), 265–285. doi:10.1007/s001480200119

Giesselmann, M., & Windzio, M. (2012). *Regressionsmodelle zur Analyse von Paneldaten*. Wiesbaden: Springer VS.

Giuliano, P. (2007). Living arrangements in Western Europe: Does cultural origin matter? *Journal of the European Economic Association*, *5*(5), 927–952.

Glaser, K., & Tomassini, C. (2000). Proximity of older women to their children: A comparison of Britain and Italy. *The Gerontologist*, *40*(6), 729–737.

Glick, P. C., & Lin, S.-L. (1986). More young adults are living with their parents: Who are they? *Journal of Marriage and Family*, *48*(1), 107–112.

Goldscheider, F. K., & DaVanzo, J. (1989). Pathways to independent living in early adulthood: Marriage, semiautonomy, and premarital residential independence. *Demography*, *26*(4), 597–614. doi:10.2307/2061260

Greenwell, L., & Bengtson, V. L. (1997). Geographic distance and contact between middle-aged children and their parents: The effects of social class over 20 years. *The Journals of Gerontology Series B*, *52*(1), 13–26.

Grünheid, E., & Scharein, M. G. (2011). Zur Entwicklung der durchschnittlichen gemeinsamen Lebenszeit von Drei- und Vier-Generationen-Familien in West- und

Ostdeutschland. Eine Modellrechnung. *Comparative Population Studies – Zeitschrift für Bevölkerungswissenschaft*, *36*(1), 3–40.

Hank, K. (2007). Proximity and contacts between older parents and their children: A European comparison. *Journal of Marriage and Family*, *69*(1), 157–173. doi:10.1111/j.1741-3737.2006.00351.x

Hogan, D. P., & Astone, N. M. (1986). The transition to adulthood. *Annual Review of Sociology*, *12*, 109–130.

Hox, J. J. (2002). *Multilevel analysis: Techniques and applications*. Quantitative methodology series. Mahwah, NJ: Lawrence Erlbaum Associates.

Iacovou, M. (2001). *Leaving home in the European Union. ISER Working Papers 2001–18*. Colchester: University of Essex.

Isengard, B., König, R., & Szydlik, M. (2017). Money or space? Intergenerational transfers in a comparative perspective. *Housing Studies*, *47*(4), 1–23. doi:10.1080/02673037.2017.1365823

Isengard, B., & Szydlik, M. (2012). Living apart (or) together? Co-residence of elderly parents and their adult children in Europe. *Research on Aging*, *34*(4), 449–474. doi:10.1177/0164027511428455

Johnson, D. (2005). Two-wave panel analysis: Comparing statistical methods for studying the effects of transitions. *Journal of Marriage and Family*, *67*(4), 1061–1075. doi:10.1111/j.1741-3737.2005.00194.x

Kalmijn, M. (2006). Educational inequality and family relationships: Influences on contact and proximity. *European Sociological Review*, *22*(1), 1–16.

Keune, M. (2009). Mittel- und osteuropäische Wohlfahrtsstaaten im Vergleich: Typen und Leistungsfähigkeit. In Ch. Klenner & S. Leiber (Eds), *Wohlfahrtsstaaten und Geschlechterungleichheit in Mittel- und Osteuropa: Kontinuität und post-sozialistische Transformation in den EU-Mitgliedsstaaten* (pp. 59–84). Wiesbaden: VS Verlag für Sozialwissenschaften.

Kiernan, K. (1999). Cohabitation in Western Europe. *Population Trends*, *96*, 25–32.

Kohli, M., Künemund, H., Motel, A., & Szydlik, M. (2005). Generationenbeziehungen. In M. Kohli & H. Künemund (Eds.), *Die zweite Lebenshälfte: Gesellschaftliche Lage und Partizipation im Spiegel des Alters-Survey* (pp. 176–211). Wiesbaden: VS Verlag für Sozialwissenschaften.

König, R. (2016). *Bildung, Schicht und Generationensolidarität in Europa*. Wiesbaden: Springer VS.

Kulu, H., & Billari, F. C. (2004). Multilevel analysis of internal migration in a transitional country: The case of Estonia. *Regional Studies*, *38*(6), 679–696. doi:10.1080/003434042000240978

Kulu, H., & Billari, F. C. (2006). Migration to urban and rural destinations in post-Soviet Estonia: A multilevel event-history analysis. *Environ Plan A*, *38*(4), 749–764. doi:10.1068/a37367

Künemund, H., & Rein, M. (1999). There is more to receiving than needing: Theoretical arguments and empirical explorations of crowding in and crowding out. *Ageing and Society*, *19*(1), 93–121.

Lauterbach, W. (1995). Die gemeinsame Lebenszeit von Familiengenerationen. *Zeitschrift für Soziologie*, *24*(1), 22–41. doi:10.1515/zfsoz-1995-0102

Lauterbach, W., & Pillemer, K. A. (2001). Social structure and the family: A United-States – Germany comparison of residential proximity between parents and adult children. *Journal of Family Research*, *13*(1), 68–88.

Lawton, L., Silverstein, M., & Bengtson, V. L. (1994). Affection, social contact, and geographic distance between adult children and their parents. *Journal of Marriage and Family*, *56*(1), 57–68. doi:10.2307/352701

Le Blanc, D., & Wolff, F.-Ch. (2006). Leaving home in Europe: The role of parents' and children's incomes. *Review of Economics Household*, *4*(1), 53–73. doi:10.1007/s11150-005-6697-z

Lee, G. R., & Dwyer, J. W. (1996). Aging parent-adult child co-residence: Further evidence on the role of parental characteristics. *Journal of Family Issues*, *17*(1), 46–59.

Leibfried, S. (1992). Towards a European welfare state? On integrating poverty regimes into the European community. In Z. Ferge & J. E. Kolberg (Eds.), *Social policy in a changing Europe* (pp. 133–156). Frankfurt am Main: Campus-Verlag.

Leopold, T., Geissler, F., & Pink, S. (2012). How far do children move? Spatial distances after leaving the parental home. *Social Science Research*, *41*(4), 991–1002.

Lin, G., & Rogerson, P. A. (1995). Elderly parents and the geographic availability of their adult children. *Research on Aging*, *17*(3), 303–331. doi:10.1177/0164027595173004

Maas, C. J. M., & Hox, J. J. (2005). Sufficient sample sizes for multilevel modeling. *Methodology: European Journal of Research Methods for the Behavioral and Social Sciences*, *1*(3), 86–92. doi:10.1027/1614-2241.1.3.86

Madigan, T. J., & Hogan, D. P. (1991). Kin access and residential mobility among young mothers. *Social Sciences Quarterly*, *72*(2), 615–622.

Malmberg, G., & Pettersson, A. (2007). Distance to old parents. *Demographic Research*, *17*, 679–704.

Michielin, F., & Mulder, C. H. (2007). Geographical distances between adult children and their parents in the Netherlands. *Demographic Research*, *17*, 655–678.

Michielin, F., Mulder, C. H., & Zorlu, A. (2008). Distance to parents and geographical mobility. *Population, Space and Place*, *14*(4), 327–345. doi:10.1002/psp.509

OECD. (2017a). LFS by sex and age – Indicators. Retrieved from http://stats.oecd.org. Accessed on April 25, 2017.

OECD. (2017b). Social expenditure – Aggregated data. Retrieved from http://stats.oecd.org. Accessed on April 25, 2017.

Pettersson, A., & Malmberg, G. (2009). Adult children and elderly parents as mobility attractions in Sweden. *Population, Space and Place*, *15*(4), 343–357. doi:10.1002/psp.558

Rabe-Hesketh, S., & Skrondal, A. (2008). *Multilevel and longitudinal modeling using Stata*. College Station, TX: Stata Press.

Rogerson, P. A., Burr, J. A., & Lin, G. (1997). Changes in geographic proximity between parents and their adult children. *International Journal of Population Geography*, *3*(2), 121–136.

Rosenbaum, E. (2014). Cohort trends in housing and household formation since 1990. In J. R. Logan (Ed.), *Diversity and disparities: America enters a new century* (pp. 181–207). New York, NY: Russell Sage Foundation.

Sciortino, G. (2004). Immigration in a Mediterranean welfare state: The Italian experience in comparative perspective. *Journal of Comparative Policy Analysis: Research and Practice*, *6*(2), 111–129. doi:10.1080/1387698042000273442

Silverstein, M. (1995). Stability and change in temporal distance between the elderly and their children. *Demography*, *32*(1), 29–45. doi:10.2307/2061895

Smits, A. (2010). Moving close to parents and adult children in the Netherlands: The influence of support needs. *Demographic Research*, *22*, 985–1014.

Snijders, T. A. B., & Bosker, R. J. (2012). *Multilevel analysis: An introduction to basic and advanced multilevel modeling* (2nd ed.). Los Angeles, CA: Sage.

Sweet, J. A., & Bumpass, L. L. (1987). *American families and households*. New York, NY: Russell Sage Foundation.

Szydlik, M. (2000). *Lebenslange Solidarität? Generationenbeziehungen zwischen erwachsenen Kindern und Eltern*. Opladen: Leske + Budrich.

Szydlik, M. (2016). *Sharing lives – Adult children and parents*. London/New York, NY: Routledge.

Tomassini, C., Wolf, D. A., & Rosina, A. (2003). Parental housing assistance and parent-child proximity in Italy. *Journal of Marriage and Family*, *65*(3), 700–715. doi:10.2307/3600033

Ward, R., Logan, J. R., & Spitze, G. (1992). The influence of parent and child needs on co-residence in middle and later life. *Journal of Marriage and Family*, *54*(1), 209–221. doi:10.2307/353288

Ward, R., & Spitze, G. (1996). Will the children ever leave? Parent-child co-residence history and plans. *Journal of Family Issues*, *17*(4), 514–539. doi:10.1177/019251396017004005

White, L. (1994). Co-residence and leaving home: Young adults and their parents. *Annual Review of Sociology*, *20*(1), 81–102.

Wilmoth, J. M. (2010). Health trajectories among older movers. *Journal of Aging and Health*, *22*(7), 862–881. doi:10.1177/0898264310375985

Withers, S. D. (1998). Linking household transitions and housing transitions: A longitudinal analysis of renters. *Environment and Planning A*, *30*(4), 615–630.

Zhang, Y., Engelman, M., & Agree, E. M. (2013). Moving considerations: A longitudinal analysis of parent-child residential proximity for older Americans. *Research on Aging*, *35*(6), 663–87. doi:10.1177/0164027512457787

Chapter 8

Below the Breadline: Families and Food in Austerity Britain

Rebecca O'Connell, Abigail Knight and Julia Brannen

8.1 Introduction

The global economic recession, rising food prices and so-called 'austerity' policies in some European countries have made food less affordable for households. In this context, food poverty and insecurity have risen across Europe, albeit there are differences between countries (Davis & Baumberg Geiger, 2017; Loopstra, Reeves, McKee, & Stuckler, 2016; Pfeiffer, Ritter, & Oestreicher, 2015). This chapter examines the case of the UK where, since 2006, food banks have proliferated (Garthwaite, 2016; Loopstra et al., 2015) and the number of food parcels handed out to families has risen dramatically (Cooper, Purcell, & Jackson, 2014; Lambie-Mumford & Green, 2015).

Whilst there is evidence that the impacts of the global financial crisis and changing social policy, including welfare reform, have hit UK families (households with children) harder than those without (De Agostini, Hills, & Sutherland, 2014; Stewart, 2015), there is a lack of systematic collection of direct data about household food insecurity or poverty in the UK and, therefore, a lack of evidence about how these economic phenomena and policy changes impact families' ability to feed themselves. However, sociological research about children, families and poverty suggests that food is compromised in low-income households (Daly & Kelly, 2015) and that parents make sacrifices to protect their children (e.g. Main & Bradshaw, 2014), suggesting that an approach to understanding families and food poverty is needed that examines differences within as well as between households.

The research on which the chapter draws (www.foodinhardtimes.org) is a mixed methods study, funded by the European Research Council,[1] that examines

[1]The research leading to these results has received funding from the European Research Council under the European Union's Seventh Framework Programme (FP7/2007–2013)/ERC grant agreement no. 337977. The authors would like to acknowledge colleagues who carried out and collaborated on the analysis of the quantitative data reported here: Charlie Owen, Antonia Simon and Matt Padley, and the MIS team at Loughborough for granting access to their data. The detailed methodology and results of this analysis are published elsewhere: O'Connell et al. (2019).

Families in Economically Hard Times, 167–185

doi:10.1108/978-1-83909-071-420191012

food practices in poor and low-income families (households with children) in three European countries, UK, Portugal and Norway. It uses qualitative methods with parents and young people aged 11–15 years from 45 families in each of the three countries as well as secondary analysis of national and international quantitative data. This chapter draws only on the UK research findings. In contrast to much other survey research on food poverty and insecurity that has focussed on the household as an undifferentiated unit, or qualitative research examining (for good reason) the views of mothers, the study is concerned with children's as well as parents' perspectives of food in the context of poverty and intra- as well as inter-household variations.

Following a discussion of the sociological conceptualisation of food poverty adopted in this study, the chapter reports on secondary analysis undertaken to identify *the types of families at risk of food poverty* in the UK. It asks what counts as a socially acceptable diet that meets needs for health and social participation and how much this costs, then compares this to actual spending on food by different family types to identify which kinds of families are spending less than expected. To examine trends over time, in the context of the changing economic context and social policies affecting the resources available to children and families, time series analysis is carried out from 2005 to 2015. To understand *how* families eat when they are spending much less than expected, and what this *means* for them, we draw on qualitative research on 45 UK households. We describe three family cases that exemplify some of the conditions under which families' food budgets are constrained, how they manage and how experiences and practices vary within as well as between households.

8.2 A Relative Deprivation Approach to Conceptualising Food Poverty

The definition and measurement of food poverty and insecurity are complex and vary across time and place (Dowler, Kneafsey, Lambie, Inman, & Collier, 2011; Kneafsey, Dowler, Lambie, Inman, & Collier, 2012; Maxwell, 2001). In this study of food poverty, we draw on the multi-dimensional definition of poverty of Peter Townsend in terms of relative deprivation and we define food poverty as encompassing social as well as material deprivation (O'Connell, Padley, Owen, & Simon, forthcoming).

Food poverty and insecurity have long been understood as dimensions and indicators of poverty (Dowler, 2002). For example, Seebohm Rowntree's (1901) definition of poverty, based on minimalist expectations of the time to establish a 'scientific' minimum income line beneath which no one could be expected to fall, included at its heart adequate food for 'physical efficiency'. As Dowler and O'Connor (2012, p. 45) note, '[w]ithin work on "poverty" [...] the ability to buy or otherwise obtain enough food is an important component, however the condition is defined'. Central to the concepts of food insecurity and food poverty, then, are 'the notion of food scarcity or deprivation in the basic need for food' (Tarasuk, 2001, p. 7) and hunger is the most severe dimension. However, as Peter Townsend

(1954, 1962, 1979) pointed out, no one could really be expected to live on Rowntree's 'primary poverty income' in real life: '[s]ocial pressures, to drink in the local pub, to buy presents for the children, to be a normal social being especially in adversity, required a higher budget' (Glennerster, Hills, Piachaud, & Webb, 2004, p. 25).

Townsend argued that people had social as well as physical needs and that these could not usefully be divided, since the ways in which seemingly 'basic' needs (for example, for nutrition) were met served social functions (Hick, 2014, p. 301). Whilst a cup of tea, for example, was nutritionally worthless, offering tea to visitors made 'a small contribution [.] towards maintaining the threads of social relationships' (1979, p. 50 in Hick, 2014, p. 301). Townsend's relative deprivation approach to conceptualising poverty thus covered a wide range of aspects of material and social living standards. In *Poverty in the United Kingdom*, Townsend (1979) identified the levels of income below which consumption and participation fell well below what might be regarded as acceptable in an increasingly affluent society. This group was seen to be in poverty (Lansley & Mack, 2015).

Research has shown that the 'social' dimensions of food and eating are widely included as part of consensually determined minimum socially acceptable standards of living (Davis, Hirsch, Smith, Beckhelling, & Padley, 2012), although there is evidence of adapted preferences (reduced expectations) in the context of austerity (Davis et al., 2012). Food poverty, as we understand it, is therefore about more than hunger or malnutrition, since, '[f]or men' [*sic*], 'food acquires a series of values other those than which hunger provides' (Richards, 2004[1932], p. 9). Food is a material resource, of course, but it is also what Winson (1993) has called the 'intimate commodity'. At one level, food provides the nutrients needed for growth and development. It plays a critical role in health and thus inequitable access to healthy food plays a role in health inequalities. But food is also fundamentally meaningful, a source of pleasure, a way of expressing care, a medium of control (O'Connell & Brannen, 2014) and a means of social inclusion and exclusion. Food is intimately linked to identity: we are what we eat (Fischler, 1988). Indeed families are reproduced as such by activities such as eating together (DeVault, 1991; Morgan, 2011). Furthermore, exercising choice in the marketplace, including what food to buy and eat, is one means of enacting agency in a consumer society. The next section describes how we have operationalised this multi-dimensional understanding of food poverty to identify UK families at risk.

8.3 Identifying UK Families at Risk of Food Poverty

In the UK study, we sought to identify families at risk of food poverty by carrying out secondary analysis of existing data. Following a relative deprivation approach, our question was 'Which types of families appear not to be meeting the lower spending threshold for a socially acceptable diet that meets needs for health and social participation and how does this change over time?' In order to answer this, the Living Costs and Food Survey (LCFS) was analysed to calculate the actual expenditure of selected different household types and compared to the food budget standard (FBS) from Minimum Income Standard (MIS) research.

The MIS, that is funded by the Joseph Rowntree Foundation and has provided annual updates since 2008, calculates the income needed by a range of different household types to achieve a minimum, socially acceptable standard of living. The definition of a minimum socially acceptable standard of living at the heart of all MIS groups is that 'it includes, but is more than just, food, clothes and shelter. It is about having what you need in order to have the opportunities and choices necessary to participate in society' (Padley & Hirsch, 2016, p. 5). Consequently, the food budget standard in MIS takes account not only of the cost of spending that is essential for health but also describes what is needed for social inclusion (Oldfield & Burr, 2008). This reflects a broad consensus that '[s]ocial participation is of high importance for social inclusion and thus should be included in the basic budgets' (Hirsch, 2009).

The FBS that is part of MIS is the amount deemed necessary for a realistic, nutritious, socially acceptable diet that allows for taking part in customary activities. It includes additional shopping for seasonal events such as Christmas and birthdays, and modestly eating out occasionally (Davis, Hirsch, & Padley, 2014; Davis et al., 2012). The FBS is constructed during the MIS research that is based on a deliberative focus group methodology. It is put together by groups of individuals looking in detail at the needs of different household types (see Davis et al., 2014, 2012). As a part of this process groups discuss and agree menus, for all individuals covered by the MIS research, which are reasonably healthy, practical in terms of lifestyle, and realistic in terms of preferences and treats. Minor adjustments to the menus by a nutritional expert are made to achieve nutritional adequacy for that particular group of the population (Oldfield & Burr, 2008) and the basket is costed using pricing from a national retailer, Tesco (as the largest supermarket chain in the UK, with a national pricing policy that means there is no need to account for regional variation in urban and accessible rural locations). MIS is calculated for 11 core different household compositions. Seven of these households are families with children (age 0–18 years).[2]

---

[2]The FBS calculates minimum costs including food (and some alcoholic beverages) consumed inside and outside of the home, for a range of different household compositions. The FBS sets out what is needed by children in four age groups, covering from birth to 18 years, recognising that children of different ages have different requirements in terms of diet and nutrition. The analysis presented here has averaged the needs of children set out by the FBS in order to enable comparisons with expenditure data. The analysis is limited to those families that include working age adults (19–65 years) covered by MIS (see Padley & Hirsch, 2016, pp. 5–7). It is based on data for a series of nine years beginning before the financial crisis, in 2005, and ending with the most recent complete data available at this time, that is in 2013. All data reported have been weighted using the 'annual weight' derived variable in the LCFS files for each data year (2005–2013). Food expenditure over time (2005–2013) has been inflated using the Retail Price Index to 2013 prices.

The LCFS collects information on spending patterns and the cost of living that reflects household budgets across the UK, the results of which are primarily used to provide information about spending patterns for the Consumer Price Indices, and about food consumption and nutrition. Using data from the LCFS we created a variable that combined a derived question in the LCFS that asks respondents about the amount spent on food and nonalcoholic drinks (inside the home) per week in pound sterling with other variables in the LCFS that quantify expenditure on food outside of the home.

Fig. 8.1 shows the results of the comparison of actual expenditure on food with the food budget standard, as a proportion of each household type not meeting the food budget standard between 2005 and 2013. The analysis shows that the proportion spending below what is needed for a minimum nutritious socially acceptable diet – the FBS – has increased over time for all of the different household compositions examined here. For all households with children the proportion with spending below the FBS has increased from 41% in 2005 to 52% in 2013. In other words, more than half of all households with children in 2013 were spending less on food than that needed for a minimum nutritious socially acceptable diet that allows for social participation.

The proportion of lone parents with one child spending less than the FBS on food each week has increased by over 50% (54.1%) between 2005 and 2013, rising from 40 to 62%. The proportion of couples with one child and couples with four children spending less than the FBS has increased by a similar order of magnitude over the same period. Lone parents with either two or three children and couples with four children are the most likely to spending less on food than that needed to provide the FBS; 71% of lone parents with two or three children and 82% of couples with four children have food expenditure below the level of the FBS in

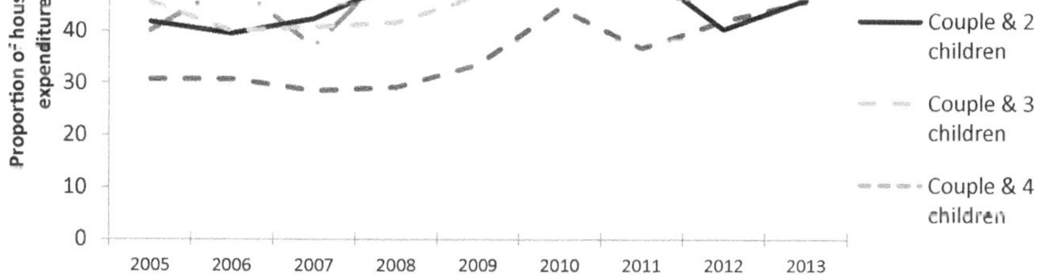

Fig. 8.1. Proportion (Percentage) Spending below the Food Budget Standard for Working-age Households with Children, 2005–2013.

2013. While there are fluctuations in the proportion of households spending below the FBS between 2005 and 2013, it is clear that the overall pattern is one of an increasing proportion of families not spending what is needed for the minimum nutritious socially acceptable diet as defined through MIS.[3]

The worryingly large proportion of all household types spending less than the food budget standard – between 30 and 82% of households with children of varying compositions between 2005 and 2013 – is perhaps to be expected for at least two reasons. First, as Bradshaw et al. (2008, p. 31) note in the first of the MIS reports, 'actual expenditure is constrained by income, whereas the MIS budgets have been derived without an income constraint'; that is, MIS is about establishing a publicly determined, socially acceptable threshold of need which reflects individuals' lived realities, but is not dictated by available resources. Second, it is clear from previous research that food expenditure is an 'elastic' part of household budgets (Dowler, 2002; Dowler, Turner, & Dobson, 2001), and in a period when the cost of other essentials, such as fuel and housing, has also risen, it is often the food budget that is dipped into in order to pay for these other things (Tait, 2015). However, these do not explain why the largest proportion not meeting the FBS is consistently found among large and lone-parent families or why this has increased over time.

Differences between households and increase over time are likely to be explained by the distributional impact of tax and benefit policies, including reforms introduced, under the cover of 'austerity', by the UK's coalition government from 2010 (Browne & Elming, 2015). Prior to these cuts, adults in households with children were already over twice as likely to be in poverty as adults without children. Households with children saw a decrease in their incomes as a direct result of government cuts and, of these households, those on low incomes fared the worst (Mack, 2017). According to the Households Below Average Income (HBAI) figures for 2013/2014 (DWP, 2015), families particularly at risk of income poverty in Britain include lone-parent families, workless households (plus those with only one adult in paid work) and those with three or more children. In the UK, one-child families do better compared to large families because child benefit is paid at a higher rate for the first child (Bradshaw & Finch, 2002, p. 152; Culliney, Haux, & McKay, 2014, p. 30). This difference is exacerbated by new policies that penalise large families further, for example, limiting state support through child tax credits and other benefits to the first two children in a household.

---

[3]Whilst these findings can give a good indication of the family types most likely to be at risk of food poverty, the ways in which people meet their food needs vary widely and there may be reasons other than economic ones that explain why households spend less than is publicly determined as socially acceptable on food. A limitation of the approach taken in this chapter compared to direct measures of food insecurity and other research about material deprivation (e.g. see Lansley & Mack, 2015), then, is that it does not tell us whether households are spending below the amount because of a lack of resources or for other reasons.

Whilst these findings tell us *which types* of families are most at risk from food poverty, and we are able to make inferences about why, they cannot tell us *how* families manage to feed themselves when they are spending much less than the FBS, what this experience *means* for them or the ways in which family members are affected. After introducing the qualitative research, the next section extrapolates from patterns found in the quantitative data by describing three cases that exemplify some of the conditions under which families' food budgets are constrained, how they cope and how experiences vary within as well as between households.

8.4 Lived Experiences of Food Poverty: Three Families

For the qualitative phase of the study, we successfully recruited 45 families at the bottom of the income spectrum in each country, including at least one 11- to 15-year-old in each family and at least one parent/carer (usually mothers). In the UK, we sought to compare how low-income families fared and fed their families in two contrasting research sites, a London borough and a small coastal town. Both are areas with high levels of deprivation and high child poverty rates, although the London borough is rapidly gentrifying with a significant rise in high- and medium-income families. Reflecting the quantitative evidence, a high proportion, two-thirds, (30/45) are lone-parent families (Table 8.1).

In the London sample, one-third (10/30) of the mothers had migrated from outside the EU, and in the total sample 6/45 were migrants from mainland Europe (Table 8.2). In the former group, there were several cases in which state support had been cut off to the parent and children as the families/mothers were in the (lengthy) process of applying for 'leave to remain'.

In each household, semi-structured interviews were conducted with parents (usually mothers) and young people that included the topics of income and outgoings, food budgets and practices, sources of informal and informal support and perspectives on managing and feeding the family on a low income. Interviews with parents (usually mothers) lasted roughly 1.5 hours on average and with young people around 45 minutes. A subsample of families (12/45) participated in two follow-up visits that used visual methods (photography and photo elicitation) to learn more about foods bought and eaten at home and elsewhere and how any changes in circumstances impacted on food and eating over time.

Table 8.1. Lone vs Dual Parent Households in the London Borough and Coastal Town (n = 45).

	Lone Parent	Dual Parent	Total
London borough	23	7	30
Coastal town	7	8	15
Total	30	15	45

Table 8.2. Mother's Ethnicity/Country of Origin in the London Borough and Coastal Town (n = 45).

	London Borough	Coastal Town	Total
White British	7	8	15
Black British/British Asian (second generation)	11	0	11
European	2	4	6
Outside mainland Europe	10	3	13
Total	30	15	45

Across our sample of 45 families in the UK, More than half (23/45) parents were experiencing the most severe dimension of food poverty, that is, they reported eating an inadequate quantity of food and experiencing hunger, skipping meals and using emergency food aid from food banks, for example. In around half of these families (13/23), the quantity of food children were eating was also compromised meaning they also went hungry at times.[4] Two-thirds (37/45) of the families, including those reporting hunger, were affected by living on a low income in a number of other ways, in regard to food and eating. These included dimensions of food poverty such as having to limit the quality and range of foods purchased and cooked (quality), not being able to participate socially by eating with family and friends at home or outside (social participation) and worrying about whether food would run out before having money to buy more (worry). Around a fifth of families (8/45) did not experience these dimensions of food poverty but did report that food budgets were 'constrained' such that they sometimes had to spend less on food to be able to afford other things (but this did not involve compromising food quantity, (nutritional) quality or social participation) (see Nielsen & Holme, 2016) (Table 8.3).

From this sample, we have selected three cases on the following grounds. The first is that they exemplify the analysis we have carried out in the quantitative datasets. Two are lone parents who as shown above are the most likely to be spending less on food than that needed to meet the FBS. One lone-parent household is also a 'large family' also shown to be at risk of food poverty. The third case, also a large family but a two-parent household, is chosen because they are not in employment; hence they have a low income in the context of bringing up four children. A second reason for selecting these low-income families in food poverty is that they are key targets of UK public policy and public discourse:

[4]All parents and children who report compromised food quantity are also experiencing some other dimensions of food poverty.

Table 8.3. Dimensions of Food Poverty Experienced by Adults and Children ($n = 45$, Categories Are not Mutually Exclusive).

	Quantity	Any of Quality, Social Participation, Worry	Food Budget Constrained Only	None
Adult	23	37	8	0
Child	13	31	0	14

migrant households without right to live in UK are at risk of deportation; lone-parent families who have long been the target of policies that have sought to reduce 'dependence' on the state; nonemployed household with parents suffering a disability; lastly, large families who are facing discrimination by reduced child allowances.

The first two cases we describe are of families living in a deprived part of the inner London borough where fresh food is readily available including in street markets. The area is also saturated with fast-food outlets whilst in the gentrified parts of the borough expensive independent shops and eateries are moving in. The third case of a large, two-parent family is living in the coastal area in South East England, where transport is expensive and there is a limited range of mainly low-budget food shops and food outlets.

8.4.1 Sahara and Tarek[5]

Sahara is a lone British Asian mother of six children, the eldest of which are young adults (aged 17 and 20 years). She is employed for 16 hours per week, which means she is able to claim benefits, such as working tax credit in addition to child tax credits child benefit and housing benefit[6]; she also has her own home-based business selling raw and organic foods and cosmetics. Receiving working tax credit means, however, that the children are not eligible for free school meals, adding to the mother's weekly food budget as school meals are mandatory at this school. The family lives in a house that is rented from the Local Authority. Sahara runs a car that she needs to take the younger children to day care and drive to work. Around 30% of the household income is spent on food (£150 per

[5]Pseudonyms are used throughout to protect the identity of participants.

[6]Working tax credit is a means tested benefit designed to top up incomes of those who work and are on a low income. To qualify, lone parents must work at least 16 hours a week; couples must usually work at least 24 hours between them per week, with one working at least 16 hours. Child tax credit is a means tested benefit designed to help parents with the costs of raising a child, including childcare costs for working parents. Child benefit was previously a universal benefit but since January 2013 is means tested where a parent earns over £50,000 per year. A higher rate applies for the first child compared to subsequent children. Housing benefit helps with the costs of renting (not mortgages) for those with a low income.

week out of £400–499) which amounts to roughly 90% of the FBS for this family type.[7]

Sahara spends less than she would like on food because the cost of other necessities squeezes her budget. She prioritises utilities, council tax and her direct debits and cuts back on food shopping to pay off the debts she has incurred doing up the house and paying for petrol to get to work. In this household the food budget is 'elastic' and often used for debts and unexpected expenses: '*I've noticed whenever I have to pay something or do something I always have to cut into my food budget*'. Whilst the cost of raising the family has grown as her children have grown, her income has remained the same: '*their needs have got more as they've grown ... they're big men now, my boys are like 6ft, 6ft 2, their diets are, you know ... but the money's just stayed the same; you know I can't feed my kids a few pieces of chicken like I would then when they're all young – I have to make sure the pot's full*'. The result of having to meet growing needs with less money is that food quality and social participation are compromised in this family.

Sahara's food practices include customary ways of cooking: she uses fresh ingredients for most dishes. However Tarek, her 14-year-old son, says food at home is monotonous: '*every now and then we'll get a take-away*', but '*most of the time*' it is '*curry and rice*'. Sahara also reports being unable to afford as much fruit and vegetables as she would like. It is fairly easy to get fresh food locally, and Sahara often resorts to buying food on credit from the local shop and paying it back when she has the money.

Even though the area is regarded as fairly unsafe by many of the children who participated in the study, and has few outdoor spaces to play, consuming fast food is a common activity for young people: '*there's a lot of chicken shops to keep us busy, there's a lot of food shops to keep us busy like*' (Tarek). However, despite the large number and wide range of restaurants (in addition to fast-food outlets) in the locality, the family is restricted in the degree to which they can participate in social activities such as 'eating out' together. Given there are five children/young people and the low budget for food, eating out only happens occasionally. Showing hospitality to guests is also restricted, and Sahara has had to impose rules about having her children's friends to play and eat '*because they don't come in ones, they come in groups*'. She said that '*I've told my kids straight 'You invite your friends round, tell them to bring their pocket money, I [can] barely feeds you lot*'.

Whilst Sahara says she has worried in the past that the food will run out before there is money to buy more no one reports going hungry in this family. Norms about the distribution food include making sure that everyone has their fair share at mealtimes '*they're quite good they'll say like now today there's chops, they'll all*

[7]The most recent FBS we have calculated for family types is 2013. Since UK food prices generally levelled off from 2012–2015/2016 (when fieldwork took place) these are valid but rough estimates. The calculations of weekly food expenditure compared to the FBS for the three cases are as follows: Sahira – has six children including one who is an adult so we compared to couple plus four children – £150/£165.20 = 91% of the FBS; Juba – lone parent plus two children – £25/£97.87 = 26% of the FBS; Peter and Diane – couple plus four children – £95/£165.20 = 58% of the FBS.

shout "Mum, how many chops each?" So I'll say "Okay, two or three"' and "one potato or two"'. However, snacks and treats are scarce and less fairly shared, and Tarek admits to taking crisps and hiding them for himself. Sahara suggests one way to manage food would be to prevent the children from being able to take it '*to a point I really thought I need to get a lock in the kitchen. Once it's done just lock up – you've had your meal*'.

8.4.2 Juba and Lewa

Juba is a lone Nigerian mother of two children, including her daughter Lewa, aged 14 years and son aged 5 years. The family has lived in the UK since 2004 and is seeking asylum. Because Juba does not have legal status, she is not allowed to do paid work and does not receive any benefits. They live in one room in a friend's council house and have limited access to the kitchen and living areas. Because she has no free bus pass she is limited in how far she can travel. The family survives on £20 a week in cash from the church and £20 a week in Tesco vouchers from the charity Kids Company (now closed down). Roughly 60% of this income (£25 out of £40) is spent on food which amounts to about 26% of the FBS for this type of family.

The family is supported by the church, friends and the food bank which involves taking two buses across London. '*And [the] food bank ... really they are really helping, they are good, can find food. They don't want me to be lack ... like tinned food, spaghetti, those things, like voucher, Tesco card, to get stuff for the children. But definitely it's not enough to live on*'. The family lives on pasta, rice, noodles, tomato sauce, tomatoes and beans on rice, cheaper fruit, such as apples and oranges, all provided by the food bank and the Tesco card. However, it is not enough, and both Juba and Lewa skip meals and go hungry. Juba goes without so the children can eat '*Yeah most of the time I always do fasting and prayer, so that I will keep the food you know safe for the children to eat. So I can ... if I want to break, I can break in the evening, take like noodles or white rice mixed with something, vegetables*'. Lewa limits what she eats so that her younger brother can eat '*there are times when I just want to leave them [any snacks] for him to eat so that you know he can eat something*'. The food is also of poor nutritional quality, with very little protein: meat is only eaten at home when gifted from people at church. The charitable food they are given does not meet social needs either and is often culturally inappropriate. As Juba says: '*Kid's Company give us like baked beans ... sometimes I don't really eat like that*'.

Juba doesn't cook much because there isn't much to cook and she has limited access to the shared kitchen: '*Yeah I don't have much to cook, because when there's no money I hardly want to do the shopping. The only thing I normally get like bread for them. ... Things that they can't... it's very easy for them to do like noodles... you know you can put the noodles in the microwave*'. As Lewa notes, meals are small, '*After school and after clubs ... probably have something really small. I'd probably have like a noodle and then I have like an apple or a fruit after that. Just for like an evening meal, and then the fruit builds me up*'. The same routine applies at weekends unless the family is given food prepared by people at the church. Lewa notes that it is 'easier' at the weekend because she needs to expend less energy as she is doing few activities '*the energy stays in you a bit longer*'. A typical weekend meal Lewa says is beans on toast with some butter '*that could last me for quite a while*'.

Occasionally they eat at people's houses (from church) but Juba says she can never reciprocate. Afraid of appearing too dependent on others Juba wanted to maintain her sense of pride; she spoke of keeping their situation secret, especially from people at school, to protect the children. Lewa was asked about friends and whether they talked about buying food and eating out. She says that this happens and that she feels upset and left out but is also a bit sceptical about these 'stories', '*I do have quite a lot of friends that do that. They'll tell me about it and I'd feel left out a bit. So I just like nod and smile, probably walk away or something. They might fake a story about them going out or something.... Cos people are like just trying to fit in and not get picked on for the way they live or the way their lifestyle is*'. Sometimes Lewa went to friends' houses where she tasted foods from different countries but she can never invite them to her home. In addition, Lewa was taken out for a meal by someone from Kids Company. While she enjoyed these trips she was not happy about being too dependent and the person always having to pay the bill for the meal.

Social participation is clearly severely restricted and Lewa talks of secrecy and shame with regard to her situation: '*I don't really talk to friends about this, cos I feel like they're going to pick on me or something like that*'. Lewa suggests that she cannot invite friends over: '*because it's not easy for me, I have to tell them I will meet you at so and so place*'. Lewa is not entitled to free school meals because of their legal status (though her little brother does because of the universal free school meal policy for under 7s). Instead her mother gives her daughter half the money she receives from the church (£10) to spend each week to combat her daughter's sense of stigma and social exclusion – so that she can be like the other children at school. '*... because I don't want her to be looking when her friends are buying things. Then she will be looking at them ... you know she would feel bad... you need to go outside there and look for job, do whatever you can do, even though it's self-employed – do whatever you can do and make money to better your children*'.

Lewa describes how she makes the most of the money that her mother gives her: she buys a meal deal in a local shop near school, for £2 and gets sandwich, drink and crisps. Sometimes, if she has run out of money, she takes bread from home. If her school is going on a trip, Lewa says '*instead of eating breakfast I'd take the breakfast I wouldn't eat, save the money that I'm going to use to buy (inaudible) and then save that say for like a week. And then I'd use the money that I've saved up to buy myself food for the trip.*

8.4.3 Peter, Diane and Bethany

Peter is aged 61 years and married to Diane, age 42, and they have four children, aged between 18 and 5 years, including Bethany who is 12 years old. They are a

White British family and live in a housing association house which is too small for them. Neither parent is in employment. The family live on a weekly sum of about £390, drawn from a number of benefits – Jobseeker's Allowance (JSA) child tax credits and child benefit, as well as additional housing benefit to cover their rent. Although the two parents are both in ill health, they have been turned down for Employment Support Allowance (ESA) and Personal Independence Payment (PiP).[8] As Peter explained: '*so neither of us are fit and able to do too much, but they went 'No you're fit'. Apparently if you can lift one finger and go like that you're fit. So there you go. So then they switched me from ESA to JSA and that changed… all the money stopped on that. Quick aren't they? Um… and we ended up with nothing for two weeks didn't we? No money at all*'.

Living in an isolated area with little transport and expensive buses with no free or subsidised child fares, as there are in London, the family prioritises the costs of running a car as this is cheaper and more convenient for them for getting the children to their various schools and colleges in the area. They spend about 25% (£90–£100 per week for a family of six) of their income on food which amounts to about 58% of the FBS for this family type. The children all receive free school meals but the parents subsidise this by giving the older two children about £9 or £10 each every week, as what the food they receive at school, they say, isn't enough.

The family's budget is squeezed by having to repay debts that have accrued over the years to pay for what parents consider to be essential items, like the car. The parents are also worried that their money is shortly going to be reduced by over £100 per week with the introduction of a new benefit cap,[9] and this results them in feeling out of control: Peter explains, '*So we're in a never ending circle of trying to pay back… so we're just in that cycle where we keep our heads above water, and then all of a sudden someone pulls the plug on us, and down the drain we go for a little while again. And then we recover, and of course it takes longer each time to recover. And after the end of this year it's going to take forever, cos there just won't be any spare money*'.

[8]JSA is a benefit paid to people who are unemployed but deemed capable to work; they need to demonstrate they are actively seeking work. Employment Support Allowance (ESA) is a benefit for people who are unable to work as a result of illness or disability but must be medically assessed as being eligible. Personal Independence Payment (PiP), which has replaced Disability Living Allowance for new claimants, is a non-means tested benefit that helps with the extra costs of having a long-term health condition or disability and is for people of working age between 16 and 64 years.

[9]As part of wider welfare reform implemented by the Conservative Government (from 2015), a benefit cap was introduced from November 2016. This benefit cap sets a limit on the total amount in benefits that most working age people can claim and was lowered from £26,000 to £23,000 in London and to £20,000 everywhere else. This means that the maximum amount a family (lone or couple parent households with children) can receive in all benefit payments, including housing benefit to cover rent, is £442.31 per week in London and £384.62 per week outside London.

The family rely on grandparents' support to cover essential and emergency costs (such as car repairs), and this includes regular dinners cooked for the children at their house and food from their allotment, *'we get a lot of fresh veg in season. So we've got marrow out there, fresh ones, we get carrots when it's time, we get all sorts of stuff… parsnips'*. The family's diet is of a mixed quality, combining some meals cooked from fresh ingredients, such as stuffed marrow or Spaghetti Bolognese with cheap frozen food, like chicken steaks, and chips, either cooked in the chip fryer or in the oven. When money is particularly tight, the family's food practices are affected: as Peter says, *'you know when you get a bigger bill come in, and that has to be paid – things like the electric and the others, then we find we're cutting down on the amount we buy, but then we're also cutting down on the quality'*. Both parents occasionally skip meals or miss out protein so that there is enough for the children; *'we'll get the chips… but we won't get the sausage or the fish'* (Diane) and as Peter adds: *'Yeah, they [the children] come first, and it's their money that we're getting it out of basically'*.

Bethany has a limited diet, partly because she is a fussy eater, yet she will eat *'like a horse'* at her grandmother's house: *'Nan's better at cooking'*; Diane adds that Bethany doesn't want to disappoint her Nan by not eating the dinner. Bethany has a cereal bar and a yoghurt drink for breakfast, and her favourite food she says is Kentucky Fried Chicken but says she only has it *'once a month if I'm lucky'*. Generally, food doesn't interest her and she has to be reminded to eat. She doesn't think her diet is particularly healthy but questions the messages given to her: *'The teachers that do it don't even believe in five a day'*.

Eating out for this family is a *'rare Chinese'* and a fortnightly bag of chips: *'The only take-away we have I think really is chips now, and it's like £2.10. But that… up until this week it used to feed all six, now they've dropped the portion down… cos someone's moaned about portion sizes at chip shops. Nice of them, thanks mate! Cos I've got to buy 1½ bags now to feed us all rather than one'* (Peter). Having friends round is something they tend to avoid, partly because there isn't much space but also because of the cost of feeding other people: *'And if we start feeding other people as well I think we'd be seriously into problems then'* (Peter). Having the children's friends to the house is also a challenge and if they do come round they adjust the meal to stretch the portions; as Peter says: *'Bethany prefers to go to other people's houses. We have had the odd one or two round but basically we don't increase the food, we just reduce the portions and still have the same… just stretch food, and we might add a couple of slices of bread to it, just to… or peel a couple more potatoes'*.

8.5 Discussion and Conclusion

The chapter began by describing a relative deprivation approach to conceptualising food poverty and addresses what counts in the UK as a socially acceptable diet that meets the needs for health and social participation and how much this costs. It then compared this to actual spending on food by different family types to identify which kinds of families are spending less than expected and may be at risk of food poverty. The main finding was that the proportion not meeting the FBS has increased over time for most families and is consistently highest for lone parent and large families. The qualitative cases of two lone-parent families, one of them large, and one large two-parent family, described how it is that families manage, and some of the consequences, when they spend much less than the FBS. The implications included compromises in food quality and quantity, social participation and socially acceptable procurement.

Given what we know about the persistent links between family structures and poverty in the UK (e.g. Culliney et al., 2014), it is unsurprising that it is large and lone parent families who are furthest from what is regarded as a minimum food budget standard. However, this situation is not inevitable and whilst many factors are well established as mediating the connection between family structure and poverty, 'the nature and extent of these links is continually changing as a result of broader demographic, socio-economic and policy developments' (Culliney et al., 2014, p. 7; Falkingham, Evandrou, & Vlachantoni, 2014). International analyses show that investment in benefit payments can successfully remove families from poverty However, in 2015 the newly elected Conservative government announced a further £12 billion cuts which included limiting tax credits to two children, a continued freezing of working-age benefits and a lowering of the level of the benefits cap. Poor households with children are set to lose up to 12% of their income (Mack, 2017, p. 90), and the recent 2017 budget has done nothing to redress this. Meanwhile, whilst efforts to 'make work pay' include encouraging more families to become 'dual earners' (Lawton & Thompson, 2013) this does nothing to help lone parents whose work opportunities are constrained in the UK by high childcare costs and low paid part-time work (Dermott & Pantazis, 2014, p. 264).

It has been established that there is a growing price gap between more and less healthy foods (Jones, Conklin, Suhrcke, & Monsivais, 2014) and when income goes down or the cost of food goes up, people switch to cheaper calories, whilst families with children purchase less fruit and vegetables (Griffith, O'Connell, & Smith, 2013). The cases of Sahara and Tarek and Peter, Diane and Bethany corroborate previous research suggesting that the food budget is 'elastic' (that is, squeezed by competing, inelastic, household expenses) and that households achieve savings through food 'coping strategies' including 'trading down' (Dowler et al., 2001; Griffith et al., 2013) involving compromises to food quality and variety. For those at the very bottom of the income distribution, like Juba and Lewa, however, further reductions in the quality of food are impossible, and in these households food quantity is reduced. Confirming previous research, the mother in this household sacrifices her own food intake to protect her children, with implications for her own health, and turns to emergency food provision such as food banks, that are socially stigmatising (Dowler, 2014; Wells & Caraher, 2014).

The research also adds to what is already known by considering intra-household variation. Whilst the mothers in both the lone-parent households manage resource distribution and, in Juba's case, sacrifice food intake, the cases show how children also play a part in resource management, reduce their own food intake for others. In the worst case, Juba's daughter Lewa goes hungry despite her mother's best efforts. Although Bethany does not appear to go hungry, largely as a result of her lack of appetite, her diet is limited in variety and her parents also reduce what they eat to ensure there is enough for her and her three siblings.

The deleterious consequences of poor diet intake and malnutrition, particularly for children, are well known and have long-term implications. The profound effects of health inequalities that are associated with poor dietary intakes and meal patterns include increasing incidence of coronary heart disease, type II diabetes and cancer. Indeed, the UK Faculty of Public Health has argued that recent evidence of increasing malnutrition and hunger constitutes a 'public health emergency'. Sub-optimal diet and food practices such as skipping meals are also associated with poor cognition and lower academic achievement as children's ability to concentrate and study is damaged by insufficient food or food of poor nutritious value. In the UK, as elsewhere, food poverty and overweight and obesity are also closely connected, a trend partly explained by the relative cheapness and wide availability of unhealthy, low-quality foods that are high in saturated fat and non-milk extrinsic sugars.

But, as noted, food is more than simply fuel or nutrition. It is fundamentally social. Exercising choice in the marketplace, including what food to buy and eat, is also one means of enacting agency in a consumer society. Individuals and households experiencing food poverty may be forced to procure culturally inappropriate foods in socially unacceptable ways (such as, in Juba and Lewa's case, from charities and food banks) and be unable to participate in ordinary social activities involving food, like eating out or offering and receiving hospitality, as illustrated by all the cases we have presented. A key finding is that children are socially excluded by being unable to participate in food occasions with peers and friends in all households. Whilst Lewa can never have friends around to her home, one room in someone else's house, Tarek's and Bethany's parents have to restrict opportunities for their friends to visit, or if they do, ask children to bring their own money or food, or stretch portions of food to feed everyone. Given that social relationships between children and their peers are an integral aspect of their development and well-being, the consequences are likely to be highly damaging. For these reasons, charitable solutions to food poverty such as food banks and food parcels, cannot 'solve' the problem and in fact may serve to further stigmatise and marginalise those already suffering material deprivation and social exclusion.

Acknowledgements

Thanks to the families who participated in the study, the UK and international research teams. The research leading to these results has received funding from the European Research Council under the European Union's Seventh Framework Programme (FP7/2007–2013), ERC grant agreement number 337977.

References

Bradshaw, J., Middleton, S., Davis, A., Oldfield, N., Smith, N., Cusworth, L., & Williams, J. (2008). *A minimum income standard for Britain: What people think*. York: Joseph Rowntree Foundation.

Bradshaw, J., & Finch, N. (2002). *A comparison of child benefit packages in 22 countries*. DWP research report 174. Leeds: CDS.

Browne, J., & Elming, W. (2015). The effect of the coalition's tax and benefit changes on household incomes and work incentives. IFS Briefing Note BN159. The Institute for Fiscal Studies, London. Retrieved from https://www.ifs.org.uk/uploads/publications/bns/BN159.pdf. Accessed on september 24, 2019.

Cooper, N., Purcell, S., & Jackson, R. (2014). *Below the breadline: The relentless rise of food poverty in Britain*. London: Church Action on Poverty, Oxfam and the Trussell Trust.

Culliney, M., Haux, T., & McKay, S. (2014). *Family structure and poverty in the UK: An evidence and policy review*. Report to Joseph Rowntree Foundation. York: Joseph Rowntree Foundation. Retrieved from http://eprints.lincoln.ac.uk/14958/1/Family_structure_report_Lincoln.pdf. Accessed on september 24, 2019.

Davis, A., Hirsch, D., & Padley, M. (2014). *A minimum income standard for the UK in 2014*. York: Joseph Rowntree Foundation.

Davis, A., Hirsch, D., Smith, N., Beckhelling, J., & Padley, M. (2012). *A minimum income standard for the UK in 2012: Keeping up in hard times*. York: Joseph Rowntree Foundation.

Davis, O., & Baumberg Geiger, B. (2017). Did food insecurity rise across Europe after the 2008 crisis? An analysis across welfare regimes. *Social Policy and Society*, *16*, 343–360.

Daly, M., & Kelly, G. (2015). *Families and poverty: Everyday life on a low income*. Bristol: Policy Press.

De Agostini, P., Hills, J., & Sutherland, H. (2014). *Were we really all in it together? The distributional effects of the UK Coalition government's tax-benefit policy changes*. London: Centre for Analysis of Social Exclusion, LSE. Retrieved from http://sticerd.lse.ac.uk/dps/case/spcc/wp10.pdf. Accessed on september 24, 2019.

Department for Work and Pensisons. (2015). *Households below average income*. London: DWP.

Dermott, E., & Pantazis, C. (2014). Gender and poverty in Britain: Changes and continuities between 1999 and 2012. *Journal of Poverty and Social Justice*, *22*(3), 253–269.

DeVault, M. (1991). *Feeding the family: The social organization of caring as gendered work*. Chicago, IL: University of Chicago Press.

Dowler, E. (2002). Food and poverty in Britain: Rights and responsibilities. *Social Policy and Administration*, *36*(6), 698–717.

Dowler, E. (2014). Food banks and food justice in 'Austerity Britain'. In G. Riches & T. Silvasti (Eds.), *First world hunger revisited. Food charity or the right to food?* (2nd ed., pp. 160–175). Basingstoke: Palgrave Macmillan.

Dowler, E., Kneafsey, M., Lambie, H., Inman, A., & Collier, R. (2011). Thinking about 'food security': Engaging with UK consumers. *Critical Public Health*, *21*, 1–14.

Dowler, E., Turner, S., & Dobson, B. (2001). *Poverty bites: Food, health and poor families*. London: CPAG.

Dowler, E. A., & O'Connor, D. (2012). Rights based approaches to addressing food poverty and food insecurity in Ireland and UK. *Social Science & Medicine*, *74*, 44–51.

Falkingham, J., Evandrou, M., & Vlachantoni, A. (2014). *Exploring the link between demographic change and poverty in the UK*. Working Paper 54. ESTRC Centre for Population Change, Southampton. Retrieved from http://eprints.soton.ac.uk/368121/1/WP54_2014_Demographic_change_and_poverty_in_the_UK_Falkingham_et_al.pdf. Accessed on september 24, 2019.

Fischler, C. (1988). Food, self and identity. *Social Science Information*, *27*(2), 275–292.

Garthwaite, K. (2016). *Hunger pains: Life inside foodbank Britain*. Bristol: Policy Press.

Glennerster, H., Hills, J., Piachaud, D., & Webb, J. (2004). *One hundred years of poverty and policy*. York: Joseph Rowntree Foundation.

Griffith, R., O'Connell, M., & Smith, K. (2013). *Food expenditure and nutritional quality over the Great Recession*. London: Institute for Fiscal Studies. Retrieved from http://www.ifs.org.uk/bns/bn143.pdf. Accessed on september 24, 2019.

Hick, R. (2014). Poverty as capability deprivation: Conceptualising and measuring poverty in contemporary Europe. *European Journal of Sociology*. [*Archives Europeennes de Sociologie/Europaisches Archiv fur Soziologie*.], *55*(3), 295–323.

Hirsch, D. (2009). Reference budgets in Europe, Keynote Lecture on "Reference budgets for social inclusion", the Final Conference of the EU Progress Project "Standard Budgets", Vienna, 20–22 October 2009. Accessed on september 24, 2019.

Jones, N. R. V., Conklin, A. I., Suhrcke, M., & Monsivais, P. (2014). The growing price gap between more and less healthy foods: Analysis of a novel longitudinal UK dataset. *PLoS One*, *9*(10), e109343, 1–7.

Kneafsey, M., Dowler, E., Lambie, H., Inman, A., & Collier, R. (2012). Consumers and food security: Uncertain or empowered? *Journal of Rural Studies*, *28*, 1–12.

Lambie-Mumford, H., & Green, M. (2015). Austerity, welfare reform and the rising use of food banks by children in England and Wales. *Area*, *49*(3), 273–279.

Lawton, K., & Thompson, S. (2013). *Tackling in-work poverty by supporting dual-earning families*. York: Joseph Rowntree Foundation.

Lansley, S., & Mack, J. (2015). *Breadline Britain: The rise of mass poverty*. London: Oneworld Publications.

Loopstra, R., Reeves, A., McKee, M., & Stuckler, D. (2016). Food insecurity and social protection in Europe: Quasi-natural experiment of Europe's great recessions 2004–2012. *Preventive Medicine*, *89*, 44–50.

Loopstra, R., Reeves, A., Taylor-Robinson, D., Barr, B., McKee, M., & Stuckler, D. (2015). Austerity, sanctions, and the rise of food banks in the UK. *BMJ*, *350*, h1775.

Mack, J. (2017). Child maltreatment and child mortality. In V. Cooper & D. White (Eds.), *The violence of austerity* (pp. 85–93). London: Pluto Press.

Main, G., & Bradshaw, J. (2014). Children's necessities: Trends over time in perceptions and ownership. *Journal of Poverty and Social Justice*, *22*(3), 193–208.

Maxwell, S. (2001). The evolution of thinking about food security. In S. Devereux & S. Maxwell (Eds.), *Food security in sub-Saharan Africa* (pp. 13–27). London: ITDG Publishing.

Morgan, D. (2011). *Rethinking family practices*. London: Palgrave Macmillan.

Nielsen, A., & Holm, L. (2016). Making the most of less. *Food, Culture and Society, 19*(1), 71–91.

O'Connell, R., & Brannen, J. (2014). Children's food, power and control: Negotiations in families with younger children in England. *Childhood, 21*(1), 87–102.

O'Connell, R. E., Owen, C., Padley, M., Simon, A., & Brannen, J. (2019). Which types of family are at risk of food poverty in the UK? A relative deprivation approach. *Social Policy and Society, 18*(1), 1–18.

Oldfield, N., & Burr, S. (2008). *Minimum Income Standard: The food budget standard.* York: University of York Department of Social Policy and Social Work. Retrieved from https://www.lboro.ac.uk/media/wwwlboroacuk/content/crsp/downloads/reports/MIS_thefoodbudgetstandard_workingpaper.pdf. Accessed on september 24, 2019.

Padley, M., & Hirsch, D. (2016). *Households below a Minimum Income Standard: 2008/09 to 2013/14.* York: Joseph Rowntree Foundation.

Pfieffer, S., Ritter, T., & Oestreicher, E. (2015). Food insecurity in German households: Qualitative and quantitative data on coping, poverty consumerism and alimentary participation. *Social Policy and Society, 14*(3), 483–495.

Richards, A. (2004 [1932]). *Hunger and work in a savage tribe: A functional study of nutrition among the Southern Bantu.* Abingdon: Routledge.

Rowntree, B. S. (1901). *Poverty: A study of town life.* London: Macmillan.

Stewart, K. (2015). *The coalition's record on the under fives: Policy spending and outcomes 2010–2015.* Summary Working Paper 12. Centre for Analysis of Social Exclusion, LSE, London. Retrieved from http://sticerd.lse.ac.uk/dps/case/spcc/WP12.pdf. Accessed on september 24, 2019.

Tait, C. (2015). *Hungry for change: The final report of the Fabian Commission on Food and Poverty.* London: The Fabian Society.

Tarasuk, V. (2001). *Household and individual food insecurity.* Discussion paper. Health Canada. Ottawa, ON: Health Canada, Office of Nutrition Policy and Promotion. Retrieved from http://www.hc-sc.gc.ca/fn-an/alt_formats/hpfb-dgpsa/pdf/nutrition/food_sec_entire-sec_aliments_entier-eng.pdf. Accessed on september 24, 2019.

Townsend, P. (1954). Measuring poverty. *British Journal of Sociology, 5*(2), 130–137.

Townsend, P. (1962). The meaning of poverty. *British Journal of Sociology, 13*(3), 210–227.

Townsend, P. (1979). *Poverty in the United Kingdom: A survey of household resources and standards of living.* Harmondsworth: Penguin Books.

Wells, R., & Caraher, M. (2014). UK print media coverage of the food bank phenomenon: From food welfare to food charity? *British Food Journal, 116*(9), 1426–1445.

Winson, A. (1993). *The intimate commodity.* Toronto: Garamond Press.

Chapter 9

Mothering and Food Acquisition in Times of Austerity: Individual versus Collaborative Responses in the UK and Italy

Benedetta Cappellini, Vicki Harman, Alessandra Marilli and Elizabeth Parsons

9.1 Introduction

This chapter provides an analysis of how women feed their family in times of austerity. It does so by comparing how Italian and British mothers have reshaped their acquisition practices to make ends meet. As a macro approach seems to have dominated the current interdisciplinary debate, studies have highlighted the impact of recession and austerity on broad consumption trends, purchase behaviour and the reshaping of the market of the so-called luxury and necessity items (Boisio, Lozza, & Novello, 2011; Leiser, Bourgeois-Gironde, & Benita, 2010; Roland-Lévy, Pappalardo-Boumelki, & Guillet, 2010). Other macro-economic studies have highlighted how recession has affected women in particular (see, for example, the edited collection by Karamessini and Rubery (2014)). As such we know that people have had to change their purchasing behaviour and that women have been at the front of such reorganisation of the overall households' finances. However, we still need more information about how women have reshaped their mundane and routinised acquisition practices in the context of austerity.

Given the current lack of an in-depth understanding of women's everyday acquisition practices, this chapter seeks to answer the following research question: How have Italian and British women changed their ways of acquiring food to cope with the financial difficulties of their households? We selected these two countries since they have been hit by recession and subsequent austerity policies impacting on the everyday life of many families (D'Ippoliti & Roncaglia, 2011; Karamessini & Rubery, 2014; O'Hara, 2015; Sassatelli, Santoro, & Semi, 2015). We collected data through interviewing 15 Italian and 12 British women and observing their food shopping. In interpreting our data, we engaged with the current feminist literature on mothering which we have summarised in the

Families in Economically Hard Times, 187–200

doi:10.1108/978-1-83909-071-420191013

following section. In this chapter, we present our findings using the narratives of Leslie, a stay-at-home mother of six from Essex and Antonella, a full-time teacher and mother of two from Florence. Their stories epitomise the differences encountered in the ways UK and Italian women have reshaped their acquisition practices. As such Leslie and Antonella summarise the main characteristics that we found in other participants. As this chapter is based on two cases only, we do not aim to provide a generalisable analysis on the two contexts of study. Our modest aim is to provide an overview of common themes emerging from amongst our limited sample, using two evocative narratives. Leslie's story echoes the stories of other British women who seem to be more reliant on the marketplace, saving money through a complex orchestration of their shopping. Similarly, Antonella's narrative reflects the narratives of other Italian women who were less reliant on the marketplace, having developed informal collaborative consumption practices through their network of family members and local friends. Theoretically this chapter shows how austerity has changed the relationship that these women have with the marketplace, with the British participants more engaged with the retail environment and the Italian ones being more engaged with forms of collaborative consumption.

9.2 Gendered Inequalities of Feeding the Family

Feminist studies have highlighted how food work plays a significant role within discourses of mothering, domestic division of labour and overall household provision. Embedded at the very heart of family life, practices surrounding the acquisition, appropriation, appreciation and disposal of the everyday meal are crucial for the doing and displaying of individual and collective identities (Cairns & Johnston, 2015; O'Connell & Brannen, 2016). The identity of women, and mothers in particular, has been argued to be crucially intertwined with the practice of feeding others (Bugge & Almas, 2006; Charles & Kerr, 1988). As DeVault famously articulated, feeding the family operates as a form of doing gender in which 'a woman conducts herself as recognisably womanly' (De Vault, 1991, p. 118). As is well documented by the literature, the strong connection between food work and good mothering is very prominent today, making the 'good mother' an idealised figure completely devoted to her role of selfless nurturer. Feminist studies have highlighted the moralistic tones of such an ideal, revealing its gendered, classed and racialised connotations (see, for example, Gillies, Edwards, & Horsley, 2016; Littler, 2013; May, 2008). These studies have also highlighted other forms of inequalities that we have summarised and called external and internal inequality. The terms external and internal refer to the practices of discourses of mothering gravitating outside and inside the home. Although this distinction is artificial as the two inequalities are interlinked and difficult to analyse separately, it is useful to tackle the challenge of disentangling them and to point out their main characteristics.

External inequality emerges from recent work on intensive mothering and the complex relationships women have with the marketplace (Lee, Bristow, Faircloth,

& MacVarish, 2014; Wall, 2010). According to Hays (1996, p. 8) intensive mothering is a 'day-to-day labour of nurturing the child, listening to the child, attempting to decipher the child's needs and desires, struggling to meet the child's wishes, and placing the child's well-being ahead of their [mothers'] own convenience.' Intensive mothering practices are 'child-centred, expert-guided, emotionally absorbing, labour intensive, and financially expensive' (Hays, 1996, p. 8). Echoing some elements of developmental psychology and the more recent so-called brain science (Gillies et al., 2016; Nadesan, 2002; Wall, 2010), intensive mothering discourses emphasise parental determinism for children's outcomes, which leads to a focus on maternal practices at the expense of structural factors. Such a child-centred understanding of mothering has put consumption at the very heart of the way women construct their own identities as 'good mothers'. In fact, intensive mothering is interlinked with the idea that caring for a child is also a matter of providing items which are both appropriate and satisfy their desires. Food is not outside this discourse and as such feeding children with the 'right' food at home and outside home is a matter of doing and displaying good mothering (Cappellini, Harman & Parsons 2018). Critical studies have highlighted the current paradoxical relationship that mothers have with the marketplace since consumption is at the same time an alleviator of women's anxieties, but also an instigator of new fears, further bouldering the discourses and practices of good mothering, which appears to be an unachievable target (The Voice, 2010). Interestingly, men seem to be excluded from the intensive parenting discourse and when they do feed their children they do not judge themselves against the hard-to-achieve standards of intensive parenting (Erickson, 2005).

Everyday lives of women and the overall organisation of their households. There is a vast literature highlighting the unequal distribution of labour in the household, and one of our studies has made a contribution showing how inequalities emerge in the management of the household's resources (Cappellini, Harman, Marilli & Parsons 2019). In borrowing the concepts of 'orchestration of power' and 'implementation of power' (Safilios-Rothschild, 1976), we have shown how decisions involving orchestration of power – which refers to 'big decisions' (for example, changing the family car or going on holiday) – are usually taken collectively or by men. Decisions involving 'implementation power' – which derive from the first ones and are more mundane and tedious – tend to be undertaken by women. Feeding the family is part of the mundane implementation of power and consists of routinised practices (from acquisition to disposal) that women undertake often without the support of their male partners or with a very limited input (Beagan, Chapman, D'Sylva, & Bassett, 2008). If male partners are now more involved in the work of feeding children, studies highlight their marginal roles and their lack of responsibility for the overall management of the household (Bianchi, Milkie, Sayer, & Robinson, 2000; Cairns & Johnston, 2015; Sayer, 2005; Szabo, 2014).

Empirical work has also highlighted how the everyday practice of feeding the family is restless work that women undertake with a sense of self-sacrifice (Cappellini & Parsons, 2012; Miller, 1998). If abnegating their own desires and prioritising those of other family members seem to be common themes in women's everyday organisation of their households, these become more prominent in the case of mothers living in poverty (Hamilton, 2012; Hamilton & Catterall, 2006; Kempson, 1996; Kempson, Bryson, & Rowlingson, 1994; Kochuyt, 2004). Women in poverty are usually the ones that sacrifice their needs in favour of their children. Examples of women having little food for themselves or going hungry in order to be able to satisfy some of their children's requests are common. Some authors have interpreted this sacrifice as an expression of parental honour (Kochuyt, 2004) and devotional love (Miller, 1998). Others have highlighted how women are not simply victims of such inequalities, but they perpetuate social relations that lock themselves into an inequitable position in the household (Harman & Cappellini, 2017).

9.3 The Study

This chapter emerges from a wider study looking at austerity and domestic food consumption in Italy and in the UK. The research project investigated the practices that women responsible for feeding their families engage in during hard times. Here, we aim to highlight the different strategies women activate for making ends meet in these two locations. We do so using two cases from a wider data set of 12 semi-structured interviews with British women (from the South East and the Midlands) and 15 semi-structured interviews with Italian women living in Florence and the surrounding area. Participants were also observed while doing their food shopping in supermarkets or online shopping. Given the limited number of women, we do not aim to provide a generalisable study of mothers' coping mechanisms in times of austerity but rather to provide 'in-depth analysis of the life stories expressed by a relatively small number of participants' (Thompson, 1996, p. 392). Women were selected on the criteria that they had experienced some financial hardship due to personal circumstances (for example, being on maternity leave) and/or due to the current crises (being made redundant or having their contracted hours reduced). Participants from the Italian context possess a more middle-class background but, having experienced a significant decline in their household income, they engaged in new coping strategies new to their families. Women from the British sample tended to identify themselves as working class, having a longer experience of coping with a limited income, which was further affected by the current recession.

Interviews lasted approximatively one hour and, with participants' permission, were recorded, transcribed verbatim and anonymised and pseudonyms have been used. The interviews conducted in Italian were translated into English by the Italian researchers in the team. Usually interviews were conducted at the participants' home, giving the researcher the possibility of gathering additional information about the organisation of domestic labour. Themes covered in the interviews included the overall organisation of financial resources in the household, the division of domestic labour and the management of food practices at home (from shopping to disposal). These topics provided a chance to unpack the emotions that women experience in their everyday juggling between domestic and work tasks, their experience of inequality at home and the overall frustration and anxiety in feeding the family with limited resources. Such reflections were analysed thematically by the research team, which followed the general guidelines of interpretive research (Hudson & Ozanne, 1988; Silverman, 2006; Spiggle, 1994).

The findings we present here are intended to provide a discussion of two ways of dealing with the crisis, based on the different relationships women have developed with the marketplace. We do so presenting the cases of Leslie and of Antonella, drawn from the UK and Italian samples, respectively. We would not wish to claim that what we represent in our findings is a generalisable representation of the consumption practices of all Italian and all British women. Our aim is more modest and consists of providing an insight into the continuities and discontinuities, similarities and differences of feeding the family in hard times in the UK and in Italy.

9.3.1 Leslie

Leslie was interviewed in the garden of her neighbour's house. She preferred to meet one of us outside her home, which she said 'is always a mess and in a terrible state'. Leslie is a 39-year-old mother, living in an owner-occupied terraced house near the town centre. She lives with her husband Brad and her six boys. Leslie's oldest son is 15 years old and her youngest is six months old. Brad has other two children with his previous wife, who occasionally visit him during weekends. Brad is a builder who usually works full time for a local company plus also working as a handyman to earn some extra cash. His company was hit by recession and consequently his working hours were reduced. As Brad was the only person working in the house – Leslie is a stay-at-home mother – the overall family income was significantly affected. At the time of the interview, Brad was temporarily out of work, doing some occasional repair jobs for cash.

Despite being immaculately made-up and wearing a crisply ironed flower-print dress, Leslie apologised for her appearance, describing herself as 'a rushed mum'. Later during the interview she admitted that buying that dress the previous weekend during the sale in a local Primark store had been the source of a considerable dilemma, one that she faces whenever she buys things for herself. As the point of the trip to Primark was to buy clothes for the children, buying something for herself as well (albeit only costing £5) left Leslie 'feeling bad'. Implicitly then, being on a budget means prioritising other family members' needs and desires over one's own. Indeed self-sacrifice of one's own pleasures is considered the 'normal' enactment of mothering. Her husband Brad, however, seems to have a different attitude toward abstinence which goes to the core of clothing choices:

> *What annoys me – well it doesn't annoy me and it does annoy me – I will just go and get three pairs of knickers for £6 but what he wears is like £15 for one pair. I do think it's a bit extravagant but it's not very often that he will do it.*

Annoyed by the different standards adopted by her husband, Leslie justifies these as being occasional, and, as she stated later in the interview, being a treat he deserves for his hard work. This narrative was not very new to us; almost all participants revealed a similar pattern of distribution of resources in the household and a very similar narrative justifying such imbalance, and indeed injustice. As others have highlighted (Daly, 2017; Kenney, 2006), women's narratives indicate that they are in charge of the mundane and thrifty practices and that their male partners, described as simply 'unable to manage resources', are excluded from such constant anxiety of saving. Considering the overall organisation of the resources in the household, it was not a surprise to learn that Leslie was the only person in charge of the food acquisition. For Leslie, along with the other women in the UK sample, getting food is a matter of shopping. School dinners consumed by the children while on the school premises are the only exceptions of food that Leslie does not directly buy and prepare for the family.

Leslie's shopping follows a well-established pattern which has been re-defined over the years to take into account the changing financial conditions of the family. For example, Leslie now shops more frequently to compensate for the limited family income. As Leslie explained:

> *Now I shop more than once a week so that it's not such a bulk in one go. It seems to work out cheaper if we try and just shop for a couple of days at a time rather than doing a big shop [...] A lot of stuff we'll get weekly. Even if we could probably in the long run save money if we bought bulk, we haven't got the money to buy bulk to start off with.*

This new way of planning the food shopping consists of visiting the shops more often and buying a limited amount of food lasting a couple of days. Because Brad's cash payment and the child benefit payments are received weekly, Leslie organises her food provision on a weekly basis, managing the money she will receive in her bank account and some extra cash that her husband might be getting. Although she is aware that this organisation of the shopping is not the most efficient because she cannot buy in bulk, Leslie is nonetheless confident it reduces costs. However, as she explains, this new way of shopping requires 'more thinking'. As she says:

> *It means you have to think more about the shopping. Whereas before you'd just go shopping and just pick up – I'd go to one shop only and pick up whatever we fancied [...] I do now shop in more than one shop because I know where there are things that are cheaper in one shop that I would want to buy, than they are in another shop. I tend to do Iceland, Morrison's and Lidl.*

Leslie's new mode of shopping doesn't simply require more frequent visits to the shops, but also a constant comparison and evaluation of the prices in three different supermarkets. We didn't grasp the full implications of this, until Leslie provided some examples.

> *I've noticed now their [Morrison's] lettuce and cucumber are cheaper than Lidl, unless Lidl have got it on offer. When they do it on offer, a cucumber is about 29p when it's on offer but when it's not on offer I think it's 69p or something like that. It's 49p at the moment in Morrison's.*
>
> *I did notice the other day that I was buying my milk in Lidl because it's 95p for four pints. Then I've noticed – because Morrison's keep advertising, 'We're dropping our prices. Everything is cheaper,' – Morrison's are now doing four pints for 84p. I've now swapped because I get through a lot of milk. We probably get through about 16 pints of blue milk a week.*

The above selected examples are simply two of the many she provides while describing her way of 'thinking more about the shopping'. The use of the verb 'noticing' is interesting as it highlights how Leslie keeps a constant eye on prices, remembers them and navigates confidently between supermarkets. The activity of 'noticing' is a never ending one; it needs to be constantly updated considering the periodic special offers, but also advice exchanged with friends and relatives. For example, Leslie has just decided to abandon her branded washing powder and conditioner since her cousin showed her how the Morrison's own brand 'is just as good as the others'. Convinced by this recommendation, she has swapped brands making what she sees as a considerable weekly saving. If cleaning products are easy to change, other branded items require more careful adjustment because of the other family members involved. As she explained:

> *I've bought cereal from Lidl and tipped it into the old branded box to see if they could tell the difference. My 15 year old could but the younger ones, because I've got a gap. My eldest is 15 and the next one down is 10 so the ones 10 and under couldn't really but he could.*

Swapping brands consumed by children is not as simple as changing washing powder. Having developed a clear preference for some branded cereals, Leslie tends to accommodate her children's desires, 'finding' some extra money to buy them. Elsewhere we have described this complex mechanism of 'finding' such extra money by saving and re-directing financial resources within the household (Cappellini et al., 2014; Cappellini, Marilli, & Parsons, 2016). Here we want to highlight how mothers orchestrate various strategies to make children happy that go beyond the practice of buying favourite items. This is indeed the case of Leslie secretly transferring Lidl's cereals into a branded box with the hope that her children will not notice the difference. We found many other examples of these mundane coping strategies that mothers use with the aim of avoiding conflicts and perhaps protecting children from some of the hardships of a thrifty life. Interestingly as well as children, fathers also seem to be relatively excluded from these strategies. Leslie admits that she would like to share more of the responsibility of the household with her husband, but she seems to consider them exclusive to her mothering role, or as she says, 'this is what mums do.'

9.3.2 Antonella

Antonella is 35-year-old full-time teacher living with her husband and two children aged two and four years. She is married to Marco who works in a legal firm as a freelancer earning what she describes as a 'very unpredictable salary'. Recession has affected Marco's firm significantly and, thus he might have months with no salary and others with a limited one. Antonella's household income is higher than Leslie's, but recession has hit Marco's firm and consequentially her family's lifestyle.

Antonella was interviewed in her home, a recently renovated semi-detached house in a quiet neighbourhood near the city. She inherited the house from her grandmother, but having done 'big renovations' to the property, she had to take a 'substantial loan' which is paid off monthly. Like Leslie, Antonella described herself as a mum who is always in a rush and who puts children's needs first. With the family's income being recently reduced, the available money is carefully managed by Antonella who administrates the 'big' as well as the small mundane household purchases. If big decisions, such as changing the old car, are made with Marco, their implementation is then orchestrated by Antonella. She sees such an unequal distribution of responsibilities as part of Italian culture and its patriarchal ideology – a mantra that all Italian participants invoke in justifying the inequalities in their households. Such an unequal division of labour and responsibility did not surprise us, as it is well documented in the literature (Beagan et al., 2008; Daly, 2017) and in line with our previous studies (Cappellini et al., 2016). Overseeing the overall management of the household includes feeding the family, an activity that she sees as her own domain. From the planning to the disposal, Antonella managed these practices with what she described as 'an eye on saving'. Such a thrifty attitude was evident in her description of the food shopping, a practice that she manages with great confidence, moving between stalls in the markets, supermarkets and small shops. Searching for bargains is an activity that, as also mentioned by Leslie, requires effort and time, two resources which needs to be 'found' somewhere in the busy daily schedule of working full time and looking after two young children.

Interestingly, shopping is not the only channel through which food is acquired in Antonella's household. Gifting, sharing and swapping are part of everyday life for Antonella, her friends and family. For example, when shopping in the market Antonella considers not simply her nuclear family, but also her extended one. As she observes:

> *The other day I went to the market and bought some boxes of fresh vegetables. It was really a lot! I divided it into portions and gave some to my parents and some to my sister… we spent very little and the quality was excellent.*

Antonella has a close relationship with her extended family whom she considers while looking for special offers. Knowing that her family members will appreciate her selection of food, she can confidently 'count on them' when she considers the value-for-money of the offers in the market. As such this sharing opens up a wider range of opportunities for saving. Other family members adopt the same strategy. For example, Antonella's sister Marta often shares bargains she has found in the market with her. Thus, we can observe a redistribution of food items amongst the members of this tightly knitted network.

However, Antonella's network of food sources goes far beyond the street market. Her parents have a little allotment where they proudly grow vegetables to be shared with their extended family and friends. The allotment has a significant impact on the way Antonella manages food in the house. Since she relies on the vegetables and fruit from the allotment her food planning needs to be carefully organised. As she explains:

> *I try to make as many things as possible: pickled vegetables like olives, tomatoes and aubergines. I'm lucky since my parents have an allotment in which they grow vegetables, they have some olive trees and keep some hens that give us nice eggs. In reality I now buy fewer things and cook much, much more.*
>
> *If I have too many vegetables from the allotment, I give them to friends. I hate throwing away food. If I have too much fruit I make a fruit salad, or some jam.*

The flow of vegetables and fruit from the allotment is unpredictable, and Antonella makes the most of the unexpected surplus of food that might appear on her doorstep. She maximises this surplus by being more flexible in her meal planning. As she explains, if too much fruit appears unexpectedly, she might decide to prepare a fruit salad for dinner. Rethinking what to do with the flow of food items coming from the allotment is an activity that also needs long-term planning. In fact in the summer, when vegetables and fruits appear in large quantities she prepares pickles or jams to be eaten later in the year. Such short- and long-term planning also involves cooking, a practice that she admits having increased considerably. As we have highlighted elsewhere (Cappellini et al., 2014), Italian women now spend more time and effort in their kitchen, as a way of maximising the reduced economic resources of their household. Antonella is not an exception, but she also admits being proud of her cooking practices, gaining satisfaction from doing a 'good job' of feeding her family with what she considers healthy food.

Sharing food with friends is another practice that Antonella undertakes regularly. The passing on of surplus fruits sits alongside more extraordinary occasions in which gift giving or sharing is practiced with friends.

> *For example, we went to pick porcini mushrooms and we found so many! We organised a dinner at my place and invited our friends and relatives. We found so many mushrooms!*

Must be consumed within a short space of time. Considered a delicacy by many, Antonella made a celebratory occasion of this unexpected surplus of food, sharing it with friends. While this might be a relatively unusual event this example shows how the redistribution of food with family and friends strengthens the bonding of the network and the mutual support that members provide to each other. We have not fully investigated the extent, structure and frequency of these exchanges, but our Italian participants highlight how being part of this network of informal swapping, sharing, lending and gift-giving is considered to be a 'big help'. Implicit in this is that as well as assisting others, Antonella will also be a beneficiary of gifts from others when their circumstances allow. What we know is that food is not the only item exchanged in the network, but other items are also exchanged. As Antonella described:

> *A relative passed me lots of clothes for the children. She passes me everything… literally everything. I receive a box full of clothes every two months. I only buy shoes for the children. It's a big help!*

We do not know if this relative was invited to the dinner party in which porcini mushrooms were served. However, it would be very unlikely that a box full of children's clothes was not reciprocated with some fresh vegetables from the allotment or some pickles. We cannot speculate much on Antonella's network, but we have observed that women have a central role in orchestrating these informal exchanges of food, clothes, dinner parties: a network in which those responsible for feeding children and managing their households support each other.

9.4 Concluding Remarks

This chapter has sought to answer the question: How have Italian and British women changed their ways of acquiring food to cope with the financial difficulties of their households? Given the focus on two cases, our answer cannot be generalised, but can offer some insights into how women's food acquisition has been modified by austerity. Despite the fact that Leslie and Antonella exhibit different cultural and social capitals, their everyday coping strategies in acquiring food present some similarities. Indeed if the comparability of the two cases might be questioned in terms of capitals, the emotional work and indeed the everyday practices of feeding their families are remarkably similar.

The first similarity is that in both cases women affirm that feeding the family in hard times is seen as their domain, and as such the overall organisation of thrifty resources presents itself as their responsibility. Both women expend considerable effort and creativity in making limited resources stretch in order to feed the family, yet they do not consider their own time within in this process. Nor do they hold their partners to account for their lack of input in their area or their own relative extravagances. This echoes previous studies and the existing literature showing how women recognise the inequality of their household organisation, but do not actively seek to change it (Beagan et al., 2008). Interestingly, Antonella and other Italian participants tended to justify their domestic inequalities evoking cultural aspects of their patriarchal culture, observing that 'it is like this for everyone' and thus comparing and aligning their situations to those of people around them. Leslie and other British participants do not evoke structural or cultural forces, but instead attribute these inequalities to the lack of organisation skills of their partners. Some go as far as attributing such a lack to 'natural' differences viewing their partners as simply unable to do food work. The evocation of nature is also an aspect that we have encountered in previous fieldwork in which participants comment on the limitations of their husbands' parenting abilities (Cappellini et al., 2014; Harman & Cappellini, 2017). In line with the discourse of intensive mothering where children are seen as 'beyond market value' (Hays, 1996; Lareau, 2003), efforts were also made to shield children from the impact of austerity.

The second main similarity between the two narratives is related to the recent reorganisation of food acquisition due to the economic circumstances. In both households stretching economic resources implies more time and labour to be spent in planning the meal. Such planning requires a greater flexibility than in the past. Leslie spends more time juggling between supermarkets, 'noticing' prices, special offers and thus changing her plans for the meals according to what she has bought. Shopping lists are carefully followed, but if special offers appear a quick recalculation of the prices and a consequent change of the menu can happen in the supermarket. Antonella has also reshaped her family meal planning. If fruits and vegetables appear on her doorstep she has to think how to maximise them, making a fruit salad or some jam. To put it simply, feeding the family in hard times has made women more anchored to their role of providing food, since changes of menu and deviations from routine often happen in order to take advantage of efficiencies. Such changes are made with the idea of saving money, a calculation that Leslie and Antonella were not able to make. Indeed, none of our participants could quantify the amount of saving that such a reorganisation of labour could provide, but they all insist that 'something' was saved.

Their modes of acquisition have some key differences, which might be explained by their different class backgrounds, with Antonella being more proactive than Leslie in using her cultural and social capitals. Leslie's acquisition is exclusively related to shopping, a practice that she executes for her own family only. Dependent on the market for acquiring food, she tries to save money by going from one discount supermarket to another, selecting products that will last. Acting on her own in the process of acquiring food (albeit acting on the occasional recommendation from trusted friends and family members), Leslie cannot fully take advantage of the offers and take the 'risk' of buying larger quantities of perishable food, including vegetables and fruit. Convenient items and ready meals – the latter significantly cheaper in the UK than in Italy – are a safe option for Leslie as they can last longer, making her flexible plans ever more flexible. Antonella's food acquisition seems to be less dependent on shopping – a practice that remains the main way of getting food – as this is combined with other informal and irregular practices including swapping, sharing, growing and gift-giving. As these practices are not performed in isolation, other consumers are involved in the food acquisition of Antonella. Even in her shopping for vegetables she considers her extended family, who can benefit from special offers that Antonella 'notices' at the markets. Swapping, sharing and gifting, although executed irregularly, involve local friends and extended family, actors that are included in a network of collaborative consumption. Such a network makes participants like Antonella less reliant on the practice of shopping and more inclined to develop her network of informal exchanges.

To conclude, recession and austerity have made the gendered work of feeding the family harder and more complex. Austerity has worsened the practice of acquiring food, forcing women to considerably reshape their routinised and taken-for-granted shopping habits in order to make ends meet. Caution should be used in generalising our study, which, as previously stated, does not aim to provide any generalisable findings. However, what we have provided here is an analysis illustrating how recession and austerity have been interpreted and acted upon by women in two contexts. In the UK, it seems that the intensive mothering discourse goes hand in hand with neoliberalism, resulting in a close association between good mothering and a competent and efficient navigation of the marketplace. In Italy, the social networks in which women are embedded make participants less reliant on the practice of shopping – instead more emphasis is placed on informal exchanges. Further work could unpack the connections between the neoliberal mantra 'being responsible for your life and your family' and the British women's dependence on the market and its convenience food. Similarly, further research could be conducted in Italy in understanding the relationships between collaborative consumption, emerging from cultural rather than political bearings, and the strengthening of existing networks making the work of feeding the family a more collaborative effort. This study has highlighted that more work is certainly needed to explore how discourses of mothering play out in different cultural and political contexts during times of austerity.

References

Beagan, B., Chapman, G. E., D'Sylva, A., & Bassett, B. R. (2008). 'It's just easier for me to do it': Rationalizing the family division of foodwork. *Sociology*, *42*, 653–671.

Bianchi, S. M., Milkie, M. A., Sayer, L. C., & Robinson, J. P. (2000). Is anyone doing the housework? Trends in the gender division of household labor. *Social Forces*, *79*(1), 191–228.

Boisio, A. C., Lozza, E., & Novello, D. (2011). La crisi dal punto di vista del consumatore. *Micro & Macro Marketing*, *20*, 51–72.

Bugge, A. B., & Almas, R. (2006). Domestic dinner: Representations and practices of a proper meal among young suburban mothers. *Journal of Consumer Culture*, *6*, 203–228.

Cappellini, B., Marilli, A., & Parsons, E. (2014). The hidden work of coping: Gender and the micro-politics of household consumption in times of austerity. *Journal of Marketing Management*, *30*(15 16), 1597–1624.

Cappellini, B., Marilli, A., & Parsons, E. (2016). Working your way down: Rebalancing Bourdieu's capitals in times of need. In B. Cappellini, D. Marshall, & E. Parsons (Eds.), *The practice of the meal: Food, families and the marketplace* (pp. 43–56). London: Routledge.

Cappellini, B., & Parsons, E. (2012). Practising thrift at dinnertime: Mealtime leftovers, sacrifice and family membership. *The Sociological Review*, *60*, 121–134.

Cappellini, B., Harman, V., Marilli, A., & Parsons, E. (2019). Intensive mothering in hard times: Foucauldian ethical self-formation and cruel optimism. *Journal of Consumer Vulture*, *19*, 469–492.

Cappellini, B., Harman, V., & Parsons, E. (2018). Unpacking the lunchbox: biopedagogies, mothering and social class. *Sociology of Health and Illness*, *40*, 1200–1214.

Cairns, K., & Johnston, J. (2015). *Food and femininity*. London: Bloomsbury Publishing.

Charles, N., & Kerr, M. (1988). *Women, food and families*. Manchester: Manchester University Press.

D'Ippoliti, C., & Roncaglia, A. (2011). L'Italia: Una crisi nella crisi. *Moneta e Credito*, *64*, 189–227.

Daly, M. (2017). Money-related meanings and practices in low-income and poor families. *Sociology*, *51*, 450–465.

DeVault, M. (1991). *Feeding the family: The social organization of caring as gendered work*. Chicago, IL: University of Chicago Press.

Erickson, R. J. (2005). Why emotion work matters: Sex, gender, and the division of household labour. *Journal of Marriage and Family*, *67*, 337–351.

Gillies, V., Edwards, R., & Horsley, N. (2016). Brave new brains: Sociology, family and the politics of knowledge. *The Sociological Review*, *64*, 219–237.

Harman, V., & Cappellini, B. (2017). Boxed up? Lunchboxes and expansive mothering outside the home. *Families, Relationships and Societies*, *7*(3), 467–481.

Harman, V., & Cappellini, B. (2015). Mothers on display: Lunchboxes, social class and moral accountability. *Sociology*, *49*, 764–781.

Hays, S. (1996). *The cultural contradictions of motherhood*. New Haven, CT and London: Yale University Press.

Hamilton, K. (2012). Low-income families and coping through brands: Inclusion or stigma? *Sociology*, *46*, 74 90.

Hamilton, K., & Catterall, M. (2006). Consuming love in poor families: Children's influence on consumption decisions. *Journal of Marketing Management*, *22*, 1031–1052.

Hudson, L. A., & Ozanne, J. L. (1988). Alternative ways of seeking knowledge in consumer research. *Journal of Consumer Research*, *14*, 508–521.

Karamessini, M., & Rubery, J. (Eds.). (2014). *Women and austerity. The economic crisis and the future for gender equality*. London: Routledge.

Kempson, E. (1996). *Life on a low income*. Social Policy, No. 97. Joseph Rowntree Foundation, York.

Kempson, E., Bryson, A., & Rowlingson, K. (1994). *Strategies used by low-income families with children to make ends meet*. Social Policy, No. 53. Joseph Rowntree Foundation, York.
Kenney, C. T. (2006). The power of the purse: Allocative systems and inequality in couple households. *Gender & Society*, *20*, 354–381.
Kochuyt, T. (2004). Giving away one's poverty. On the consumption of scarce resources within the family. *The Sociological Review*, *52*, 139–161.
Lareau, A. (2003). *Unequal childhoods: Class, race, and family life* (second edition with an update a decade later, 2nd ed.). Berkeley, CA, University of California Press.
Lee, E., Bristow, J., Faircloth, C., & MacVarish, J. (2014). *Parenting culture studies*. Basingstoke: Macmillan.
Leiser, D., Bourgeois-Gironde, S., & Benita, R. (2010). Human foibles or systemic failure – Lay perceptions of the 2008–2009 financial crisis. *The Journal of Socio-Economics*, *39*, 132–141.
Littler, J. (2013). The rise of the 'yummy mummy': Popular conservatism and the neoliberal maternal in contemporary british culture'. *Communication, Culture & Critique*, *6*, 227–243.
May, V. (2008). On being a 'good' mother: The moral presentation of self in written life stories. *Sociology*, *42*, 470–486.
Miller, D. (1998). *A theory of shopping*. Cambridge: Polity Press.
Nadesan, M. H. (2002). Engineering the entrapreneur infant: Brain science, infant development toys, and govermentality. *Cultural Studies*, *16*, 401–432.
O'Connell, R., & Brannen, J. (2016). *Food, families and work*. London: Bloomsbury Publishing.
O'Hara, M. (2015). *Austerity bites: A journey to the sharp end of cuts in the UK*. Bristol: Policy Press.
Roland-Lévy, C., Pappalardo-Boumelki, F., & Guillet, E. (2010). Representation of the financial crisis: Effect on social representations of savings and credit. *The Journal of Socio-Economics*, *39*, 142–149.
Safilios-Rothschild, C. (1976). A macro and micro-examination of family power and love: An exchange model. *Journal of Marriage and Family*, *38*, 355–362.
Sassatelli, R., Santoro, M., & Semi, G. (2015). *Fronteggiare la crisi: come cambia lo stile di vita del ceto medio*. Bologna: Il Mulino.
Sayer, L. C. (2005). Gender, time and inequality: Trends in women's and men's paid work, unpaid work and free time. *Social Forces*, *84*, 285–303.
Silverman, D. (2006). *Interpreting qualitative data; methods for analysing talk, text and interaction*. London: SAGE Publications.
Spiggle, S. (1994). Analysis and interpretation of qualitative data in consumer research. *Journal of Consumer Research*, *21*, 491–503.
Szabo, M. (2014). Men nurturing through food: Challenging gender dichotomies around domestic cooking. *Journal of Gender Studies*, *23*, 18–31.
The Voice. (2010). Buying into motherhood? Problematic consumption and ambivalence in transitional phases. *Consumption, Markets and Culture*, *13*, 373–339.
Thompson, C. (1996). Caring consumers: Gendered consumption meanings and the juggling lifestyle. *Journal of Consumer Research*, *22*, 387–407.
Wall, G. (2010). Mothers' experiences with intensive parenting and brain development discourse. *Women's Studies International Forum*, *33*, 253–263.

Conclusions: Lives of Families in Face of Economic Crisis in Europe

Gerardo Meil and Vida Česnuitytė

Introduction

The economic crisis of the recent past has had a profound impact on the material and subjective wellbeing of many citizens and families in Europe. Its plainest effects have been a rise in unemployment and a reduction of salaries, with the ensuing reduction of available income and increase in the risk of poverty and unequal income distribution. According to Eurostat, the proportion of people at risk of monetary poverty in the EU 27 rose from 16.6% in 2007 to 17.2% in 2014, whilst the Gini coefficient of inequality rose from 30.6 to 31.0. The effects of the crisis were also reinforced by social policy reforms aimed at slowing the rate of growth in social spending, especially in the countries hardest hit by the economic crisis. In many cases, that led to cutbacks in family support policies, turning the families most afflicted by the crisis into victims twice over.

Of course, not all countries have been affected the same way or at the same intensity; the differences between countries are vast. Nor are all people affected the same way; family circumstances and a family safety net play a decisive role in what impact the crisis has on individual wellbeing. This edited collection of papers *Families in Economically Hard Times: Experiences and Coping Strategies in Europe* takes an analytical look not into national and regional differences, but into the heterogeneity of the impact the economic crisis has had on different family circumstances and family dynamics. The main aim formulated in the book was to provide readers with novel and unique sociological knowledge on European families' experiences and behavioural strategies in the decade after economic crisis that ensued at the beginning of twenty-first century. The research studies focus on hardships, functional solidarity and issues of vital human needs, including practices of co-residence, sharing of money, food acquisition. The main questions that the book seeks to answer are the following: how challenges emerged during recent economically hard contexts influenced way of life of European families? Which known and unusual behaviour strategies are specific to families of various

Families in Economically Hard Times, 201–208

doi:10.1108/978-1-83909-071-420191014

configurations in solving vital issues caused by the latest economic crises? So, what lessons can the reader learn from findings based on analysis of situations in over 10 European countries?

Family Structure and the Impact of Economic Crisis

Single-mother families are traditionally the type of household most frequently at risk of poverty, social exclusion and lower overall quality of life (Maldonado & Nieuwenhuis, 2015). Using 60% of the median equivalised income after social transfers as the cut-off point, monetary poverty in the EU 28, at least since 2005, has been around twice as much amongst single-parent families as amongst other households, according to the Eurostat database. The economic crisis has increased the vulnerability of single-parent families, especially in the countries that have seen the severest effects of the crisis and enacted the greatest cutbacks in social spending.

This book illustrates the consequences of this process in the specific case of Lithuania. Lithuania numbers amongst the countries where single-parent families are the most widespread. It also has one of the highest poverty and social exclusion rates in the European Union. The reasons why a high proportion of single-parent families are unable to attain a socially acceptable standard of living are traced by Maslauskaitė and Platūkytė (Chapter 4), primarily to the neoliberal reform of social benefits that took place in the wake of the 2008 economic crisis. The end of universal family benefits (replaced by family benefits dependent on previous social security payments), the authors argue, pushed many single-parent families outside the income redistribution system, especially those struggling under unemployment and job insecurity. The consequence is that, for single-parent families, unlike other households, the risk of poverty hardly varies at all in terms of available income before and after factoring in social transfers.

Based on a specific survey designed to study single-parent families, the authors expand the concept of social exclusion used by the European Income and Living Conditions Survey to include other subjective indicators of physical wellbeing, thus revealing that the vast majority of single-parent families endure economic hardship or cannot consume many of the goods and services included in a normal standard of living. The degrees of material deprivation vary, however, according to each mother's human capital and her possibilities of capitalising on it in the job market. This material deprivation has a high impact on the mother's personal wellbeing. Higher levels of material deprivation lead to more severe feelings of depression, accompanied by a general loneliness, thoughts of life as a failure, sadness and other depressive feelings. Additionally, whilst the majority of women are exposed to stress linked with various aspects of being the sole carer and provider, this stress is strongly related with their lack of resources. As a consequence, the authors see an urgent need for adequate social policy measures aimed at reducing the single mother's deprivation and raising her quality of life.

Chapter 8 by O'Connell, Knight and Brannen delves into the consequences material deprivation has on family nutrition and how food poverty also leads to social exclusion. Focusing on the UK, this chapter explores how food poverty is a fact in developed countries and moreover grew during the economic crisis as a consequence of, amongst other things, the reduction in spending on social protection for families. The proportion of households with children whose food spending was below the basic standard increased from 41% in 2005 to 52% in 2013, with lone parents with two or more children and couples with four children feeling the impact the most.

Since the food demand is elastic and changes with income level, the in-depth interviews on which the study is based reveal quite a wide range of strategies for adapting diets to available income. The most vulnerable families interviewed reported eating an inadequate quantity of food and experiencing hunger, skipping meals and using emergency food aid from food banks. The variety and quality of the food purchased and prepared was compromised, too, resulting in a narrower variety of foods, lower fruit and vegetable consumption and recourse to cheap calories. The authors also show that food poverty results not only in poorer nutrition, which has negative effects on children's health and cognitive development, but also in social exclusion for all members of the family. Since a fair share of socialising revolves around eating and drinking, a food-poor family cannot invite relatives or friends over. This constraint tends to isolate the family socially and curb children's engagement in friendships. Teens are barred from their regular leisure practices, which largely involve going out to eat and drink. Since peer contact is a fundamental part of teen development and individual wellbeing, the consequences of food poverty are potentially highly damaging, as they affect health, cognitive development, performance in school and social integration.

The work by Mazzuchelli and Parise (Chapter 1), on the case of Italy looks into the problem of the economic crisis' negative consequences on family dynamics from an entirely different yet complementary viewpoint. Based on survey data, this paper reveals how having a stable partner and a family support network improves families' economic situation by facilitating savings and avoiding family indebtedness. The authors' analysis shows that, besides the well-established relevance of employment and educational qualification for avoiding the risk of falling into debt, having a stable partnership and being able to count on the help of the family network are key determinants of family members' wellbeing.

These papers therefore illustrate that family structure is important in palliating poverty and its devastating consequences on present and future personal wellbeing. Family structure alone is not enough to provide an escape route from poverty, though. Family policies play a large role in this sense. That is why the authors underline the need for family policies to be designed specifically to combat poverty. Family solidarity may help palliate the consequences of poverty somewhat, but it too has been compromised by the economic crisis.

Family Solidarity and Economic Crisis

For some time it has been held that, as the welfare state has taken on more and more functions once belonging to the family, the state has increasingly worn away at family solidarity. This has been termed the 'crowding out' hypothesis: The welfare state crowds out family obligations, thus eroding family solidarity (Künemund & Klein, 1999). The process is, also, thought to be more intense in those welfare states that have more generous work–life balance and family policies that actually seek to outsource dependent relative care, removing it from the family circle. Then there is the weakening of social control over family life plans as a consequence of growing individualisation and the increased fragility of family relationships that this involves (Beck-Gernsheim, 2002), which are thought to result in an even greater weakening of the standards of family solidarity and a diminished transfer of aid.

Many national and country comparison studies (Daatland & Lowenstein, 2005; Künemund & Klein, 1999, among others) have proved that family solidarity in advanced industrial societies is not on the wane, at least in times of economic plenty. However, a substitution relationship has been found between a generous family aid policy in terms of childcare services and dependent adult institutionalisation services and intergenerational care. This does not mean aid among generations of this sort has vanished in developed welfare states, but that it has become more sporadic and less time intensive. Financial aid, on the other hand, is more frequent in strong welfare states (Albertini, Kohli, & Vogel, 2007). The better the economic situation and aid capabilities of senior generations, the more likely they are to help out junior generations; and if they give, they are also more likely to receive when they need it.

Česnuitytė and Widmer in Chapter 5 investigate behaviours of Lithuanians concerning solidarity creation. Family practices contributing to creation of personal and family networks that are ready to provide informal support are explored. Findings reveal rather extended involvement of individuals into solidarity through their personal and family practices, and certain family practices. Therefore, in case of sudden need for help in services and care, or financial, material or emotional support, individuals would have larger or narrower personal networks ready to contribute. Nevertheless, it is evident that in face of economically hard times and problematic situations, Lithuanians do not exploit all the possibilities: sharing with support mainly is going within the family of procreation, and the family of orientation.

The economic crisis puts the ability of family networks to help out their weakest members to the test. As said before, unemployment, the risk of poverty and economic inequality have risen whilst social spending has undergone cutbacks. In this socioeconomic context, it is to be expected that intergenerational aid would try to offset these processes' negative effects. The contributions addressed in this book analyse the characteristics of and constraints on intergenerational transfers of time and cash in times of economic hardship.

The work by König, Isengard, and Szydlik (Chapter 2), based on 2013 data from the Survey of Health, Ageing and Retirement in Europe (SHARE), shows that social inequalities (including gender inequality) at the micro, meso and macro levels alike have an important influence on the flow of regular intergenerational aid in the forms of cash and time. Children's neediness and parents' ability to help are both factors in the frequency and direction of aid flows; thus, joblessness and lack of resources affect the possibility of both receiving and giving aid. The family situation of both generations, their frequency of contact and the physical distance between their homes also prove to be relevant, as already thoroughly evinced by earlier studies. At the macro level, analysis shows that in countries where the risk of poverty is greater, aid in the form of money and time given by parents to their emancipated children is more frequent, but not aid from children to their parents. Furthermore, in countries where the welfare state affords the family greater social protection, aid in the form of time for grandchildren and dependent adults is lower, and transfers of cash between generations are more frequent, although top-down transfers prevail. The authors conclude that 'living in difficult and uncertain circumstances such as higher unemployment and an increased risk of poverty can lead to more stress and strain on family members and reduce functional solidarity from children to parents'.

Deindl and Brandt's contribution in Chapter 6 runs in the same direction. Its advantage is that it takes a three-generational perspective, focusing on flows of aid the sandwich generation gives and receives from the generation before it and the generation after. Based also on data gathered in SHARE' wave 5, the study reveals that aid is not all that frequent; only one in three households provides or receives aid. In the typical solidarity pattern, middle-aged parents support their adult offspring (mostly with money and grandchild care) and their older parents (with practical hands-on help and care). The main factors in aid flow intensity include not only the country's overall poverty level (as shown by König, Isengard, and Szydlik), but, also, how the countrywide poverty level affects the risk of poverty at the individual level. When people in the sandwich generation experience material or social deprivation, their ability to help their children and parents is compromised, and they change from providers of aid to receivers of aid from their emancipated children. If moreover they live in a region of high economic inequality, they are less likely to provide aid or receive it, regardless of the region's wealth level. The authors thus show that poverty risk and economic inequality strengthen each another by eroding the patterns of traditional family solidarity and doubly victimising the weakest people. This may be due, the authors maintain, to the fact that these circumstances create a subjective perception of a higher risk of impoverishment or dependency. Since the aid indicator the authors use in their analysis draws no distinction between aid in the form of money and aid in the form of time, it is impossible to say whether there is a substitution relationship between the two types of aid, where an inability to deliver cash aid might be offset by aid in the form of time.

These studies therefore reveal that the decay of the economic situation has a big impact on the possibility of giving aid and the need to receive aid, for individuals and collectives alike. If emancipated children are experiencing economic hardship and their parents can help, the children will probably receive help. If the parents themselves are experiencing material and/or social deprivation, it is they who will probably receive help from their children. If social inequality increases and the welfare state's ability to redistribute income declines, the possibilities of intergenerational aid will decline as well. Where all generations of a given family network have entered material and social deprivation, family solidarity will lose its compensatory function, thus heightening social inequality.

These two papers address the forms family solidarity takes in terms of flows of aid in cash and time between generations that do not share the same household, but there are other kinds of solidarity, too. One of the leading ways family solidarity manifests itself is for more than one generation to share the same household, as typically happens during certain phases of the life cycle. With the rise in unemployment and temporary employment, especially amongst young adults, offspring have in many cases put off their emancipation from the parental home. In some cases offspring unable to maintain an independent lifestyle have even temporarily moved back in with their parents; they are what have been termed 'boomerang kids'.

The second paper by Isengard, König and Szydlik (Chapter 7) in fact addresses the issue of generations' household moves and the factors behind moving house. The authors find that unemployment does indeed affect mobility decisions. Based on data from waves 1 (2004/2005) and 2 (2006/2007) of the Survey of Health, Ageing and Retirement in Europe (SHARE), the authors show that roughly two-thirds of older Europeans (50+) live near their children (less than 25 kilometres away) or in the same household as their children. No signs of any trend towards putting distance between generations have been spotted. Emancipation from the parental home and moving depend primarily on life cycle phases (couple formation, parenthood and breakup), career and parents' circumstances, but it also depends on the current economic situation and the degree of social protection available. The higher the unemployment rate, the more likely offspring are to put off emancipation from the parental home or, if already emancipated, to move house. Nevertheless, in stronger welfare states the pressure to remain in the parental home or to move house is lighter because new adults can draw on greater social protection.

Gender Inequality in Family Relations

The economic crisis has also affected gender relationships within the family, yet its effects are not necessarily limited to making gender relationships more traditional; there is the potential for making them more egalitarian as well. A high degree of occupational segregation by gender, where women are overrepresented in the service industry and underrepresented in all other economic sectors, has proven to be a protective factor in times of crisis (Eurofound, 2016). Inasmuch as the crisis mainly hit jobs in the industrial sector and construction and had less of an impact on the service industry, women's employment rate has been less affected by the rise in unemployment.

The paper by Dueñas-Fernández and Moreno-Mínguez (Chapter 3) reveals how the crisis has worked to wear down the patriarchal family model espoused by a significant share of Spanish families. The profound job crisis afflicting Spain from 2008 to 2015 affected partnered men much more than partnered women; women lasted much longer in their jobs and joined the job market in a larger proportion, especially women with children. In addition, partnered mothers increased the number of hours they worked, and the proportion of partnered mothers working part-time declined, whilst in all other cases the trend ran in the other direction. A significant proportion of mothers nonetheless have continued to fall back on part-time work as a work–life balancing strategy, and women do leave their jobs on becoming a parent much more frequently than do men, whose behaviour in respect of work is not influenced by parenthood. The crisis has thus partly helped reduce the scope of the traditional family model, although the change pertains only to the distribution of paid work. The impact on the distribution of unpaid work and the overall burden of housework has yet to be analysed. The authors interpret this behaviour as an 'added worker' effect, i.e. as a compensating strategy women use to neutralise the risk of poverty or income reduction stemming from losing their partner's job. The data the authors present on the development of female employment, however, show that this behaviour falls within a more general trend of women taking paid work independently of their family situation, as can be observed in all countries of the European Union (Eurofound, 2016).

On the other hand, the paper by Cappellini, Harman, Marilli and Parsons (Chapter 9) with which the book closes illustrates the traditionalising effects the crisis can have amongst families with unstable incomes, regardless of the mother's employment status. On the basis of an in-depth analysis of the life histories of two groups of families in the UK and Italy that have had to cope with a reduction of their income and uncertainty over whether they will continue to receive an income, the authors examine how women are affected as the people responsible for feeding their families. As argued in the chapter, feeding the family is an essential part of family life, and it is a responsibility traditionally assigned to women. Accordingly, practices associated with this task are a way of doing gender and generating individual and collective identities: The image of good mothering is closely linked to how a mother feeds her children. The authors' conclusion is that income reduction and uncertainty about income regularity has strengthened mothers' role as the people responsible for feeding their families and has made their job much more complex. In an environment like this, the task of feeding the family requires more time and effort plus continuous changes in food acquisition and preparation strategies in order to make ends meet, which results in greater gender inequality in affected families.

References

Albertini, M., Kohli, M., & Vogel, C. (2007). Intergenerational transfers of time and money in European families: Common patterns – Different regimes? *Journal of European Social Policy*, *17*, 319–334.

Beck-Gernsheim, E. (2002). *Reinventing the family: In search of new lifestyles*. Bristol: Polity Press.

Daatland, S. O., & Lowenstein, A. (2005). Intergenerational solidarity and the family–welfare state balance. *European Journal of Ageing*, *2*(3), 174–182.

Eurofound. (2016). *The gender employment gap: Challenges and solutions*. Luxembourg: Publications Office of the European Union.

Künemund, H., & Rein, M. (1999). There is more to receiving than needing: Theoretical arguments and empirical explorations of crowding in and crowding out. *Ageing and Society*, *19*, 93–121.

Maldonado, L. C., & Nieuwenhuis, R. (2015). Family policies and single parent poverty in 18 OECD countries, 1978–2008. *Community, Work & Family*, *18*(4), 395–415.

Index

Printed and bound by CPI Group (UK) Ltd, Croydon, CR0 4YY

13/09/2026

14961031-0001